Interactive Introduction to Theatre

Improving Life One Act at a Time

Second Edition

Daisy Nystul

Cover Design by Justin Stier

Back Cover Photos:

Top Row Photograph:
Ben Jonson's *The Silent Woman*,
adapted and directed for Oregon State University Theatre by Scott Palmer.
Costume design: Kim Decker.
Set design: George Caldwell, May, 2006.
Photograph Courtesy of Scott Aaron Palmer.

Second Row Left Photograph:
Proof, directed by Matt Nesmith.
Photograph by Dennis Chandler.
Photograph Courtesy of the University of South Dakota.

Second Row Right Photograph:
Pterodactyls, directed by Daisy Nystul.
Photograph by Daniel Smith.
Photograph Courtesy of the University of Central Oklahoma.

Bottom Row Photograph:
The Unsatisfactory Supper by Tennessee Williams.
Directed by Jack Heller.
Photograph by Danielle Weeks.
Cast from left to right: Grady Lee Richmond, Eve Sigal, Jolene Adams.
Produced by Jolene Adams, Actors Art Theatre.

Kendall Hunt
publishing company

www.kendallhunt.com
Send all inquiries to:
4050 Westmark Drive
Dubuque, IA 52004-1840

Copyright © 2008, 2010 by Kendall Hunt Publishing Company

ISBN: 978-0-7575-6507-6

All rights reserved. No part of this publication may be reproduced,
stored in a retrieval system, or transmitted, in any form or by any means,
electronic, mechanical, photocopying, recording, or otherwise,
without the prior written permission of the copyright owner.

Printed in the United States of America
10 9 8 7 6 5 4 3 2 1

This book is dedicated to Mary E. Nystul

Contents

Foreword by A. Max Weitzenhoffer   xv
Prologue   xvii

Act I: Scene I   1
Viewing and Critiquing a Play   1

Theatre: What Is It?   2
Audience   3
The Playscript   4
How Can Production Affect the Playscript?   5
Theatrical Conventions   6
The Critic   7
The Excellent Critic   8
Writing the Critique   10
Critiquing a Production for a Class Assignment   11
  Suggested Outlines   12
Theatre Critic Robert Hurwitt   14

   Feature Section: An Interview with Theatre Critic Robert Hurwitt   14

  Theatre Review, by Mr. Robert Hurwitt   16
Networking   17
  Summary   18
  Theatre in Your Career   18

Active Learning Assignment: "Bringing Theatre to Life"   19
  I. Tasting Theatre/Getting Involved   19
  II. Breaking the Ice-Improvisation   19

Act I: Scene II   21
Theatre: In the Beginning—The Development of the Western Theatre   21

Rituals: An Early Form of Theatre   22
Theatrical Ritual in Modern Society   22

Active Learning Assignment: "Bringing Theatre to Life"   23
  I. Tell a Story   23
The Greek's Spiritual Beliefs   23
The Religious Celebration of Dionysus   24
Thespis, of Icaria, in Attica   25
Dionysian Festivals   25
Selection of the Poets (Playwrights) and Actors   25
The Theatre and Its Scenic Elements   26

Dramatists   27
Aristotle (384/3 B.C.–322 B.C.)   29

Active Learning Assignment: "Bringing Theatre to Life"   30
   I. Writing and Performing Your Own Greek Tragedy   30
      Critical Thinking in Class Discussion   30
Roman Theatre   30
Roman Comic Playwrights   32
Medieval Europe   34
Liturgical Drama   34
Cycle Plays   36
Folk Drama: May Games   37
Folk Drama: Mummings   38
Non-Cycle Plays   38
End of the Middle Ages—Birth of the Renaissance   39
   Summary   39

Active Learning Assignment: "Bringing Theatre to Life"   40
   I. Remembering Greek, Roman, and Medieval Theatre   40
      Critical Thinking in Class Discussion   40

Act I: Scene III   41

The Renaissance (Italy, England and France) Through the Restoration   41

The Renaissance   42
Italy   42
French Playwrights   44
Commedia Dell' Arte (comedy of the profession of skill)   47

Active Learning Assignment: "Bringing Theatre to Life"   50
   I. "World of the Lazzi"—Non-object/physical lazzi (Inspired by John Dennis)   50
   II. "World of the Lazzi"—Prop lazzi with stock character traits
     (Inspired by John Dennis)   50
      Critical Thinking in Class Discussion   50
England and the Theatre   51
Shakespeare's Plays and Sonnets   51

Active Learning Assignment: "Bringing Theatre to Life" (Inspired by Kelly Kiernan)   54
   I. Write a Sonnet   54
      Critical Thinking in Class Discussion   55
Puritan Revolution 1640–1660   55
The Restoration-Charles II (1630-1685) King of England, Scotland, and
   Ireland (1660-1685)   56
     Summary   57
     Critical Thinking in Class Discussion   57

Act I: Scene IV   59

Romanticism and the Battle of the "ism" (Naturalism/Realism vs. Symbolism, and Modern Experiments)   59

The Political Climate   60
Romanticism   60
Symbolism "Art for Art's Sake"   61

Naturalistic Theatre Movement 62
Expressionists 63
Naturalism vs. Symbolism 63
Dada 65
Surrealism 65
Antonin Artaud (1896–1948) and The Theatre of Cruelty 66
Absurdist Movement 67
Happenings 67
The Living Theatre 68
The Living Theatre's Judith Malina 68

Feature Section: An Interview with The Living Theatre Creator, Judith Malina 69

Jerzy Grotowski (1933–1999) 71
Bertolt Brecht 71
Brechtian Acting 72
Other Experimental Theatre Companies 73
Performance Artist Cita Ricardo 73

Feature Section: Cita Ricardo Comments on Performance Art 74

Melodrama 74
Summary 75

Active Learning Assignment: "Bringing Theatre to Life" 75
I. Reenacting History 75

Critical Thinking in Class Discussion 76

Act I: Scene V 77

American Musical Theatre: Storytelling through Song and Dance 77
Robin Carr
Assisted by Adam Schelski

The Evolution of Musical Theatre 78
Types of Musical Theatre 80
Influences on Musical Theatre 82
Contemporary Trends in Musical Theatre 84
The Musical Theatre Team 85
Tony Awards for Best Musical 86
Feature Section: An Interview with Robert Dusold 88

Active Learning Assignment: "Bringing Theatre to Life" 89
I. Create your own Musical 89

Critical Thinking in Class Discussion 90

Act I: Scene VI 91

Theatre around the World 91

Theatre on the Continent of Africa 92
Arabic Theatre 94
Australian Theatre 95
English Speaking Canada 98
French Speaking Canada 100

Chinese Theatre 101
Indian Theatre 103
Japanese Theatre 104
Mexican Theatre 107
　　Summary 109

Active Learning Assignment: "Bringing Theatre to Life" 109
　I. Reenacting Theatre from a Variety of Nations 109
　　Critical Thinking in Class Discussion 109

Act I: Scene VII 111
The Theatre in You 111

Humanity in the Theatre 112
Censorship 112
Diversity in the Theatre 114
Theatres Created by Specific Groups 114
Working Together 115

Active Learning Assignment: "Bringing Theatre to Life" 116
　I. The Final Group Project—Writing and Producing a Play 116

Act II: Scene I 119
Dramaturgs and Stage Managers 119

Researching and Running the Show 120
The Dramaturg's Responsibilities 120
Dramaturg Liz Engelman 121

 Feature Section: An Interview with Dramaturg Liz Engelman 122

Active Learning Assignment: "Bringing Theatre to Life" 123
　I. Researching for the Final Group Project—Writing and Producing a Play 123
The Theatre in Your Career 123
Stage Management 123
The Stage Manager's Responsibilities 124
Stage Manager Rick Cunningham 126

 Feature Section: An Interview with Stage Manager Rick Cunningham 127

　Summary 128
　Theatre in Your Career 128

Active Learning Assignment: "Bringing Theatre to Life" 129
　I. Creating a Prompt Book for the Final Group Project—Writing and Producing a Play (Inspired by Rick Cunningham) 129

Act II: Scene II 131
The Art of Playwriting 131

The Playwright in You 132
Crucial Ingredients in a Play 132
Coming up with an Idea for a Play 132

Writing Exposition   134
Naming the Characters   135
Foreshadowing   135
The Plot   136
Locations—Where to Set the Scene   136
Staged Readings   136
Influential Playwrights   136
Playwright Edward Albee (1928–   )   142

Feature Section: An Interview with Playwright Edward Albee   144

Playwright Nicky Silver   144

Feature Section: An Interview with Playwright Nicky Silver   145

The Lifestyle of a Playwright   146
    Summary   146
    The Theatre in Your Career   147
        I.   Brainstorming   147
        II. Story Development   147
Active Learning Assignment: "Bringing Theatre to Life"   147
    I. The Final Group Project—Playwriting Section   147

Act II: Scene III   149

Producing and Directing the Play   149

Financial Classifications of Theatres   150
The Producer's Role in Theatre Production   150
Commercial Producer A. Max Weitzenhoffer   151

Feature Section: An Interview with Commercial Producer A. Max Weitzenhoffer   151

Executive Director Louis G. Spisto   152

Feature Section: An Interview with Executive Director of The Old Globe Theatre, San Diego, California-Louis G. Spisto   153

History of Directing   154
Director's Role in Theatre Production   155
Typical Schedule of a Four-Week Rehearsal Period   157
Director John Doyle   158

Feature Section: An Interview with Director John Doyle   159

Director Scott Aaron Palmer   159

Feature Section: An Interview with Director Scott Aaron Palmer   160

    Summary   163
    The Theatre in Your Career   163
Active Learning Assignment: "Bringing Theatre to Life"   164
    I. Staging Techniques to be used in the Final Group Project   164

Act II: Scene IV   167

Whether or Not You Want to Be an Actor, Achieve Your Personal Best   167

Personal Preparation: Improving Your Self-Esteem, Appearance, and Interpersonal Communication Skills   168
Networking   171
Agents   171
Actors Labor Union: Actors Equity Association   173
Training   174
Arthur Lessac, the Creator of the Lessac Kinesensic Voice and Body Training   178

Feature Section: An Interview with Arthur Lessac, the Creator of the Lessac Kinesensic Voice and Body Training   178

Acting Coach Jolene Adams   179

Feature Section: An Interview with Acting Coach Jolene Adams   180

Actor/Acting Coach Larry Silverberg   181

Feature Section: An Interview with Actor/Acting Coach Larry Silverberg   182

Actors/Actresses   185
Actress Kaitlin Hopkins   190

Feature Section: An Interview with Actress Kaitlin Hopkins   190

Actor/Acting Teacher Steve Eastin   193

Feature Section: An Interview with Actor Steve Eastin   194

Luis Salgado—Actor, Dancer, Choreographer   195

Feature Section: An Interview with Actor/Dancer/Choreographer Luis Salgado   196

Summary   197
The Theatre in Your Career   198
  I. Getting the Job—No Matter What Your Vocation   198
Active Learning Assignment: "Bringing Theatre to Life"   198
  I. Character Analysis and Voice and Body Warm-Up   198
    Note: How Hollywood Got Its Name   199

Act II: Scene V   201

Designing   201

The Performance Space   202
Traditional Theatrical Spaces   202
Black Box Theatre   203
Other Theatrical Spaces   203

Contents **xi**

    The Classroom as a Theatre   203

Active Learning Assignment: "Bringing Theatre to Life"   204
    I. The Theatrical Space   204
        Critical Thinking in Class Discussion   204
    Designing the Production   204
    Commonalities—Designers and the Realization of the Director's Concept   205
    An Overview of the Techniques Used by Designers   205
    Scenic Designer Eugene Lee   207

    Feature Section: Eugene Lee Comments on His Art and Career   208

Active Learning Assignment: "Bringing Theatre to Life"   212
    I. Designing Your Set   212
    II. Building Your Set   212
    III. Using Computer Images as Backdrops   212
    IV. Scene Changes   212

    Costume Designers   213
    Building the Costumes   213
    Costume Running Crew   214
    Costume Designer William Ivey Long   214
    A Quote by William Ivey Long Regarding Costumes   215
    Costume Designer Theoni Aldredge   215

    Feature Section: Thoughts on Costume Design by Theoni Aldredge   215

Active Learning Assignment: "Bringing Theatre to Life"   216
    I. Designing the costumes for the final project   216
    II. Collecting, Building, and Altering the Costume Pieces for the Final In-Class Project   216
    III. Costume Running Crew   217
        The Theatre in Your Career   217
            I. Color and Clothing   217
            II. Styles for Job Interviews   218
    Lighting Designers   218
    Lighting Designer Jennifer Tipton   220

    Feature Section: An Interview with Lighting Designer Jennifer Tipton   221

Active Learning Assignment: "Bringing Theatre to Life"   222
    I. Designing the Lights for Your In-Class Production   222

    Sound Design   222
    Sound Designer Bruce Ellman   223

    Feature Section: An Interview with Sound Designer Bruce Ellman   223

Active Learning Assignment: "Bringing Theatre to Life"   225
    I. Designing Sound for Your Production   225

    Hand Properties   225
    Properties Master Paul James Martin   226

Feature Section: An Interview with Properties Master
Paul James Martin   226

Active Learning Assignment: "Bringing Theatre to Life"   228
    I. Designing the Props for Your Production   228
    II. Using Props During the Production   228
        Summary   228

Act II: Scene VI   229

Getting an Audience   229

Publicity and Promotion   230
Marketing Director John Zinn   230

Feature Section: An Interview with Steppenwolf Marketing Director
John Zinn   231

Programs (Playbills)   232

Active Learning Assignment: "Bringing Theatre to Life"   232
    I. Make a Program   232
The Wrap Up   233
Partial Listing of Regional Theatres   233

Bibliography   235

Glossary   243

Index   253

About the Author   261

"All the world's a stage;
And all the men and women are merely players;
They have their exits and their entrances,
And one man in his time plays many parts . . ."

William Shakespeare
As You Like It
Act II, Scene VII

Foreword

written by A. Max Weitzenhoffer

I began going to the theatre over 60 years ago, first with my parents, then as a drama student, and finally as a professional. Throughout my career, three elements have always been central for me: first, the history of the theatre; second, and even more important, the mentoring of my peers (which continues even today with the current generation of theatre artists because the theatre is a dynamic business and is constantly changing); third, and perhaps most important, I believe nothing can take the place of doing theatre because practical experience is the ultimate learning tool.

Whenever I have lectured to non-theatre majors, I have never had the benefit of a textbook to reinforce my comments. Usually, I have ended up just telling amusing stories about my experiences in the theatre. Had I had this text for assistance in the preparation of just one or two lectures, it would have made an enormous difference. What is truly remarkable about this book is that, in a single introductory course, the novice is taken completely through the entire process of producing theatre and, thus, can clearly understand how the art of theatre is created. First, the book presents the history of the theatre. Next, it includes numerous examples of top professionals explaining their ideas and approaches to writing, acting, directing, and designing. Last, the text ingeniously involves the students in the creation of a 10-minute play in which they write, direct, design, and act.

In a single course, students are able to gain a complete basic knowledge of the way the theatre works. Naturally, this can only lead to a deeper understanding of what the students experience when they attend any theatrical event. But most important, these students will develop the desire to continue going to the theatre for the remainder of their lives.

Daisy's text is really a giant step forward in the development of the next generation of theatre audiences.

Prologue

Traditionally, "Introduction to Theatre" is presented in a lecture format. The first time I taught an "Introduction to Theatre" course was at Rio Hondo Community College in California. I began to lecture on theatre. One day, a student came up to me and said, "Teacher, your lectures are interesting, but when are we going to experience theatre?" I went home and thought about what he had said. The next day, I came to class with an abridged version of my lecture and an in-class "hands-on" theatre activity which brought my lecture to life.

The students were very excited about the change of activity and atmosphere in the classroom. The students were now experientially learning about theatre—appropriate because theatre is an experiential art form. One of my students became so excited that he applied to Central Drama School in London and got accepted.

When I began teaching at the University of Central Oklahoma, I offered to teach "Introduction to Theatre" and the students were very enthusiastic about my experiential approach. The Chair of my department, Dr. Robert McGill, suggested I write a paper on my methodology. The paper was presented, in a workshop form, at the Hawaii International Arts and Humanity Conference and the International Conference on Arts in Society in Edinburgh, Scotland. After receiving positive responses at these conferences, I began writing this textbook.

This textbook offers the basic information covered in most "Introduction to Theatre" texts—a brief history of theatre including acting, design, and playwriting—but my book sets itself apart from other texts by "bringing theatre literally to life" through active-learning in-class assignments that teach students the skills used by theatre practitioners and shows how these skills can be effectively utilized in other vocations.

While writing the text, I began to contact several theatre professionals in the hopes that they might be willing to share their experiences and advise students on how to pursue careers in theatre. Most of the individuals that I contacted were more than happy to share their expertise. I would like to take this opportunity to thank those artists who gave their time to be interviewed for this book: Jolene Adams, Edward Albee, Theoni Aldredge, Rick Cunningham, John Doyle, Steve Eastin, Bruce Ellman, Liz Engelman, Kaitlin Hopkins, Robert Hurwitt, Eugene Lee, Arthur Lessac, William Ivey Long, Judith Malina, Paul James Martin, Scott Aaron Palmer, Cita Ricardo, Luis Salgado, Nicky Silver, Larry Silverman, Louis Spisto, Jennifer Tipton, A. Max Weitzenhoffer, and John Zinn.

When reading the interviews, keep in mind that the statements that appear within parenthesis are mine.

This textbook also features moving animation. An anime character appears on the far right hand side of each page. When the pages are flipped, the anime characters appears to move, thus reminding students that theatre is a dynamic, living art form. I would like to thank artist Justin Stier for his illustrations and introduce his anime character.

Additional thanks go to the Head of the UCO Theatre Design Program, Christopher Domanski. Professor Domanski is responsible for the illustrations of the thrust, proscenium and arena stages as well as the plan of an ancient Greek theatre, the diagram of the stage areas and an example of a lighting plot.

The keynotes, text bank for instructors, glossary, and index were created by my hard-working research assistant, Theatre Education major, Sharin Burke.

I would like to acknowledge and thank the following for their support and for providing production photographs: University of Central Oklahoma, UCO College of Arts, Media and Design, the UCO Jackson College of Graduate Studies and Research, UCO Department of Theatre, Dance, and Media Arts, UCO Art Department, the University of New Hampshire, McNeese State University, University of Southern Mississippi, Oregon State University, University of South Dakota, Kendall/Hunt Publishing Company, and Southwestern Oklahoma State University.

My thanks also to the following for their support and assistance: Nels Anderson, Michelle Bahr, Dr. T. H. Baughman, Sharin Burke, Dr. George Caldwell, Robin Carr, Dr. John Clinton, James Dickson, John Dennis, Peter Ellenstein, Jaafar Gassid, Dr. Charlotte Headrick, Kelly Keirnan, Dr. Gayle Kearns, Deb Kinghorn, Brian Mear, Charles McNeely, Dr. Robert McGill, Matt Nesmith, Dr. and Mrs. Michael Nystul, Dr. and Mrs. Oliver Nystul, Luke Southern, Justin Stier, Steven Strickler, Stephanie Waley, Keith Webb, and Colleen Zelinsky.

Last, I would like to express my deep appreciation to Don Bristow for serving as the historical advisor for the text and for painstakingly editing each chapter.

Viewing and Critiquing a Play

Theatre: What Is It?

It's Fun

First and foremost theatre is FUN! There are many ways to enjoy this art form—from Broadway musicals to dinner theatre to interactive murder mysteries. Each play has a different plot line and unique characters. In fact, every production has something new for you to discover even if you have seen the same play before. With all of this variety, there is almost certainly a play being produced nearby that will suit both your artistic taste and your budget. You do not have to be a scholar to appreciate the theatre, but having a basic understanding of its development and the elements that make up a production will make your experience more enjoyable.

It's Inclusive

The theatre is a place to share, learn, and stimulate our ideas.

Learning about the theatre can also help us to become more appreciative of it as an art form. We can acknowledge that the theatre is a place to share, learn, and stimulate our ideas. It helps to strengthen community by celebrating the unique and beautiful differences of us as individuals and to illuminate the cultural backgrounds that make up our world. The theatre can promote understanding and encourage inclusiveness. At times we can all be ethnocentric—feeling that our own culture is better than others. When we strive to be inclusive, we become genuinely interested in our unique differences. This is not simply being tolerant or accepting, it is about becoming appreciative. Theatre is a marvelous way for us to learn about ourselves and others because it "holds a mirror up to life." Theatre allows us to see ourselves and others as we truly are—our strengths and weaknesses, our hopes and fears. It challenges our beliefs and it celebrates our individuality.

It's Art

Theatre is an art, and the joy of art is that we do not have to love all of it in order to gain something from it. There will undoubtedly be some plays that we do not care for, but we will gain a new perspective because we attended the play and participated in the theatre experience. All of our reactions to theatre, positive or negative, expand our knowledge of the human condition and the human experience. Understanding and appreciating others and their varying points of view can make us more successful in our own careers. As we shed our ethnocentricity, we become capable of considering the needs and desires of others.

It's Communal

Theatre is different than film in that it is a shared communal experience. The audience and the performers "bond" with one another during a production. For example, the actors will stop speaking if the audience begins to laugh and the actors will wait to speak until the laughter has subsided. Actors do this because they do not want the audience to miss the next line and because they want to give the spectators time to laugh and enjoy themselves. This bond between the audience and the actors intensifies the level of empathy that the audience members have toward the characters onstage. While we watch a play, we can evaluate our lives and the lives of people we know. This can be a cathartic experience for us and the actors who themselves have "become" the characters.

It's Composed of Four Essentials

These four essentials are the **performers,** the **audience,** the **space,** and the **message** to be conveyed. In some cases, the message may be indefinable and the space may not be a traditional theatre. Most often, the performers present scripted material, although in some instances, the performers may use improvisation. Improvisation is the art of creating lines and/or physical actions during the performance. Because no one knows what may happen during an improvisation, there is no guarantee how effective it will be. There is, however, something exhilarating about watching a performance develop in front of one's eyes. The spontaneity present in improvisation makes it interesting to watch—even if the dialogue does not turn out brilliantly.

*The four essentials crucial to theatre are the **performers,** the **audience,** the **space,** and the **message** to be conveyed.*

Audience

Image © Robert Zywucki, 2008. Used under license from Shutterstock, Inc.

Probably the most important aspect of theatre is the audience. Theatre would not be theatre if no one were there to experience it. If we are unaccustomed to going to the theatre, we may be unfamiliar with theatre etiquette. It is not necessary to "dress up" to see a play, although we may if we wish to make it an extra special affair. It is important to arrive at least 15 minutes before the production begins to find our seats and get comfortable. In large professional theatres there may be ushers to show us to our seats; but if the production has already begun, we may not be seated until the intermission since seating during the performance is disruptive to the actors and the other audience members. As audience members, we want to be attentive, so we need to turn off our cell phones and other electronic devices before the play begins. Also, open all candy wrappers before the play begins and try not to chew loudly during the production. If the show is longer than an hour and a half, there will probably be an intermission (a break—like the half time during a football game, less the half time show). The intermission will allow us to stretch, have refreshments, and make phone calls. Unless there is an emergency, it is polite to stay seated during the production. The production may be exciting and we may wish to share our enthusiasm with neighboring audience members

Probably the most important aspect of theatre is the audience.

while the play is underway, but it is best to refrain from discussion until the intermission or after the show. If writing a review of the play, we need to take notes as quietly and discreetly as possible.

It Has Its Own Jargon

As in most businesses, theatre has its own jargon. Take the word "theatre." Theatre is a building, but it can also be the play itself. Someone may ask you, "Have you seen any good theatre lately?" The "play" is the playscript—a piece of dramatic literature—"Did you read the play?" But when you go to a theatre or a non-traditional space to see "theatre" or a "play," someone may ask you, "Did you like that production?" or "Did you like that show?"

The Playscript

*The key elements that constitute a play are the **characters** and **characterization**, **plot**, **dialogue**, and **theme**.*

Playscripts or scripts are other names for the dramatic pieces of literature that we also call plays. Plays cover an almost endless list of subjects including social issues, politics, religion, love, sexuality, jealously, hatred, fear, etc. There are almost as many different genres (literary classifications of drama) as there are subjects. Major ones include musical, tragedy, comedy, melodrama, and tragicomedy. We will learn more about these and other genres in later chapters. There are several key elements that constitute a play. These are the **characters** and **characterization, plot, dialogue,** and **theme.**

Characters and Characterization

When performers are acting onstage, they become the characters in the play. In order for them to become these characters, they assume certain vocal and physical characteristics to depict the way they believe their characters would walk and speak. For example, the CEO of a high profile company has a different gait and vocal pattern than a homeless person. Performers take on the physical and vocal characteristics that they feel are appropriate to the characters because this makes their characters more lifelike. The creation of realistic characters helps the audience become more emotionally invested in the play.

Fefu and Her Friends

Production from University of Southern Mississippi. *Photograph courtesy of Steve Rouse.*

Plot

*Plot is the structure of the dramatic action which constitutes the play and contains seven elements: **exposition, point of attack, inciting incident, rising action, climax, crisis,** and **denouement** or **falling action**.*

Plot is the structure of the dramatic action which constitutes the play. In some plays there is a main plot and one or more subplots. Most theatre scholars agree that all play scripts have similar patterns using these seven elements: **exposition, point of attack, inciting** incident, rising action, climax, crisis, and **denouement** or **falling action.** The plot begins with an **exposition** which introduces us to the characters in the play and relationships that they have with one another. The exposition also "exposes" us to the series of events that led up to the characters' present situation. The **point of attack** is the beginning of the new adventure in the characters' lives. It is where the story in the play begins. The **inciting incident** propels the characters into the struggle to obtain their objectives. The **rising action** arouses our curiosity and intensifies the suspense as we observe the characters striving to accomplish their objectives despite seemingly insurmountable obstacles. These obstacles create conflict, a crucial element of drama. Characters can have internal conflicts such as struggling to reevaluate one's belief system or they can be in conflict with one another. The **climax** is the highest peak of the dramatic action during which the characters make final attempts to achieve their goals. The **crisis** is an event or discovery which ends in a final resolution. The final part of the pattern is the **denouement** (a French word meaning unraveling) or **falling action** when everything "falls into or out of place" giving the story sense of closure. Regardless of whether or not the characters have achieved their objectives, they all will have gained a better sense of who they are.

Dialogue

The dialogue is all of the words spoken by the characters. In most cases characters talk to each other, but there are some exceptions such as soliloquies. A soliloquy is a speech that a character delivers when there is no one else on stage. It is directed to his/herself, to a higher power, or the audience depending on the director's interpretation of the soliloquy. The dialogue may be written in either verse or prose. Verse is more poetic. Prose is a more commonly used style of language—everyday speech. A monologue is a long speech given by a character in the presence of other characters and it provides the speaker an opportunity to divulge personal history and present state of mind. Overall, dialogue is very important because it moves the action along and it helps to define the world in which the characters live.

Theme

The theme of the play refers to the overall meaning of the play, and a director spends a great deal of time analyzing the script in an attempt to define it. Sometimes the meaning of the play can be easily identified in the dialogue. But unless the director is the playwright or asks the playwright what he or she intended, the director's interpretation may not be exactly what the playwright intended. Theme and how it pertains to the director's concept for the production will be addressed in the following section.

How Can Production Affect the Playscript?

The production of a play is the final product that you see in the theatre. In a truly outstanding and memorable production, the **theatrical conventions** are clearly defined. There is a sense of **unity** between the design elements, the concept is **original,** the characters evoke **empathy** from the audience members, and some aspect of the **human condition** is investigated.

Act I: Scene I

Theatrical Conventions

Coyote on a Fence
Production from the University of Southern Mississippi, directed by Robin Carr. *Photograph courtesy of Fred Lloyd.*

Probably the most important theatrical convention is willing suspension of disbelief.

Probably the most important theatrical convention is willing suspension of disbelief.

It is the unspoken understanding between the audience members and the performers in which everyone pretends that what happens on stage is real. It is this agreement that allows the audience to become involved in the production and have an emotional investment in the characters.

Unification

Unification is important to a production because it ties all of the production elements such as the costumes, make-up, style of acting, pace of the production, and the scenic design—lights, sound, and set together.

Unification is important to a production because it ties all of the production elements such as the costumes, makeup, style of acting, pace of the production, and the scenic design—lights, sound, and set together. In some cases, particularly in the non-realistic theatre genres, the director works to create a production that celebrates little or no unification. However, in the majority of mainstream productions, unification is very important to the production. For example, if a play is set in the America wild west, the production would lose credibility if an actor drove a Porsche on stage. If this were to happen, the audience would stop their involvement in the lives of the characters and spend time pondering the relevance of the sports car.

Originality

Originality seems an easy element to achieve in a production, but it is more difficult than one might think. As we all know from personal experience, it takes courage to vary from the norm. Large professional theatres are sometimes skeptical about taking chances with new ideas because there is so much at stake. Broadway plays can cost millions of dollars to produce and those involved have their reputations to consider. Thus, commercial producers tend to rely on familiar genres, revising successful plays, or using well-known stars in the leading roles to sell tickets.

But the theatre needs new ideas to grow, and progress, so producers and directors occasionally take risks, some of which turn out to be very profitable. Frequently, innovative productions open at small regional theatres in order to test their popularity and make adjustments before going on to Broadway.

Empathy

Audience members want to become emotionally connected to the characters. We want to feel what they are feeling, become intimately involved in their lives and in some cases "escape" from our own lives for a while. In order to immerse ourselves in another person's life circumstances, we must have empathy for them or "step into their shoes" as the adage goes. Having empathy may be difficult, particularly if the character lives in a way that is different than our own, or if they are, in our opinion, immoral. Well-trained actors and directors are able to make even the most despicable characters empathetic.

The Silent Women

May, 2006, directed by Scott Palmer. *Photograph Courtesy of Oregon State University.*

Human Condition

As our life experiences expand, we begin to understand more about the human condition and, as we all know, one constant characteristic of human beings is imperfection. Despite one's desire to do the right thing and to improve, one cannot help but make mistakes. Since theatre "holds a mirror up to life," it can be an inspirational and encouraging experience for the audience members. They will have an opportunity to see others, not unlike themselves, meet unknown challenges, struggle and suffer, become tenacious, search for a solution, and after much persistence, come out victorious or fail miserably, all the while learning invaluable lessons.

The Critic

Constructive Criticism

Everyone is a natural critic. It is easy to say "I like it" or "I don't like it" but there are some techniques that we can employ which can make us better critics. No matter what the vocation, one of the most important attributes of a good leader is the ability to use constructive criticism. Truth be told, no one likes to be corrected. Constructive criticism first means giving at least one

genuine complement to the individual being corrected and then stating what needs to be changed. It is always best to give the correction in a way that does not put the person on the defensive. For example, people are more responsive to change when the suggestion does not begin with, "you"—"You need to file those papers." The entirety of the conversation, using constructive criticism, might go like this: "Thank you for all of your hard work. I can see how thoughtful you have been in organizing these papers. It would help me a lot if you could put them into files."

But what does constructive criticism have to do with the theatre? The theatre is like any business. It depends on teamwork in order to be successful. People need to feel as though they can trust one other and that they are safe. Using leadership techniques such as constructive criticism encourages others to improve their work habits and their self esteem. Constructive criticism is a useful skill to utilize in any business because it keeps morale high and promotes ownership of the job. The most effective professional theatre critics balance constructive criticism with critical thinking in their reviews.

Critical Thinking

As a critical thinker, it is not enough to say you liked something or you did not like something. It means specifying what you liked or disliked and giving detailed reasons as to why you felt that way. Many times, particularly in the professional theatre, the success of a production depends on a positive review from a theatre critic. If the theatre critic writes a critique of a play that isn't favorable, it can still be very useful to the production provided that it is based on critical thinking and constructive criticism. The director may read the critique and decide to make adjustments in the production, thus improving the overall quality.

The Excellent Critic

The following can improve your ability to critique a production: ethics, open-mindedness, excellent writing skills, and familiarity with the theatre.

Regardless of whether or not you intend to become a professional theatre critic, the following can improve your ability to critique a production: **ethics, open-mindedness, excellent writing skills and familiarity with the theatre.**

Ethics

It is crucial for a theatre critic to be ethical when writing critiques. Ethical means that one is honest, forthright, and conscientious. Certainly, having high ethical standards is important no matter what your career path. Sometimes in striving for success, we meet situations that challenge our ethics. We may be tempted to take short cuts that, although unethical, seem the easiest way to attain a goal, so we justify inappropriate choices and lose integrity. There are many consequences associated with unethical behavior. The most obvious is losing a job. This can make getting another job difficult or impossible, since many employers share employee work histories with other businesses. Some indiscretions can even mean fines or imprisonment.

Open-Mindedness

A theatre critic must be open-minded. Being open-minded means not judging but instead being tolerant, understanding, and emphatic. Many times a critic may not agree with the subject addressed in a play. He or she may find it morally indecent or simply inappropriate for one reason or another. But the critic cannot afford to be judgmental; instead, he or she must analyze the production for its quality. Open-mindedness is an excellent quality to have, no matter what your vocation. If colleagues are open-minded in the workplace, it allows them to take their focus off of one another's shortcomings and improves their ability to work as a team.

Excellent Writing Skills

A critic must have excellent writing skills. He or she must not only have mastered the techniques of writing but also be able to bring their review "to life" by conjuring up intriguing images and captivating readers. A well-written review will give the reader a feeling for the overall production. He or she must skillfully weave metaphor, research, opinion, and observation into the critique. The better the quality of the writing, the more credible a critic will seem.

Familiarity

Critiquing a play becomes easier as one's familiarity with theatre deepens. Some may say that theatre is a dying art form. If you have not seen or read a play before, you can probably understand why some hold that opinion. Theatre has a great deal of competition—DVD, TIVO, the Internet, reality television, film, etc. Today's generation is part of an interactive, instant society, a group who has high expectations and who demands immediate gratification. Ironically, the theatre is an ideal source of entertainment for this savvy generation.

The theatre offers what this generation craves. It is interactive, instant, and LIVE (unlike reality television shows); it is really LIVE in front of the audience so it is even more exciting than the electronic media. The more theatre you are exposed to, the more familiar you will become with it and this will improve your critical ability. Activities such as watching or reading plays, reading theatre magazines, acting in or writing plays, and watching plays on video are some ways to expose you to the theatre experience.

To appreciate the theatre, you must also have an overall knowledge about past, present, and upcoming theatre productions and the talent responsible for them. It is helpful to know what productions the artists have worked on in the past and what was said about these productions. If the artist working on a project is new to the professional world, how they become involved in the production is also valuable information. The Internet and the library will provide much of this information, but it is also helpful to read trade magazines and newspapers, particularly when the production and/or the talents are new.

Your ability to critique theatrical productions will improve as you encounter more and more theatre. This exposure gives you a standard of excellence on which to base your analysis of new productions. Most sports have a Hall of Fame where the most outstanding players are honored. These

athletic "giants" sometimes seem to defy the laws of physics and do with ease what seems humanly impossible. The theatre has similar "giants," those actors who immortalize a role, such as Laurence Olivier's portrayal of Hamlet. There are directors and designers who bring to life the world of a play so memorably that audiences have a difficult time imagining it any other way. It is the quality of these "All-Star" interpretations that all theatre artists strive to match.

Concept

Many times it can be the director's concept that creates an award winning production. The critic will carefully evaluate the concept when he or she watches a production. The concept of the play is the director's means of conveying his or her interpretation of the playwright's theme (message) to the audience. But in order to develop a concept, the director must first determine the theme of the play. The director reads the play and asks numerous questions: What is the play about? Does it have a subtle message hidden in a more obvious plot? How does the text relate to the audience? How do I want the audience to respond to the play? After the director determines the message of the play, he or she works with a design team to produce the play so that the look, the sound, and the rhythm, in their collective opinion, most effectively communicate this message to the audience.

In the first pages of a playscript, the playwright usually gives a description of the setting—where and when the play takes place. Many times a director will strive to be as truthful to this description as possible and critics frequently praise replication of the playwright's vision. But just what is the playwright's vision? It is usually impossible to know exactly what the playwright had in mind. Each person's perceptions, internal truths, and backgrounds are unique, and these differences affect the production process, thus making theatre an interpretive art form. Even if everyone working on the play has the same vision, the production can never be completely authentic because of the nature of theatre—it is not real life, it is only a play.

Sometimes critics favor a director whose concept for a production is unlike the one obviously intended by the playwright, provided, of course, that such a concept enhances the meaning of the play. Directors frequently place Shakespeare's plays in settings which are more familiar to a modern audience. The intention is to help the viewer relate to the plays. The only danger with deviating from the playwright's elected time and place is that many plays have conflicts associated with a particular time period and/or social norm. That is the case, for example, with Moliere's *Learned Ladies*. The play concerns a mother who begins one of the first salons (schools) for women in the 1600s. This premise is filled with conflict because women did not receive formal educations in the 1600s. If a director selects to set the play in the year 2009, much of the conflict is lost.

> The concept of the play is the director's means of conveying his or her interpretation of the playwright's theme (message) to the audience.

> Each person's perceptions, internal truths, and backgrounds are unique, and these differences affect the production process, thus making theatre an interpretive art form.

Writing the Critique

If the play has previously been produced, the critic will probably research (read past reviews and books that cover the play) before watching the production. He or she will research the director's, designers', and actors' professional credits. He or she will also investigate the theatre company to get an idea of what types of plays they generally produce and how successful the productions have been. When a critic watches the production, he or she will discreetly take notes. At the end of the performance, he or she may interview a few of the artists.

Soon after the production, the critic will write his or her review (critique) of the production. In most cases, the first part of the critique will generally give a brief description of the plot. Then, it will cover the other production elements such as the acting, the choices that the director made (such as the concept), the overall continuity of the production, and the scenic, costume, lighting, and sound designs. He or she may compare the production to previous productions. If the critic has a strong opinion about a past production, it is possible that objectivity may be lost in critiquing the current production.

The critique will generally give a brief description of the plot. Then, it will cover the other production elements.

Critics often make comments about the playscript in their critiques. Perhaps they feel that the characters are undefined, that the script is predictable, or that it lacks dramatic action. He or she may have an opinion about the dialogue—too prolific or too abstract. Of course, he or she may have only positive things to say about a production. Certainly, that is what the producers want. The better the critique, the more the public will come and encourage their friends to join them.

Critiquing a Production for a Class Assignment

You may want to begin by doing research, similar to the professional critic. You may even want to read the play before seeing the production. Reading it may help you gain a better understanding of the characters and remember the plot. Keep the program that you receive when you go to see the play. It will give you a list of the names of the characters and the names of the actors, designers, and the director. The program also tells you about the play's setting, and, in some cases, there are "Director's Notes" which discuss the concept and other pertinent information. The program generally contains information about upcoming productions and, if you are very lucky, coupons for these productions or nearby food establishments.

Write the paper as soon as possible after watching the play because you will want to have the production fresh in your mind. Write the paper as if you were writing for a professional journal. Have someone else proofread your paper and check your grammar and spelling (even if you used spell-check.) Reviews are best when written analytically. If you bring up an idea, the sentences that follow should give detailed examples defining your idea.

As in a professional critique, your paper should be written in two parts. The first section is a brief overview of the story line; the second is your assessment of the production—direction, acting, lighting, sound, costumes, make-up, special effects, properties, and setting. You may want to begin your review, as you would any well-written paper, with a catchy opening statement reflecting the production. Ideally, a well-written review should find some worth in the production. The following includes two outlines that are intended to encourage constructive criticism and the use of imagination, problem solving techniques, and critical thinking.

Suggested Outlines

Outline for a Play that Has Been Read

I. Brief Summary of the Plot
   A. Point of attack
   B. Inciting incident
   C. Crisis
   D. Climax
   E. Falling action

II. Theme
   A. What is the message that the playwright is trying to convey?
   B. How do you think the audience should respond to the play?

III. Main Characters
   A. Who would you cast in each of the principle roles?
   B. What characteristics and emotional qualities make these actors the best choice for the roles?

IV. Set
   A. How do you visualize the scenic elements?
   B. How does your set design enhance the production?

V. Costumes
   A. How do you visualize the principle characters' costumes?
   B. How will your costume choices enhance the performers' characterizations?

VI. Sound Effects and Music
   A. Are any sound effects needed for the production? What are they?
   B. What type of music, if any, would complement the production?

VII. Special Effects
   A. Are any unusual hand or furniture props needed? If so, what are they?
   B. Are there dance numbers or fight scenes?
   C. Are any fire, water, fog or special lighting effects needed?

VIII. Conclusion (Do not to introduce new information in the conclusion. The conclusion should summarize what you have talked about in the paper.)

Outline for a Play that Has Been Seen on Stage

I. Brief Overview of the Plot

II. Evaluating the Acting
   A. Select an actor/actress in the play and discuss a **positive** quality of his/her acting. (For example, actor Bob Smith used a high pitched voice when portraying his character, and the high pitch emphasized the emotional stress of the character.)
   B. For the same actor/actress, discuss an acting quality that could have been **improved** upon and describe why.
   C. Select another actor/actress in the play and discuss a **positive** quality of his/her acting.
   D. For the same actor/actress that you selected to talk about in "C," discuss an acting quality that could have been **improved** upon and describe why.

III. Evaluating the Set
   A. How did the set **enhance** the overall production?
   B. How could the set have been **improved**?

IV. Evaluating the Costumes
   A. How did the costumes **enhance** the portrayal of the characters? (Pick one or two costumes on which to focus your evaluation.)
   B. How could the costumes have been **improved**? (Pick one or two costumes on which to focus your evaluation.)

V. Evaluating the Lighting
   A. How did the lighting **enhance** the overall production?
   B. How could the lighting have been changed to **improve** its overall effectiveness?

VI. Evaluating the Sound (music and sound effects)
   A. How did the music and sound effects **enhance** the production?
   B. How could the music and sound effects been **improved**?

VII. Conclusion (Do not introduce new information in the conclusion. The conclusion should summarize what you have talked about in the paper.)

Theatre Critic Robert Hurwitt

Mr. Robert Hurwitt was the 1994–1995 recipient of the George Jean Nathan Award, one of the most distinguished theatre critic awards in the country. He has also received a Woodrow Wilson Fellowship. Currently he serves as theatre critic for the *San Francisco Chronicle*.

FEATURE SECTION
An Interview with Theatre Critic Robert Hurwitt

Please give a brief history of your background leading up to your becoming a theatre critic.

The short answer is that I became a critic because I was unemployed, recently separated from my wife and had two young children to feed, clothe and shelter. I turned to freelance journalism as a quick way to make money while I looked for a full-time job and, by the time I found one, I was earning more as a freelancer than the job would have paid. But, though I never planned to become a theater critic, there were many factors in my life that led to that result.

I was born in New York and grew up nearby, so I was exposed to theater at an early age. By the time I was in high school, in the 1950s, I was acting in school plays and would often take dates to Broadway shows, almost as often as movies (a front-row balcony seat cost $5 in those days). I did a lot of acting in college, at New York University, both on campus and off. I was also very active in politics, particularly in the Civil Rights Movement, and spent the summer of 1964, after graduation, as a civil rights worker in Louisiana. I did a year's graduate work at the University of California, Berkeley, receiving a Master's Degree in English Literature in '65.

After receiving my degree, I became very involved in the anti-Vietnam War movement before returning to the theater. I was a member of the San Francisco Mime Troupe as an actor, and later co-founded and directed a radical street theater company in London. At the same time, in the late '60s, I began writing for some of the new so-called "underground" papers (free weeklies, the ancestors of the "alternative" weeklies of today) and then, in London, for magazines. When my then-wife and I returned to the United States—and eventually to Berkeley—and began to raise a family, in the early '70s, I took a job with Oxford University Press for most of the rest of the decade.

I returned to the theater briefly toward the end of the '70s, as an actor and as a theater manager, then returned to weekly journalism as a freelance writer as stated above. Because of my experience, I began as a theater critic and continued to focus primarily on theater, though I wrote about a variety of other subjects (especially book reviews and coverage of science issues) to add to my income.

I was the theater critic and arts editor for the *East Bay Express* from 1979 to 1992, during which time I freelanced for many other outlets, including the *Los Angeles Times, San Francisco Examiner, California Magazine* (in which I had a monthly column on theater) and *Focus Magazine*. I also edited several volumes of a quarterly new plays anthology called "West Coast Plays." I became the theater critic for the *San Francisco Examiner* in 1992, received the George Jean Nathan Award for theater criticism and moved to the *San Francisco Chronicle* when the Hearst Corporation bought the *Chronicle* and merged the staffs of the two papers in 2000.

Theatre students are often asked to write reviews of the plays they see. Their reviews often lack organization. Could you recommend a generic outline that might serve as a guide?

I think generic outlines are dangerous and can easily lead to lazy or wooden writing. The important thing about criticism, in my view, is for the writer to engage as immediately as possible with the subject of the review.

That said, I think it's important to let your readers know within the first couple of paragraphs what it is that you're covering and what you think is the most important aspect of the production. In other words, you want to let them know—up front—the name of the play, the author, the name of the company producing it or the theater where it's playing (and when it opened), and any other essential fact. If this is a new play, that might be the most newsworthy aspect, and you'll probably spend more time analyzing the writing than the direction or acting. If it's a classic, the reverse is true. If a well-known actor is involved, you may want to lead off by talking about his or her work—which may also be true if a particular performance strikes you as more important to write about than any other element of the production.

Every review is a matter of making choices, usually some very hard choices, because you never have enough room to get into all the aspects of the show. When watching the performance, you'll want to be both as thoroughly involved in it as you can be and also keep part of yourself in reserve, so that you remember to take note of every aspect you can. Is the set working properly to support the drama in every scene? Does it create odd traffic flow problems for the director to solve? Does it lend itself to creative stage tableaux? How well does the director use it? (I've seen sets for musicals that left no room for the choreography.) How about the lighting? How well does it enhance or distract from the mood of a scene? (You'll notice some lighting designers have lit the stage without regard to the costumes, leaving actors' faces in the shadows of their hats or wigs.)

Those are just examples of things to look for. You'll almost always find that some of your observations, however well they inform your opinion, have to be left out of your review for sheer lack of space. The most important thing, I think, is to figure out what the primary theme of your review is, to state or indicate it early on, and to weave your review around that theme. Every writer is different, but I find that I can't really begin to write until I know what my first two sentences are. Once I've figured out my lead, I also pretty well know where I'm going with the rest of the review. One of my colleagues tells me he can't begin writing until he knows what his final sentence will be. It's the same principle.

University programs aspire to teach students critical thinking skills. Students who write theatre reviews have an excellent opportunity to practice using these skills. Do you agree? Is critical thinking important in your profession?

I absolutely agree. Critical thinking is the essence of my work.

If a student is interested in a career as a theatre critic, what steps should they take?

I'm really torn about how to answer this. Given the current state of the industry, with newspapers folding all over the place and the rest repeatedly downsizing their staffs, my knee-jerk reaction is to say: Don't! Run as hard as you can in the opposite direction. Take up plumbing, beekeeping, acting, psychic healing—anything but journalism. On the other hand, I certainly understand the desire to respond to an artistic experience by engaging with it verbally, and I think the practice of intelligent criticism is an important part of the cultural conversation. Critics have played a role in the development of theater for perhaps 300 years (not counting Aristotle),

and their writings serve as important resources for theater historians as well. It may be that we'll never again see so many people gainfully employed as theater critics as we did during the 20th century, but nobody knows at this point what the future of journalism will look like as it increasingly moves from newsprint to cyberspace.

Anyone interested in becoming a theater critic should give this matter serious thought, unless he or she is independently wealthy. Apart from that, I have to say that I know of no standard way of becoming a theater critic. From the 1960s through '90s, when many papers and magazines were hiring critics, some simply looked within, moving a writer over from another department; others looked to recent j-school graduates; still others, and it's my impression that this increasingly became the norm in the late '80s and early '90s, hired critics who'd distinguished themselves in the weeklies. It's my impression that the weeklies are often the best place to get started, and frequently the only place looking for new writers. That's usually freelance work, however, which means the aspiring critic has to be prepared to write about a variety of topics, to earn a living, and put in a lot of work seeking outlets for his or her work.

Apart from that, there are, I think, two key requisites for theater criticism. One is to know your subject as best you can, but never expect to feel as if you're an expert in the field. Familiarize yourself with the literature. Read all of Shakespeare, closely, and be prepared to reread the plays until you know them well. No other writer is performed a tenth as much as Shakespeare is in America. Get out and see as much theater as you can, and it's even better if you can see it from a number of angles—as an actor, stage manager, stage hand, or any other kind of participant. You want to know what goes into creating the effects and the art you see onstage. Read criticism, not just to seek models but also to think about how others have practiced the craft and what you might bring to it. And always remember, the more you learn about the art and mystery of theater, the more you'll be aware of how little you really know.

Two, is to practice your craft. A critic is first and foremost a writer. The act of criticism is one of continuous learning, as a writer as well as a student of life and the art form.

Theatre Review Written by Mr. Robert Hurwitt

Johnny watches as Mom's world unravels in 'Cryptogram'

Monday, May 14, 2007

The Cryptogram: Drama. By David Mamet. Directed by Patrick Dooley. (Through June 17. Shotgun Players, Ashby Stage, 1901 Ashby Ave., Berkeley. 75 minutes. Tickets: $17-$25. Call (510) 841-6500 or go to www.shotgunplayers.org).

It's no wonder John can't sleep. The 10-year-old is supposed to go on a weekend fishing trip with his father in the morning, and Dad hasn't come home yet. He also can't help but be aware of the unspoken tensions in a household where his mother is about to find out that her husband is leaving her. The mysteries that earn David Mamet's masterfully intense "The Cryptogram" its fitting title derive less from what transpires than from its child's-eye view of the bewildering, exciting, ominously unsettling and inexplicably secretive world of adults.

Short, dense and both deeply humane and startlingly emotionally brutal, "Cryptogram" is one of Mamet's most perfect scripts, on a par with "American Buffalo" and "Glengarry Glen Ross." The author didn't do it much justice when he staged it in New York in 1995. Barbara Damashek's West Coast premiere, two years later at the Magic Theatre, was a dramatic tightrope stretched between comic miscomprehension and tragic misunderstandings that remains one of the decade's theatrical high points in my memory.

The Shotgun Players revival that opened Friday, staged by Artistic Director Patrick Dooley at the company's Ashby Stage, doesn't plumb the script's riches as deeply nor rise to the same level of unsettling tension. But it's a more than credible effort that captures more than enough of the play's, yes, cryptic undercurrents to make for strong, edgy and bracingly evocative theater.

Mamet's most autobiographical play, "Cryptogram" is made up of three short, subtext-crammed scenes that contain one of the best parts for a woman and one of the most demanding for a child in contemporary theater. It's also disarmingly simple on the surface. It takes place on three evenings in 1959, when family "normalcy" was at a premium, divorce was a relative rarity and many matters weren't openly discussed, especially in front of the children.

John (seventh-grader Gideon Lazarus) can't sleep. His mother Donny (Zehra Berkman) is distracted with his problems, the pending fishing trip and the underlying tensions in a marriage she doesn't know is ending. Her and her absent husband Robert's best friend, the ineffectual, well-meaning closeted gay Del (Kevin Clarke), is hanging about trying to help deal with John while nervously attempting to conceal how much he knows of Robert's plans.

Dooley and his actors had trouble on opening night establishing the rhythms of the crisp, tentative broken sentences and pregnant pauses with which Mamet builds the mostly unspoken drama (the sometimes rushed performance came in a good five minutes short of its usual 80). But the script's masterfully edgy, disturbing undercurrents broke through soon enough, with Clarke providing ably awkward, guilt-ridden support to Berkman's perplexed, then stunned and increasingly angry Donny and Lazarus' engagingly smart, probing, dumbfounded and deeply worried John.

Dooley frames it well on Lisa Clark's black-walled living room set adorned with '50s furnishings and kitsch. Berkman is gripping as Donny wrestles with mounting anger at the betrayals of all the men in her life. The sight of the pajama-clad Lazarus at the top of the dark stairs becomes the increasingly fraught focus of an elliptically acute drama of the terrors of childhood and the cruelties we inflict on those we love.

Credit Line: From *San Francisco Chronicle*, May 14, 2007 by Robert Hurwitt. Copyright © 2007 San Francisco Chronicle. Permission conveyed through Copyright Clearance Center.

Networking

Networking is getting to know and befriend a lot of different people so that you can share information with one another. It is through networking that people hear about job openings and, if you think about it, wouldn't you rather work with your friends? We have often heard, "It's who you know."

Networking is one of the principle ways that theatre practitioners obtain new jobs. In many cases, new productions are developed during meals, receptions, and other social gatherings. Competition is stiff no matter what your career so you want to "be in the know" as much as possible. This means being outgoing and greeting everyone with an upbeat and positive attitude. The hours are long and there are many difficulties to resolve when a production is in progress, so those with the most agreeable personalities are the most valuable employees.

Networking is a little intimidating at first, especially if you are shy or if you find it difficult to remember others' names. When a person hears his or her name, it is music to their ears. With that in mind, you want to work on becoming a person who remembers names easily. When you meet a stranger, say his or her name as many times as you can during your initial conversation. When you get a chance, write the name down or collect a business card from the person. Put the name and any other information you learn about the person in an index card file. That way when you see that person again, you will be able to have a personal discussion.

Summary

Theatre is a fun, interactive art form that is diverse and inclusive. Theatre reveals our history and celebrates our continuing development as a global society. It creates ongoing opportunities for audience members to examine humanity—its strengths and its weaknesses. Theatre bridges the gaps between people who have different interests and beliefs. The theatre, in its diversity, can teach us how to think "outside of the box." It helps us to devise new solutions for existing problems in our society, in our homes, and in our workplace.

The audience is a key player in the theatre. Without the audience, theatre would not be the communal experience that has been its hallmark for many centuries. Together, audience members and theatre artists embrace a willing suspension of disbelief in order to bring intriguing stories to life on stage. In order to produce a play, it takes many artists such as playwrights, directors, performers, and designers.

Many of the techniques that theatre practitioners use are beneficial to anyone striving toward success in another career—critical thinking, constructive criticism, and networking. In addition, qualities associated with well-respected theatre professionals—high ethical standards, open-mindedness, and excellent writing skills—are appreciated in all vocations. All of these qualities will enhance career development; and, after a long day at work, we can all go to the theatre and find a haven in which to relax, meet new people, and celebrate life.

Theatre in Your Career

Networking can be beneficial to your career both as a student and as a working professional. The following is a daily in-class activity that reinforces networking.

   I. Students are to spend a moment before class thinking about a recent positive or negative experience they would like to share with their classmates.
  II. During the calling of the roll, the instructor will ask if anyone has something to share. Many times there will be another student who has a solution to a problem that is presented. For example, a student may be having difficulty in one of his or her other courses. There may be someone who can recommend a study group.

This activity reinforces networking, builds ensemble, and encourages students to be inclusive, thereby creating an atmosphere of trust and support.

Active Learning Assignment
"Bringing Theatre to Life"

I. **Tasting Theatre/Getting Involved**

Since the roots of the theatre came from of the necessity to relay stories to one another, the first thing we need to establish in class is a communal atmosphere. The following is an in-class theatre assignment:

A. Pair up the students.

B. Have them ask each other some questions such as:

   1. What is your favorite food, music, hobby?

   2. What is your major field of study and what year are you?

   3. What made you take this class?

C. Finally, have the students come to the front of the class in their pairs and tell the class about each other.

This and other exercises in the text will help to foster teamwork, networking, community, a sense of belonging, ownership in one's education, interpersonal communication skills, pride, empathy, and the reduction of public speaking anxiety, while also demonstrating theatre to the entire group, in its most basic form—storytelling.

II. **Breaking the Ice-Improvisation**

Other important aspects of theatre include: being disciplined, following directions, trusting, using the imagination, committing, listening, and entertaining others. The following is an in-class assignment:

A. Invite two students to the front of the class who are willing to play a game similar to the games played on "Whose Line Is It Anyway?".

B. Explain the rules of our game, *Breaking the Ice-Improvisation*.

   1. You can't ask questions of your partner during the game because it forces them to come up with all the information and questions do not help the scene to progress. For example:

      Student One: "I am your mother, you took my car without asking and while you were driving it you got in an accident!"

      Student Two: "What?"

2. You can't leave the room.

3. You have to accept what the other person has told you to be the truth. For example:

   Student One: "I am your mother, you took my car without asking and while you were driving it you got in an accident!"

   Student Two: "I am sorry, Mom. I promise I'll never do it again."

   Student One: "You're grounded!"

4. This would be an example of not accepting the truth:

   Student One: "I am your mother, you took my car without asking and while you were driving it you got in an accident!"

   Student Two: "You're not my mother!"

5. The scene should always begin with a clear objective and a clear relationship in the first sentence. An example would be:

   Student One: "I am your mother, you took my car without asking and while you were driving it you got in an accident!"

6. Another example is:

   Student One: "I know we have been married for ten years, but I really think getting divorced would be best."

7. Before the students begin, remind them to speak loudly, clearly, and attempt to keep their face toward the audience/class during the "game"/improvisational scene.

C. Now you are ready to begin.

1. The first student speaks the opening line, "I am your mother, you took my car without asking and while you were driving it you got in an accident!"

2. The scene continues until it reaches a natural peak or "tag line," then the instructor calls freeze and another student in the class takes the place of one of the two students.

3. The new student begins the scene with an opening line that clearly states an entirely different conflict and relationship than the previous scene.

4. The scene continues until it reaches a natural peak or "tag line," then the instructor calls freeze and another student in the class takes the place of one of the two students.

5. After the students have caught on to the game they may want to call freeze without the instructor prompting.

6. Play as long as you like.

This exercise stresses conflict and relationship—two of the most important components that make up dramatic action.

Theatre: In the Beginning— The Development of the Western Theatre

Rituals: An Early Form of Theatre

In modern terms theatre can be defined as one or more actors using their bodies and voices to rehearse an activity mimicking real life behavior and performing what they have rehearsed in front of an audience. Primitive man's speech was rudimentary; thus, the primary form of communication was mime. This dramatic "acting out" of daily events or tribal needs may be considered an early form of theatre. The primary difference between the modern concept of theatre and the rituals of primitive man is that the latter was intended to accomplish a specific end result beyond entertainment.

For example, early civilizations living off the land relied on hunting and gathering to survive. These early people did not comprehend life's inevitable mortality. They assumed that they were investing annually in a "new lease on life" which was dependent upon the seasons and supernatural forces. Spring and summer brought the bounty which insured their survival; fall and winter destroyed much of the food supply and created hardship. In an effort to insure their bounty and stave off hardship, the tribal communities performed seasonal ceremonial rituals.

These rituals were intended to rejuvenate the humans and their environment through the assistance of supernatural forces. Theses ritualistic activities can be divided into two categories: *Kenosis* (Emptying) and *Plerosis* (Filling). *Kenosis* involved fasts and mortification which symbolized the end of the previous "lease on life." *Plerosis* symbolized the renewal of life through ceremonial mass mating and special incantations intended to promote both human fertility and fertility of the land. These seasonal rituals were meant to represent an ideal existence for both the living and the supernatural. The representational aspects of the ceremonies make them an early form of drama.

Even the manner in which these early humans performed rituals had a theatrical quality. They decorated themselves by painting their faces and bodies and wearing special articles of clothing. For example, a man performing a hunting ritual might cover his entire body with an animal hide and don a mask bearing the likeness of the same animal. These rituals typically included music, dancing, and chanting and were usually performed before or around a fire. All of these ritualistic elements have modern theatrical equivalents.

Theatrical Ritual in Modern Society

Religious and ceremonial rituals still play an important part in modern culture. They may be termed rituals because, similar to ancient rituals, they are performed in order to achieve a specific goal, such as a wedding in which the result is spiritual and legal partnership. Other modern rituals include baptism, graduation, funerals, and social fraternity/sorority inductions. Most of these modern rituals involve the wearing of special articles of clothing, appropriate music, and the decorating of the location, all of which give them a representational dramatic quality.

Theatre as we know it grew out of the rituals celebrated by primitive tribes. Those tribes that settled in a particular location achieved more stability than nomadic groups and eventually began performing their rituals for

Theatre, as we know it grew out of the rituals celebrated by primitive tribes.

pleasure rather than for survival. As these stable communities multiplied, the tribes became aware and concerned with their lineage. Thus, theatre became a means of imparting their history and culture to others.

The ancient Greek society is a prime example of primitive tribes developing into a highly sophisticated civilization. Their prosperity allowed them the time to express themselves through the arts. Many Greek literary works have survived and portions of these are based on the ceremonial rituals that were performed in the early stages of Greek societal development. Theodor H. Gaster uses this example from Euripides' *The Baccahae*. Lines 64–169 are essentially a stylized version of a ritual chant:

> Who walks upon the road? Who walks upon the road?
> Who bides within his house? Let every such make way; let
> every mouth be hushed in hallowe'd devotion;
> for I will chant the old time-honored hymn of Dionysus!
>
> O happy he, by fortune blest,
> who knows the mystic rites divine,
> who makes his life one long austerity,
> who steeps his soul in scared revelry,
> who, amid the sacred ceremonies of purgation,
> serves as bacchanal on the hills
> and as a votary in the revels of Cybele, that Great Mother,
> who tosses high the thyrsus, his head with ivy crowed,
> who ministers unto Dionysus!

The ancient Greek society is the prime example of primitive tribes that developed into a highly sophisticated civilization. Their prosperous settlement allowed them time to express themselves through the arts.

Active Learning Assignment
"Bringing Theatre to Life"

I. **Tell a Story**

This in-class learning activity reminds us that storytelling (one of the early forms of drama) is still an important part of our culture. A few days prior to this activity, each student should recall a cherished memento from home, such as a picture, a childhood toy, or an article of clothing. The memento should summon up a story that has special meaning or significance for the individual. On the day of the in-class assignment, the student is allowed some class time to outline a story based on his or her memento. The story's outline should include a clear beginning, middle, and end. With the outline (in hand, if desired) each student is encouraged to share his or her story with the class.

The Greek's Spiritual Beliefs

The Greek Gods

The ancient Greeks believed that there were 12 all powerful gods and goddesses who controlled their destinies; and, if they were not respectful toward these supernatural beings, they would be reprimanded for their insolence. The twelve gods and goddesses included: Zeus, the sky god and leader of all of the deities; his wife, Hera, the goddess of marriage; Aphrodite, goddess of love; Artemis, the

goddess of nature; Athena, the goddess of wisdom and war; Demeter, the goddess of grain and the harvest; Apollo, the god of the sun; Ares, the god of war; Hephaestus, the god of fire; Hermes, the messenger of the gods; Poseidon, the god of the sea; and Dionysus, the god of wine and fertility.

These gods and goddesses did not love humans unconditionally; they expected to be worshiped. In return for protection and good fortune, the ancient Greeks attempted to please the gods and goddesses. They sacrificed animals, offered prayers, built beautiful sanctuaries, and held elaborate festivals in the god's honor. Oracles were located in major cities in an attempt to communicate with the deities. Seers and priests consulted these oracles seeking divine advice and intervention on matters of marriage, children, and finances. The gods and goddesses always answered in riddles, but the ancient Greeks readily accepted these curious responses because it was believed mere mortals were incapable of fully understanding the powerful beings.

The gods and goddesses were thought to possess human qualities in appearance, emotional capacity, and personality. For example, quick temper and jealously were thought to be characteristics of all these deities. Mythological stories detailing love affairs between gods and goddesses and humans underlined the belief that these deities were all powerful. One myth involves Zeus and his wife, Hera. The story says that Zeus fell madly in love with a mortal Theban princess, Semele. Wanting to prove to Semele that his love for her was true, Zeus swore by the river Styx that anything Semele asked of him he would do. Hera overheard his promise to the river Styx and, realizing that no god could reverse an oath made to the river Styx, used her powers to have Semele request that Zeus show himself in his majestic, god-like form. Zeus knew that Semele would be killed by the bright burning light of his true form but could not break his oath. Semele, pregnant with Zeus' child, died as she gazed upon his image; but Zeus saved the child who became the god Dionysus.

The Religious Celebration of Dionysus

Dionysus was believed to be the god of nature and, like nature, he died every winter and was reborn the following spring. The winter Dionysian rituals symbolize the god's suffering and death while the spring rituals rejoice in his rebirth with the worshippers imbibing wine and frolicking in ecstasy. Dionysus was highly revered and inspired a cult of women worshippers called Maenads (or Bacchantes) who took special pains to honor him. These women would begin their celebration of Dionysus by reveling in the woods, eating nuts and berries, and drinking fresh milk and wine. As their ritual continued, the women, impassioned with wine and their love of Dionysus, would scream in high pitched voices, tear apart live creatures with their bare hands and devour them.

Dithyrambs

Dithyrambs were originally passionate lyrical poems that were sung and danced by choruses of 50 men or boys to honor Dionysus, but they were eventually extended to praise other gods, goddesses, and even mortal heroes.

The Greek historian, Herodotus, credits Arion of Lesbos (c. 620 B.C.) as being the first poet to introduce spoken lines into the dithyramb.

Thespis, of Icaria, in Attica

The Greek poet, Thespis, is considered to be the "father" of drama since he introduced the first lines for an actor into one of his plays, which included a traditional chorus and its leader. Although none of Thespis' plays survived, his name is a part of our modern vocabulary—Thespian, meaning actor. He also won the prize—possibly a goat—at the first tragic play contest in Athens. The word *tragedy* or *tragos* means "goat-song" in Greek.

Dionysian Festivals

Festival Fees and Events

There were four Dionysian festivals each year, and since festivals were the only places where plays were produced, they were essential to the development of drama. Two festivals were especially important. The City Dionysia was the spring festival and it seems to have featured tragedies; The Lenaea was the winter festival and it spotlighted comedies. Each festival lasted five or six days, and originally no admission fee was charged. A few years after the festivals' beginnings, a small admission fee was instituted; but, in order to insure that everyone could afford to attend the festivals, the government established a fund which provided tickets for anyone who applied. Once an audience member was admitted into the theatre, he could sit anywhere he wished except for the center seats in the first row. These were reserved for the priests of Dionysus, the city officials, and their guests.

The first day of the City Dionysia began with a processional to the theatre. On each of the three days that followed, a trilogy with its accompanying satyr-play was performed in the morning and comedies were played in the afternoon. The last day or two of the festival was dedicated to dithyrambic contests. The entire festival was judged by an elected jury who awarded the prizes.

The salaries of the "supers/dumb persons" (background actors) and the three principal actors were paid by the state. The other expenses such as the chorus were underwritten by a *choragus*. The *choragus* was chosen from a group of wealthy citizens who were called upon to finance public projects such as equipping a warship or funding a play. It was an honor to be selected as the *choragus,* and when a tragedy won the competition, the prize was given jointly to the poet and the *choragus*.

The Greek poet, Thespis, is considered to be the "father" of drama since he introduced the first lines for an actor into one of his plays, which included a traditional chorus and its leader.

There were four Dionysian festivals each year, and since festivals were the only places where plays were produced, they were essential to the development of drama.

Selection of the Poets (Playwrights) and Actors

It was a distinct honor to be chosen as one of the three poets competing at the City Dionysia. First, an official evaluated submissions from numerous poets. If the poet's work was well-known, he could present the official with a short scenario of his work, but if the poet was a newcomer, he needed to provide the entire script. Once the three poets were selected, they would draw lots for a *choragus*.

In the early festivals, the poet was also his own chief actor (the plays had only a single actor and the chorus). Acting became a profession shortly after Aeschylus added a second actor; Sophocles added a third; and the number of actors in tragedy never exceeded three. Naturally, an actor could play multiple roles. The first professional actors always worked with the same poets, but eventually the actors were assigned to the poets by lot.

Acting became a profession shortly after Aeschylus added a second actor; Sophocles added a third actor; and the number of actors in tragedy never exceeded three.

Censorship

No formal rules were in place to censor a dramatist's works, but if a play seriously offended a public official, the writer could receive a special punishment. For example, Phrynichus' play, *The Capture of Miletus,* recalled a very painful historical incident. The playwright was fined and the play was not allowed to be produced again. Comedy frequently lampooned public figures, but there is no definitive evidence that it was ever censored. Certainly, it would have been possible for the officials to censor plays by simply not selecting them for production, but it appears that the choices were fair and based strictly on literary merit.

The Theatre and Its Scenic Elements

The Stage and the Theatre

Early Greek theatres in the 5th Century B.C. consisted of the orchestra, a large flat circular area at the base of a hill, a small building, the *skene,* at the back of the orchestra, and the hill itself where the audience sat (the *theatron*). In the beginning, audience members sat on the ground, later on wooden benches, and finally, in the Hellenistic Age, on stone benches. The largest and best known theatre was in Athens. It was located at the bottom of the hill where the Acropolis was built. This theatre was called the Theatre of Dionysus.

The area where the actors performed was probably on ground level in the orchestra, thus allowing the chorus members and the actors to interact more easily. In the later Hellenistic period, the chorus' role diminished and the actors' playing space was a raised stage. The *skene* in the back of the orchestra served primarily as a dressing room, but it had at least one door which made it possible for the building to double as scenery. The actor could indicate that he had to go into the "palace" or the "cave" and exit through

Greek theatres in the 5th Century B.C. were composed of the orchestra, a large flat circular area at the base of a hill, and the hill itself where the audience sat (the theatron). The best-known theatre was in Athens and was located on the slope of the hill where the Acropolis was located. It was called the Theatre of Dionysus.

Illustration by Christopher Domanski

the door. Eventually, three doors became the norm, and additional entrances and exits could be made by using the *paradoi* (entrances into the theatre) on either side of the *skene*. The actors could also access the roof of the *skene* by means of a ladder.

There was no scenery, as we think of it, but rather a permanent painted background that was used for the duration of the play. Scene-painting was called *skenographia* and was done on large panels which were hung on the *skene*. It is probable that new *skenographia* were created for each production, and they may even have been changed during the production in order to add variety.

The Flying Machine

Special effects were used and were undoubtedly popular with audiences. One of the most exciting effects was the *mechane*. This was a large crane that could raise actors into the air so that they could "fly" as if they were gods. Its overuse led to the term *deus exmachina* or "god of the machine." The term has since come to mean a contrived ending.

Costumes for Tragedies

All actors wore masks constructed of linen and cork or wood. These helped to clarify personality traits and to indicate the sex of the character (all actors were male.) The principal tragic characters wore two-layered, elaborately decorated robes. The chorus members' costumes reflected nationality and occupation. Actors in the fifth century wore soft boots that extended up their legs. It is thought that Aeschylus may have been the first to include shoes as a part of the costume.

Costumes for Comedies

Old Comedy actors wore masks for the same reasons that the tragic actors wore them. They also wore a short *chiton* (tunic) with a red leather phallus attached. The chorus members wore costumes that defined their role in the play. For example, the chorus was dressed as wasps in Aristophanes play, *The Wasps*.

Dramatists

Aeschylus (525–456 B.C.)

Aeschylus is considered one of the greatest and most influential dramatists of all time. He added a second actor to his plays which made his tragedies more theatrical than others. In earlier plays, the chorus had been the focus, but because he added a second actor and reduced the chorus from fifty to twelve, the focus shifted to the actors and resulted in more complex plots. Aeschylus' tragedies dramatized a crisis within a particular myth rather than simply retelling the entire myth. The characters and their relationships with other characters in his plays were by no means subtle. In every scene, the characters are thrust into intense conflict. Good examples of these character-driven conflicts are seen in *Agamemnon*. *Agamemnon* is one part of the only extant Greek trilogy, *The Orestia*.

Sophocles (496–406 B.C.)

Sophocles created a balance between the chorus and the actors (it is thought that he added the third actor) and championed character-driven conflicts in his plays—between two characters, between a circumstance and a character, or between a character and an inner struggle. These conflicts infused his plays with tension. Sophocles' characters are carefully crafted with complex inner lives and diverse personality traits. His plays have great depth but also maintain continuity so that all of the intricate details fit together beautifully. His use of the chorus (he used a fifteen-member chorus and later dramatists retained the number) was reduced, but the choral contributions that remained were pertinent and emotionally charged. Sophocles wrote numerous plays including *Oedipus Rex, Oedipus at Coloneus, Antigone,* and *Electra.* He was a popular poet and won 18 prizes at the City Dionysia.

Euripides (484–406/7)

Euripides won only five prizes but wrote a total of 92 tragedies. Seventeen of these are extant and include *Alcestis, Medea, Hippolytus, Children of Heracles, Andromache, Hecuba, Heracles Furens, The Suppliants, Ion, Electra, The Trojan Women, Iphigenia in Tauris, Helen, The Phoenician Women, Orestes, The Bacchae, Iphigenia and Aulis,* and *Cyclops* (the only surviving complete satyr-play.) His dramas are anchored in the emotional plight of an individual—loves, losses, jealousies, hatreds, and passions. Euripides probably preferred these kinds of topics because of his unconventional interest in what is now called abnormal psychology. His plays are inventive in style—in fact, some are considered tragicomedies or romantic drama rather than tragedy. Euripides invented the formal "prologue," which essentially relays to the audience what has happened between the characters up to the point when the drama begins. It was not until after Euripides death that he was appreciated. Sophocles honored him by costuming a chorus in black to mourn his passing.

Aristophanes (c. 448–c. 380 B.C.)

The "revels" were an important part of fertility rites and included singing, dancing, and the use of defamatory or vulgar language to joke with the audience. The fact that the word comedy means "revel-song" implies that comedy was derived from early fertility rituals. In fact, Old Comedy has many qualities associated with the "revels." The only remaining Old Comedy plays are those of Aristophanes. His early plays were based on anything and everything in the Athenian society from prominent public servants to religious beliefs. All subjects and people were fair game for Aristophanes' satire. His plays combine obscenity, fantasy, burlesque, wit, and parody but also possess a lyrical quality. In *The Clouds,* Socrates was personally attacked and it is said that the philosopher responded by standing up in the theatre so that the audience might compare the real Socrates with the stage version.

The Ecclesiazusae (392 B.C.) and *The Plutus* (388 B.C.) were Aristophanes' last two plays and they show a much different style than his previous comedies. They are still very political but are less personal. The satire shifts from individuals to social and political ideas such as feminism. Some scholars categorize these plays as Middle Comedy; but, by the middle of the fourth century, Greek comic writing had morphed into what is called New Comedy.

Menander (c. 342–292 B.C.)

Menander was the most prominent writer of New Comedy. Fragments of four of his plays were found in 1905 and a complete play, *The Grouch*, in 1959; but before these discoveries, the only knowledge of Menander was from his influence on succeeding authors such as the Roman playwright Terence. New Comedy is essentially situation comedy with hints of intrigue and romance. It focuses on contemporary life and has an urban feel and philosophy. Unlike Old Comedy, it did not indulge in satire or burlesque. The plays are fluent in form and overall style and include sympathetic characters. The eloquence of Menander's story line leaves no room for a chorus. In fact, Menander did not find choruses to be of much value except for transitions between the acts of his plays. His plays may lack choruses but they include numerous stock characters often used by later writers of comedy.

Hellenistic Age

The period from fourth century B.C. to the first century B.C. is referred to as the Hellenistic Age in order to note the passing of Greek culture to the non-Greeks that Alexander the Great (356 B.C.–323 B.C.) had conquered. During the Hellenistic Age, the major theatrical contribution was the preservation of the classical Greek tragedies, but there were several notable changes in theatre production. For example, the actors' footwear changed from the soft boot with a flat sole to a boot called a *kothornos* which had a sole that was eight to ten inches high. The use of theatrical spectacles within a performance became more frequent. Most important, the theatres were constructed of stone and the actors were confined to a raised stage while the chorus used the orchestra.

The fourth century B.C. to the first century B.C. is referred to as the Hellenistic Age. There were several notable changes in theatre production. Most important, the theatres began to be constructed of stone and the actors were confined to a raised stage while the chorus used the orchestra.

Aristotle (384/3 B.C.–322 B.C.)

The philosopher Aristotle was born in the small village of Stagira located on the eastern coast of the peninsula of Chalcidice in Thrace. His father, Nicomachus, was the court physician. When Aristotle was eighteen years old, he was sent to Athens where he spent time at the Academy of Plato. When Plato died, Aristotle went to the court of Hermias, the ruler of Assos, and Atarneus in Mysia in Asia Minor.

He became Alexander the Great's tutor at Phillip the Great's request in 343/2. Alexander studied with Aristotle until becoming regent for his father in 340. After Phillip died in 335/4, Aristotle returned to Athens, and over the next twelve years, devoted himself to his studies and to teaching. It was during this time that he composed the works that have become his legacy. Most important to the theatre was *The Poetics*.

The Poetics analyzes the function and structure of tragedy and is thought to be one of two books. The other is thought to have focused on comedy, but it did not survive.

In *The Poetics*, Aristotle defines tragedy as possessing the following elements: Plot, characters, thought, diction, melody, and spectacle, with plot being the most important. Plot is action. According to Aristotle, plot must be a complete "whole" made up of several incidents so closely connected that, if two of these incidents are reversed or if one incident is removed, the "whole"

becomes disconnected and confusion ensues. Aristotle considered spectacle the least artistic element because it has to do only with the arrangement of the actors on the stage.

Neo-classical critics, particularly French critics of the seventeen and eighteen centuries, bent Aristotle's theories to suit themselves. In fact, their interpretations of *The Poetics* are often so far removed from Aristotle's original intention that they appear ludicrous. Even the most rudimentary of Aristotle's ideas were misinterpreted—for instance, "The Three Unities." Aristotle clearly discusses one of these in *The Poetics*. He insists on the "Unity of Action," but his brief comments regarding "The Unity of Time" and "The Unity of Place" were twisted by the seventeenth and eighteenth century neoclassicists.

Active Learning Assignment
"Bringing Theatre to Life"

I. Writing and Performing Your Own Greek Tragedy

This activity begins by first viewing in class approximately three-fourths of a video of one of the Greek tragedies. Next, the class will be divided into groups of 10 to 15. Each group is to invent its own ending for the tragedy and then write and stage that conclusion—paying close attention to the major Greek conventions such as the chorus. Then, each group will perform its conclusion for the class. After the performances, the class will vote on its favorite ending. Finally, the entire class will watch the conclusion of the play and compare the original ending with the student creations.

Critical Thinking in Class Discussion

I. How close were you to the real ending?

II. Did one of the groups have a better idea of how the play should end?

III. What was it like to create a dramatic story for your peers?

IV. How did you feel about working in a group?

V. Are there any rituals or performances in modern society which compare to the Greek theatre?

Roman Theatre

After the Romans conquered Greece in the third century B.C., the Roman gods and goddesses merged with those of the Greeks. For example, the Greek goddess Aphrodite and the Roman goddess Venus became one and the same, and Dionysus became known as Bacchas. Like the Greeks, the Romans instituted public celebrations honoring their gods and goddesses. These were known as "The Games" (*Ludi*) and contained a variety of entertainments such as boxing, rope-dancing, and eventually, performances of plays. In 240 B.C., Livius Andronicus translated the first Greek tragedy into Latin and presented it at the public games; but Romans were fond of performances that included comedy and a substantial amount of spectacle. As a result, it is thought that Livius Andronicus rewrote parts of the play to suit Roman tastes. His introduction of Greek tragedy was very well received and it quickly became a popular form of entertainment. Many Roman writers began to translate Greek tragedies and comedies, but they took a good deal of artistic license and reconfigured them to please their audiences. The great comic playwright Terence was the exception. Even while molding the plays for Roman audiences, he took great care to preserve the artistic merit of the originals.

The Games (Ludi)

Roman religious festivals were called games or *ludi*. Since the Romans believed that their gods enjoyed the same things that they enjoyed, the festivities included religious ceremonies, sacrifices, animal baiting, acrobatics, and chariot races, as well as plays. The performances began in the early morning and concluded by mid-day. There was no admission fee and anyone could attend, including slaves, women, and children. The audiences tended to be unruly because numerous entertainments were presented simultaneously. In his prologue *The Carthaginian*, Plautus gives an idea of the typical Roman audience:

> Let no worn out prostitutes sit in the front part of the auditorium, nor the guards make any noise with their weapons, nor the ushers move about in front of spectators or show anyone to seats while the actors are onstage. . . . Don't let slaves take up seats meant for free men . . . , let nursemaids keep little children at home. . . . Let matrons . . . refrain from gossiping.

The Amphitheatres (Amphitheatrum)

Roman amphitheatres were elliptical shaped structures with tiered seating similar to modern football stadiums. The seats surrounded a center arena which was used for gladiatorial combats, chariot races, wild beast hunts, and even sea battles (aqueducts were used to flood the entire arena to accommodate small warships). The first amphitheatre was built by Julius Caesar in 46 B.C., and in 80 A.D. the Coliseum was constructed in Rome. It held 87,000 spectators and much of it still stands, but amphitheatres did not accommodate theatre performances. These were performed in front of other public buildings such as temples.

Roman amphitheatres were elliptical-shaped structures with tiered seating similar to modern football stadiums. Amphitheatres did not accommodate theatre performances. These were performed in front of other public buildings such as temples.

Roman Actors

The most important quality the actor possessed was his voice (all actors were male.) It was imperative that he be heard and understood. Many Roman actors complained of the strain to their voices caused by performing in huge open air theatres filled with large crowds of unruly and loud audience members. Acting was not a highly respected vocation, but some actors became quite famous and, as a result of their fame, wealthy. Roscius was the most highly respected actor in Rome.

The Costumes

A theatre company staff member known as the *choragus* made all of the arrangements for the costumes. The actors wore *persona* (masks) so that a

single actor could play multiple roles. For the most part, the costumes reflected clothing worn in daily life, although alterations were made for comic effect. Since most of the characters were stereotypes, certain colors became associated with certain characters. For example, slaves were costumed in red and courtesans were dressed in yellow—both wore matching wigs.

Producing the Play

The authorities responsible for the public games designated a producer who commissioned the play and also arranged all of the necessary details for its performance. Of course, the Greek tragedies were very popular but so were new Roman plays. New plays were purchased outright from their authors. If a Greek drama was performed, it was sure to be one that included an exciting plot, ostentatious characters, and horrifically gory scenes.

Roman Comic Playwrights

The Romans may have relied heavily on the Greeks for their tragedies, but two of their own poets, Plautus and Terence, made significant contributions in comedy. Both used Greek New Comedy (usually plays by Menander) as their model. Their innovative approaches, equal in quality yet different in style, have been used as models for comedy throughout the centuries.

Plautus (?–184 B.C.)

Plautus was the son of a poor Umbrian farmer. At one time he worked as a miller and it is said that he wrote three of his plays while at the mill. Plautus' world demanded that everyone respect and obey the *Patria Potestas* (the Father's Authority.) In most of his comedies, sons are ridiculed by their fathers because of intolerable behavior. Edith Hamilton provides an example in Platus' *Comedy of Asses*. The basic premise is that a young man is in love with a girl to whom his father is also attracted. Here is a short section of dialogue:

> *Father:* Come, my boy, you don't mind, do you if she sits 'longside o' me?
> *Son:* (dolefully) I am your son. I know my duty, father. I'll not say a word.
> *Father:* Young men must be modest, son.
> *Son:* Oh, yes, I do know what you want.
> *Father:* (briskly) Well, fill up—good wine, good talk. No filial awe, my boy, for me. It's your love I want.
> *Son:* (more doleful) Of course, I give you both as a son should.
> *Father:* I'll believe it when you take that look off.
> *Son:* Father, I am sad. It isn't that I don't wish everything you wish. But I really love her. Any other girl I wouldn't mind.
> *Father:* But it happens I want this one. Come, tomorrow she'll be yours. That's not much to ask.
> *Son:* (wretchedness complete) You know I want to please you first.

Ms. Hamilton also notes that Plautus makes fun of every person and every one of the gods. And if one of his jokes did not receive a laugh, he might have one actor call out to another.

> "Softly now, speak softly.
> Don't disturb the pleasant slumbers of the audience
> I beg."

Plautus' comedies have little plot. They typically begin with a prologue that reveals the simple plot to the audience and mentions that the characters are completely unaware of the plot. Although this approach made it impossible for suspense to build or surprise to occur, Plautus' comedies were certainly not devoid of irony. His *Menaechmi* provides an example of this. The story revolves around identical twins that are too dim to see the resemblance. The audience is in a superior position because it can clearly see that it is the characters' similar physical appearance that is causing the ridiculous confusion and frustration. Shakespeare makes use of comic irony in most of his comedies, including *Measure for Measure* and *The Comedy of Errors* (based on Plautus' *Menaechmi*.)

The use of irony is easily traced back to the Greek tragedies and to Menander who appears to utilize irony as a means of creating comic situations. This suggests that Plautus copied Menander, but Plautus is usually given credit as the first playwright to use irony as a comic device. It is one of the most effective ways to create comedy and has been used by many playwrights throughout the centuries.

Terence (185 B.C.–159 B.C.)

Terence was born a slave in one of the Roman colonies in Africa. He was fortunate to grow up in a house in which his master recognized his talents, provided him an education, and freed him. Terence was so talented that he won a place in a small circle of wealthy, well-educated, young men. It was this group for which Terence wrote his plays. Sometimes, outsiders, jealous of his success, accused his friends of writing the plays for him. Terence, however, was a graceful individual and responded by simply praising his friends for their help and encouragement.

Like Plautus, Terence was raised in a world where a father's wishes were expected to be honored; but, unlike Plautus, Terence's fathers are admirable and considerate. Terence admired well-bred, congenial persons, and the fathers in his plays exhibit these qualities. Edith Hamilton provides this example in *The Roman Way:* "Does my darling son want that pretty flute girl? The dear boy—I'll buy her for him at once. Extravagant do you call him? Well, all young men are like that. I was myself. I'll gladly pay his debts." Terence based his plays on Greek New Comedy, particularly the work of Menander, whom he strived to equal in his writing. Unlike Plautus, Terence's comedy derives from the suspense in his plots and the surprise that each character experiences when he learns the true seriousness of the situation that he is in. Of course, Terence was a talented comic writer who was capable of writing jokes, but his care and concern for well-bred, considerate people resulted in a sophisticated style of comedy. Terence's use of suspense has influenced comic writing for centuries.

The First Female Playwright: Hrotswitha (935–c.1001)

Terence's comedies were read in European monasteries and inspired a nun named Hrotswitha, from the Benedictine monastery at Gandersheim in northern Saxony, to write her own plays and poems. She was the niece of the Emperor of the Holy Roman Empire, Otto I (912–973). Thus, she was educated and had a great deal of access to the outside world. This has led to the suggestion that she was not a nun but a canoness (one who lives in a religious community without taking vows.)

Hrotswitha wrote six short plays "after Terence" including *Dulcitius*. *Dulcitius* features a farcical scene depicting an evil governor named Dulcitius and some dirty kitchen utensils. The play centers around three virgins who are commanded by the governor to denounce Christ and consent to court-arranged marriages. The women refuse and Dulcitius goes to the women's apartment to rape them. But a miracle occurs and, instead of raping the virgins, he makes love to the greasy pots and pans. Although the women are executed for their insolence, their virtue is preserved and this would have pleased a medieval Christian audience. It is, however, unlikely that her plays were produced. They were probably read aloud with only minor sections acted out.

Medieval Europe

The Emperor Nero (A.D. 37–68) severely persecuted the early Christians in Rome. Although his predecessor, Constantine the Great (A.D. 274–337) had issued the Edict of Milan demanding tolerance for all religions, Nero did not tolerate Christianity. The early Christians condemned the theatre which had degenerated into spectacles such as bloody chariot races and gladiatorial combats. Roman theatres were closed in the sixth century and theatre, as least in the formal sense, disappeared for approximately 400 years. Casual performances still took place such as tumbling, singing, dancing, and early fertility rituals. The existence of these rudimentary performances enhanced the theatre when it was reborn as part of the mass of the Christian church.

Liturgical Drama

Drama Inside of the Church

The church brought the theatre back to life in the form of liturgical drama. Although they began as separate entities, dialogue (chanting/singing), and physical reenactment were in themselves valuable components of the ceremonial mass that eventually evolved into liturgical drama. The first of these realized dramas was an Easter play depicting the resurrection of Christ. The *Regularis Concordia* includes directions for staging and singing an Easter production and it was probably performed in 970. The script includes special notes on costumes and a cast of four characters—one angel and three Marys.

The popularity of the *Regularis Concordia* and other more elaborate Easter plays created a desire for a Christmas play to depict the birth of Christ. This Christmas play, the *Praesepe*, introduced the most popular character in medieval liturgical drama, the evil Herod, who is desperately seeking the location of the Christ Child. Thus was precipitated a series of liturgical drama to teach the mostly illiterate congregations about original sin and the entire plan of salvation.

During most of the thirteenth century, liturgical dramas remained the property of the clergy and were performed only in the church. By the end of the century, because of their popularity, the plays were being performed outside on consecrated church grounds. At first, while the plays were produced in the church, the scenic elements were essentially the church architecture itself, but when it was determined that the Easter play was in need of a representation of the sepulcher, a model of the sepulcher was built. This model was the forerunner of the medieval *mansion*.

The *mansion* provided the audience with a visual representation of the play's location. Mansions were large enough to contain some properties and costume pieces, but they were too small to accommodate the actors. In order to rectify the problem, a platform (*platea*) was placed in front of the mansion and used as the stage. As time passed on and the liturgical dramas became more complex, several different mansions might be needed to perform a single play; so a *platea* was placed in front of each mansion and the audience moved from one mansion to the other. As the complexity of the settings grew, so did the need for special machinery, such as a flying machine to create the sudden appearance of the star of Bethlehem. The plays grew in number and eventually resulted in the great medieval Cycles—a series of religious plays outlining the Church's plan for salvation.

The early Christians condemned the theatre which had degenerated into spectacles such as bloody chariot races and gladiatorial combats and theatre, as least in the formal sense, disappeared for approximately 400 years. The church brought the theatre back to life in the form of liturgical drama. The plays grew in number and eventually resulted in the great medieval Cycles—a series of religious plays outlining the Church's plan for salvation.

Actors

During most of the thirteenth century the actors were all clergy; but toward the end of the century, so many characters had been added to the plays that choirboys, theological scholars, and their young male students were all invited to perform. These non-clerical actors were partly responsible for the transition from liturgical drama to secular drama.

Costumes

Originally, all of the actors were dressed in traditional Church vestments, but as the plays developed, small symbolic items were added: the angels were given wings made of gauze and the three Kings wore non-clerical, richly-made costumes. As the plays grew in number and complexity, the costumes became more elaborate.

Drama Outside of the Church

The complexity of the stories, the need for numerous scenic elements, the addition of characters, the added costumes, and the public's demand for the productions grew so large that the liturgical drama literally outgrew itself and began to become more secular. Many changes were made to the original form in the years between the first recorded Cycle play in 1204 and the plays performed in the early fourteenth century. One major change was the time of year when the plays were performed. Since warmer weather was more conducive to outdoor drama, spring and summer were chosen as the times for productions. Pope Urban IV solidified this when, in 1264, he decreed that Corpus Christi Day would be celebrated on the Thursday following Trinity Sunday (which occurs between May 23 and June 24.) Most of the cycles were performed on or around Corpus Christi Day.

When the plays began to be performed outside of the Church, the persons who took them over exercised a good deal of artistic license. These new producers spiced up the plays with farcical comedy. For example, Herod, frustrated and embarrassed that the Wise men had escaped, entertained the audience by ranting and tearing his hair. An earlier example of a farcical approach to a biblical story appears in Chaucer's *Wife of Bath's Tale*, based on Noah and the Arc. This version focused on the relationship between Noah and his wife rather than the original Biblical tale. In Chaucer's version, the audience enjoyed seeing the couple fight for control of their relationship.

Cycle Plays

Cycle plays or (mystery plays) were short dramas that dramatized the entire Biblical history from Creation to the Last Judgment. The Wakefield Cycle, written between 1440 and 1485, is the best known collection of English Cycle plays. Originally called the Towneley Cycle, the Wakefield Cycle includes 32 plays along with production notes and indicates the specific guilds that produced the plays.

The author of the Wakefield Cycle plays is unknown, but is believed that he was somehow connected with the Church since he knew Latin and was quite familiar with the Church liturgy. This author, referred to simply as the Wakefield Master, exhibits a superior style of writing including distinctive stanzas, several proverbs, and much wit. One of the plays, *The Second Shepherd's Play*, concerns the shepherds who visit the Christ Child and is considered one of the best of the English Cycle plays. In this little drama, the author uses dialect to add humor. For example, one of the principal characters has a southern accent, and when the shepherds curse, they curse in Latin. The *Second Shepherd's Play* remains popular with modern audiences.

The Guilds and the Cycle Plays

The scope of the plays continued to grow to the point that some cycles took several days to perform and involved hundreds of actors. In order to afford these enormous productions, trade or craft guilds within a community took over the financing and development of the plays. Each guild was assigned the play that best suited their trade. For example, the shipwrights would handle the Noah episode and the bakers would produce "The Last Supper." In the English Cycles, each play was performed several times at different locations along a predetermined route, and the city sponsoring the cycle was responsible for the overall supervision.

The Spectacle of the Cycle Plays

Cycle Plays depended on mansions to provide the audience with a visual reference for the play. Mansions were constructed of wood and fabric, brightly colored and elaborately decorated. If a play had more than one setting, several mansions were built. The plays would be presented in one location and the audience would move from one mansion to another in order to follow the story. By far the most popular mansions were those depicting heaven and hell. These were given the prominent end positions—heaven was located on the far left and hell was on the far right. Also, heaven was built several feet higher than the average mansion while hell was built several feet lower. Heaven was the largest mansion and it had special lighting to depict a heavenly aura; whereas, hell was enveloped with a giant "hell-mouth" containing sharp teeth, fire, and billows of smoke.

In England and a few other countries, wagons were used to present productions. They were called pageant wagons in England, and the mansions were mounted on them. Each mansion was painted, decorated, and held flying machines and properties. The primary advantage with these was that they were easily transported. No wagons or parts of wagons survive, but the pageant wagon probably consisted of a one-story unit with a loft. There was a flat bed wagon at each performance site that the pageant wagon drew up to so that the actors could perform on it. Whether the audience was watching a play produced on a wagon or in a stationary setting, they gathered around on three sides very much as the ancient Greek audience did.

> In England and a few other countries, wagons were also used to present productions. They were called pageant wagons in England, and the mansions were mounted on them.

Actors in Cycle Plays

In most locations, the actors were men and boys, except in France where women performed occasionally. Since the plays were performed seasonally, professional actors could not make a living by appearing in religious plays. The vast majority of actors were amateurs who were merchants and craftsmen. Some peasants acted, but they apparently were not very reliable. In an attempt to remedy the problems, actors were required to sign a legal form requiring them to be present for rehearsals and performances. The actors that followed through on their agreement received a lavish dinner including beef, ale, and roast goose as payment for their services.

As with the Greeks and Romans, the most critical component of performing was the actor's voice and how he used it. It was particularly important that the role of God go to an actor with a rich voice. Herod, on the other hand, was normally played by an actor with a less refined, grating voice. The actors probably tried to match their physical movements to the characters that they were playing.

Costuming in Cycle Plays

Costumes in the Cycle Plays were modeled after medieval dress, regardless of the character's origin. If a Roman solider were one of the characters, he would wear medieval armor. Actors generally provided their own costumes unless the role required a special article of clothing. Judas, for example, was always dressed in a red wig and a yellow robe. Probably the most innovative costume was that of the devil. The devil's costume changed slightly with each production, but most devil costumes consisted of a deformed body covered with hair, a terrifying mask with large fangs, hooves on the feet, and a pointed tail. This made him a theatrically terrifying character. It is interesting to note that modern portrayals of the devil use similar characteristics.

Folk Drama: May Games

May Games were very popular with medieval peasants and the day's celebrations included Maypole dances and the crowning of a May Queen. In the evening, the village youths would go into the woods to "search for

may-blossoms." While these young people were away from watchful eyes, they would take the opportunity to flirt and kiss. It was this association with the woods that inspired the tale of Robin Hood and Maid Marion. There are many versions of this story, but the first to receive literary attention was written by a Frenchman, Adam de la Halle, and it was called *Le Feu de Robin et Marion.*

Folk Drama: Mummings

European folk dramas derived from Celtic and Teutonic rituals, were adapted to Christian beliefs, and continued as popular forms of entertainment until the twentieth century. The rituals were easily adjusted to suit Christian values by changing some of the characters and the time of year that they were performed. For example, the principal character in the English hero-combat play, originally performed as a spring fertility rite, was changed to feature St. George as the central character and performed during the Christmas season (Christmas mummings). Folk dramas may not have influenced liturgical drama, but they helped to maintain theatre as part of the culture during the medieval period.

Non-Cycle Plays

Miracle Plays

The Miracle play had its roots in religion. These were plays based on the lives of martyrs or saints.

The Miracle or Saint Play had its roots in religion. These were plays based on the lives of martyrs or saints. The most beloved character in the French Cycle Plays was the Virgin Mary. The national library in France, the *Bibliothe'que Nationale,* has two manuscripts from the late fourteenth century that contain over forty plays about the Virgin Mary—these are known as the *Quarante miracles de Notre-Dame.* St. Nicholas is the second favorite character and the *Fleury Play-Book* contains four plays in his honor. As time passed, many of the saints were honored in plays featuring their lives.

Morality Plays

Morality plays were allegories which began to develop in the fourteenth century and remained popular throughout the sixteenth century.

The best known of Morality Plays was *Paternoster,* based on the Lord's Prayer. It contains seven distinct sections and depicts the conflict between the Seven Deadly Sins and the Seven Moral Virtues. The format and storyline of *Paternoster* greatly influenced the subsequent development of the medieval morality play. Morality plays were allegories which began to develop in the fourteenth century and remained popular throughout the sixteenth century. The play *Everyman* is the most famous of all Morality Plays. It is one third of a longer play written in the fourteenth century and it was based on either a Dutch play entitled *Elckerlijk* or St. John Damascene's *Barlaam and Josaphat.*

Everyman begins with God summoning Death to take Everyman to his grave, but Everyman, not wanting to die, attempts to find someone to accompany him. He asks Fellowship, Kindred, Cousin, and Goods, but all decline to travel with him. He then seeks the company of Knowledge, Confession, Discretion, Strength, Beauty, and Five-Wits to follow him. They agree but soon desert him. Everyman is left with Good Deeds who, in the end, enters the grave with him. The moral to the story is explained by a Doctor at the end of the play. Other morality plays include didactic dramas such as John Rastell's *The Nature of Four Elements* which was intended to encourage students to study nature.

End of the Middle Ages—Birth of the Renaissance

Medieval drama was very popular throughout Europe, but when Henry VIII broke with the Roman Catholic Church in 1530, the interest in religious drama in England waned. There were, however, many practicing Catholics in England who enjoyed the dramas. In 1558, Queen Elizabeth banned all religious plays because she feared a civil war between Protestants and Catholics. The Catholic Church, at the Council of Trent, also withdrew its support of religious drama.

Probably another reason medieval plays were abandoned was the renewed interest in classical literature and art. The Renaissance began in Italy in the fourteenth century and made its way to England by the early sixteenth century. The combination of the rebirth of classical study and the adoption of the Protestant religion by Queen Elizabeth effectively ended medieval drama in England by 1570.

The Renaissance began in Italy in the fourteenth century and made its way to England by the early sixteenth century. The combination of the rebirth of classical study and the adoption of the Protestant religion by Queen Elizabeth effectively ended medieval drama in England by 1570.

Summary

Early man participated in seasonal rituals which were meant to represent the ideal existence of both the living and the supernatural. The representational aspects of the ceremonies constitute an early form of drama. The ancient Greek society developed into a highly sophisticated civilization. Their prosperity allowed them time to express themselves through the arts. Many of the ancient Greek dramatic literary works from playwrights such as Sophocles, Aeschylus, and Euripides have survived and portions of these are based on ceremonial rituals performed in the early stages of Greek societal development. Religious celebrations such as The Festival of Dionysus featured the presentation of plays. The Romans adapted Greek dramatic literature to suit their own tastes and performed the plays at their own religious festivals called the games or *ludi*. Religious-based plays were popular during the Middle Ages in Europe. The most popular genres include Cycle Plays, Morality Plays, and Miracle Plays. In 1558, Queen Elizabeth banned all religious plays in England, and effectively brought an end to the Cycle Plays in that country. This, together with the Church's ban on religious plays, ended the religious drama of the Middle Ages.

Active Learning Assignment
"Bringing Theatre to Life"

I. **Remembering Greek, Roman, and Medieval Theatre**

Each group (10 to 15 people) selects four pieces of information from the keynote sections of the Greek, Roman, or Medieval periods. Then, the group devises a short play (five to seven minutes in length) and performs them for the rest of the class. One example: a talk show might feature Sophocles as the host's special guest, and the two could discuss the opening of his new play, *Oedipus Rex*. Euripides and Aristophanes could be other special guests on the show.

Critical Thinking in Class Discussion

I. What were the four main points that each of the groups covered?

II. Were other important facts missed? If so, what were they?

III. What are the most surprising facts about the Greek theatre, the Roman theatre, Medieval church theatre, and the Cycle Plays?

IV. If you could travel back in time, which one of these cultures would you like to be a part of and why?

The Renaissance (Italy, England and France) Through the Restoration

The Renaissance

The Renaissance is that period of European history spanning the fourteenth through the sixteenth centuries. Many of the ideas associated with the Renaissance grew out of the culture and ideals of the Middle Ages and classical literature. The period marks the beginnings of modern science and geographical discovery and is defined by a renewed interest in and study of classical literature and philosophy.

Three major factors were responsible for the gradual transformation from the Middle Ages to the Renaissance: the growth of cities, the increased power of the nobility, and a renewed interest in life and the *humanist* ideals of the classical world. The *humanists* were scholars who found value not just in the preparation for an afterlife, but also in the individual's earthly life. The *Humanists* celebrated both classical and Christian virtues such as loyalty, courage, integrity, and caring for oneself and others. The *humanists* felt it was important for a person to develop his or her potential to the fullest. To that end, they championed study in the sciences, politics, sports, and the arts.

Italy

The Renaissance began in Italy.

The Renaissance began in Italy for several reasons. One was that the country was a vital stopping point on the trade route to Asia and Africa. Italy's prime location along this route brought a great deal of intellectual and financial wealth from the eastern Mediterranean, Byzantium, Islam, and other cultures. A second reason was because it was the seat of the Roman Catholic Church. Controversies in regard to the Pope had been under scrutiny since the late fourteenth century. The Italian city-states removed the focus from religious scandal by supporting and praising artists, scholars, and writers. The third reason for Italy's importance in the Renaissance was the fall of Constantinople. This brought many scholars with Greek and Roman manuscripts to Italy. For example, Seneca's tragedies had been previously unknown and their moral lessons were popular with the Italian people. In 1429, 12 of Plautus' plays were discovered and provided models for oral style. The introduction of the printing press facilitated the distribution of these and other classical works.

Neoclassical Ideals

Italian literary theory was based primarily on two manuscripts—Horace's *Art of Poetry,* well-known because it was written in the first century, and Aristotle's *The Poetics.* The translation of *The Poetics* into Latin in 1498 made it readily accessible, and *The Poetics* quickly became the authority on dramatic style and structure. *The Poetics* gained even more popularity and respect when it was translated into Italian in 1549. Most scholars of the time accepted Aristotle's theories. A number of these scholars set down their own versions of Aristotle's theories on tragedy. Some of the most influential were Antonio Minturno (?–1574), Julius Caesar Scaliger (1494–1558) and Lodovico Castelvetro (1501–1571). Their dramatic treatises became quite influential and epitomized neoclassical ideals. The neoclassical ideals included a series of "rules" to be followed when writing or evaluating dramatic literature. One

The neoclassical ideals included a series of "rules" to be followed when writing and evaluating dramatic literature.

basic rule was that playwrights had to keep the subjects of their plays as close to real life as possible. As a result, fantasies and supernatural events were to be avoided in neoclassical works. In line with creating dramas that mimicked "real life," theatrical conventions such as soliloquies and the use of a chorus were discouraged since they were not "real." It was also important for a neoclassical drama to teach the audience a moral lesson.

Neoclassicism completely separated comedy and tragedy. Comedy could not be at all serious. It had to have a happy ending and the characters needed to be from the lower classes. Tragedy could not be at all humorous. It had to be based on history or mythology, and all the tragic characters had to be from the upper classes. Since all drama was supposed to teach as well as to please, comedy ridiculed behavior that should be avoided, and tragedy revealed the horrifying consequences of mistakes in judgment or deed.

Lodovico Castelvetro introduced the "three unities" in 1570. They were defined as the unity of action (only one plot), the unity of place (all of the action had to take place in one location) and the unity of time (all of the action had to occur in 24 hours or less). Castelvetro's three unities were celebrated by critics and, for many years, plays that did not follow all of the neoclassical ideals were regarded as substandard and not worthy of serious consideration. By the sixteenth century, enthusiasm for the neoclassical rules was waning. Audiences responded to the neoclassical tragedies only half-heartedly. They much preferred the neoclassical comedies, largely because of the *intermezzi* sandwiched between the acts.

Intermezzi

Intermezzi provided audiences with a treat. They were filled with visual spectacle including colorful costumes, scenery, lighting, exciting special effects, music, and dance. These lavish productions were presented primarily at the courts to celebrate a special event—weddings, births, etc. Often the plots of the intermezzi were especially written for the person or persons being honored. Because intermezzi were laden with special effects and lavish scenery, new scenic devices constantly needed to be invented. This popular art form eventually gave way to opera, first in Italy and then elsewhere.

Intermezzi provided audiences with a treat, because they were filled with visual spectacles which included colorful costumes, scenery, lights, exciting special effects, music, and dance.

Opera

Opera is defined as a play in which the dialogue is sung or chanted to instrumental accompaniment. The scenery and costumes are typically extravagant. At first, Italian opera was performed only at the courts or in academic settings, but when a public opera house opened in 1637, opera quickly became Italy's most popular form of entertainment. The first public opera house was so successful that from 1640 to 1700 four additional opera houses were opened. Opera became immensely popular in Italy and then began to spread throughout Europe.

Opera is a drama in which the dialogue is sung and chanted to instrumental accompaniment.

Italian Scenic Design

Italian scholars (Humanists) and artists were the first to embrace the rebirth of classical drama. The nobility and the Humanists collaborated in order to make the revival of the classics part of the court festivities which had traditionally taken place outdoors. In 1491, as a part of court festivities, a play

> *In order to rectify the scenic problems, perspective painting was used in order to make the small room look larger than it actually was.*

was produced inside a building for the first time. However, producing indoors presented many scenic difficulties; the old scenic methods were simply not condusive to an indoor venue. In order to solve some of the scenic problems, perspective painting was used to make a small room look larger than it actually was. Perspective painting was a relatively new technique that was being employed by such painters as Leonardo da Vinci (1452–1519), Raphael (1483–1520), and Bramante (1444–1514). Bramante was regarded as a specialist in the art of perspective painting, having successfully used the technique to decorate a church in Milan in 1480.

Baldassare Peruzzi (1481–1537) was influenced by Bramante and began to use perspective painting to decorate theatres. Peruzzi's student, Sebastiano Serlio (1475–1554) used his teacher's notes to write his own book, *De Architettura*. The section of this work dealing with perspective appeared in print in 1545. Serlio's *De Architettura* also recommended three stage sets, one each for tragedy, comedy, and pastoral. The drawings accompanying the text included houses lining both sides of a street, all of which receded at right angles to the front of the stage.

Bartolomeo Neroni (c. 1500–71/3) expanded on Serlio's ideas in 1560 by constructing a proscenium arch (a variation of the picture frame) in a great hall located behind the Palace of the Senate in Siena. He then decorated it with scenery based on Serlio's drawings.

French Playwrights

Pierre Corneille (1606–84)

> *In France, Corneille, Racine, and Moliere were the best dramatists.*

Pierre Corneille's first play was a comedy entitled *Melite*. It was produced in a tennis court that had been converted into a theatre (a common practice in the seventeenth century). The play deviated from the neoclassical "unities" of action, place, and time; and this caused the play to be subjected to harsh criticism. Despite negative reviews, the play was successful. Corneille's next play, *Clitandre*, adhered to the neoclassical standards, but the critics disliked the play, although they did concede that Corneille's original style was better. Corneille went on to write four more comedies in his original style and in 1635 he wrote his first tragedy, *Medea*.

Corneille had the honor of being invited to write plays for Cardinal Richelieu in Paris; but he declined, saying that he did not want to be placed in a position of servitude. Richelieu was furious and Corneille returned to his birthplace in Rouen. In Rouen, he immersed himself in Spanish literature, including Guillen de Castro y Bellvis's *Las mocedades de Cid*. Corneille based his next play, *Le Cid*, on the Spanish classic and it was an immediate success. Corneille, however, was an egotistical man and bragged about his talent and the supreme quality of *Le Cid* in published pamphlets. His arrogance alienated him from his contemporaries. Ironically, the play and its production at the Theatre du Marais are still regarded as outstanding dramatic achievements.

In 1647, Corneille, having made peace with Cardinal Richelieu, came to be elected a member of the French Academy and was regarded as one of the most respected dramatists in France. Corneille went on to write numerous successful plays including *Nicomede* (1651) which the great comic writer

Moliere later revived, although unsuccessfully. Moliere admired Corneille and was inspired to write his play *Le Misanthrope* after seeing Corneille's most successful comedy, *Le Menteur*.

Corneille enjoyed great popularity and success during his lifetime. Although he was shy and at times egotistical, he seems to have been a man of good character. His younger brother, Thomas, was also a talented dramatist, but Thomas's works had been overshadowed by his brother's, however, but not because of Pierre's lack of support and encouragement. Pierre was never one to succumb to petty jealousy when it came to his younger brother. Thomas married Pierre's wife's younger sister and the two couples lived their lives, happily, side by side, in either the same or adjoining homes.

Jean Racine (1639–99)

Jean Racine, probably the best of the French tragic playwrights, was orphaned at the age of four. He was educated at the College de Beauvais and, although he was an excellent scholar, he was considered to be undisciplined. He admired the Greek tragedies and, by the time he was 19 years old, he was regarded as an exceptional poet. Moliere produced one of his first plays, *La Thebaide, ou les freres ennemis*. Because the play was well received, Moliere produced another of Racine's plays. When the second play opened, Racine allowed a rival theatre to produce it at the same time. It was in production at Moliere's theatre and Moliere lost ticket sales to the other theatre's production. Racine claimed that the second theatre possessed a better reputation than Moliere's theatre for producing tragedies. Moliere remained sympathetic, but then Racine hired Moliere's leading actress to play the lead in his next tragedy. This ended the friendship between the two.

Racine wanted to be revered as a greater playwright than Corneille, who won great acclaim for his play, *Andromaque* (1667). Perhaps his success can be attributed to his "hands on" writing method. When writing, he would work directly with the actors and recite his work aloud at rehearsals. This system allowed him to make necessary improvements in his dialogue and plot. *Iphigenie* (1674) was a huge success and it seemed to many in the theatre community that he would indeed become the most successful playwright of the era.

Unfortunately, by the time *Iphigenie* was produced, Racine had made many enemies, particularly other playwrights; and his enemies devised a plan to publicly insult Racine. When it became known that Racine was writing *Phaedra*, another dramatist was encouraged to write a play on the same subject. Both plays opened simultaneously at different theatres, and Racine was embarrassed that the public praised the other work over his own.

Shortly after the *Phaedra* incident, Louis XIV selected Racine to be the historiographer-royal. Racine then left the theatre, married, and had seven children. He was invited to write a couple of plays for Mme de Maintenon's school for ladies. They were well received by academic audiences, but Racine did not allow them to be played in public.

Racine was self-centered, inconsiderate, and angry, but despite his personality, he was an exceedingly talented playwright. His strength was by his ability to remain true to the neoclassical rules while creating fascinating characters and using poetry to bring lyricism and interest to his plays.

Jean-Baptiste Poquelin—Moliere (1622–73)

It was assumed that the young Jean-Baptiste Poquelin would take his father's place as an upholsterer to the king. Instead, he became one of the greatest comic playwrights in the entire history of the theatre. There is little information about Jean-Baptiste's childhood except that he was a good mimic and enjoyed going to the theatre. In approximately 1631 he enrolled in the Jesuit College of Clermont, where he was known as a good student, particularly in Latin, and where he performed in the school's plays. One of his classmates was Prince de Conti who later became his patron. Poquelin also met Cyrano de Bergerac while attending Clermont. They became lifelong friends.

Poquelin left the school in 1639 and studied law for a short time before finally pursuing a career in the theatre. In 1643, he and a few friends formed the Illustre-Theatre and performed their plays in an abandoned tennis court. The most notable member in the group was Madeleine Bejart. It was suspected that the young Moliere, as Poquelin had renamed himself, was her lover. Unfortunately, the company failed miserably in less than a year and Moliere was imprisoned for debt.

Failure and debt did not dissuade Moliere and many of the former Illustre-Theatre members from organizing another theatre company. Moliere wrote improvised farces, similar in style to those performed by commedia dell' arte troupes, for his new company and the audiences loved them. Moliere's talent helped bring success to the newly formed company and they spent several years performing in the provinces. It was during this time that Moliere's boyhood friend, Prince de Conti, became his patron and occasionally offered the company some financial relief.

On October 24, 1658, Moliere's company was given the opportunity to perform in Paris for the twenty-year-old Louis XIV. They performed Corneille's popular tragedy *Nicomede*, but the audience was unmoved by the production. Fortunately, Moliere then offered an afterpiece consisting of one of his own farces, *Le Docteur amoureux*. The little play was well received and the king invited the company to continue performing in Paris at the Petit-Bourbon. Afterwards, Moliere's company shared performance nights with a commedia dell' arte troupe at the Palais-Royal. He had to pay the commedia troupe rent and a fee for the use of their sets, but the young Moliere was appreciative of the arrangement. Within a few years, Moliere's company became so successful that the commedia troupe had to pay rent to Moliere in order to perform at the Palais-Royal.

The close relationship between Moliere and Louis XIV was very beneficial in that it provided the playwright with financial security, but it also created a great deal of responsibility and pressure for Moliere. He was expected to write a series of plays for court presentation, and the plays were required to have music and ballet dance intervals so that the king and his court could dance.

Moliere was so favored by the court that he was often ridiculed by other less popular acting companies that were jealous of his success. Some of his private affairs were also publicized including his marriage to the youngest sister of Madeleine Armande Bejart. She was a 20-year-old who was spoiled, capricious, and self-centered. She was rumored to be Madeleine's daughter and the actor/manager Montfleury went so far as to suggest to the king that she was not only Madeleine's daughter but also Moliere's daughter from an affair that the two had had when they were touring the provinces. Fortunately for Moliere, the king's reaction to Montfleury's insulting accusation was to become the godfather of the couple's first child.

Moliere is credited with raising French comedy to the heights of French tragedy. He was a talented actor, playwright, and producer. As an actor, his forte was comedy. It is thought that, perhaps his slight speech impediment kept the public from admiring him as a tragic actor; however, he was renowned in comedy and his success did not keep him from encouraging other playwrights. He was a strong supporter of Racine, whose first play was produced by Moliere at the Palais-Royal in 1664.

Moliere wrote many great comedies, including *Tartuffe, The Learned Ladies, The Misanthrope, The Doctor in Spite of Himself, The Bourgeois Gentleman,* and *The Imaginary Invalid*. On February 17, 1673, Moliere collapsed on stage during a production of *The Imaginary Invalid* and died shortly after the performance.

Commedia Dell' Arte (comedy of the profession of skill)

Commedia Dell' Arte derives from the ancient Roman Atellan farce which had been preserved by wandering mimes during the middle ages and by Byzantine troupes who fled to the west when Constantinople fell in 1453. Commedia Dell' Arte developed into an art form in Italy in the sixteenth century; but, since the Commedia Troupes were company, France, Spain, Germany, and England shared in its growth and prosperity. Commedia reached its height of popularity in 1650, and continued to be regularly performed until 1775.

The two principal traits indicative of commedia are stock characters and improvisation. The performances were improvised from a scenario which was tacked up for reference in the stage wings during the performance. The scenario gave a rough plot line and the actors improvised around it. These scenarios were based on central themes such as love, intrigue, disguises, and misunderstandings. The actors and actresses played the same characters throughout their careers and developed proven physical comedy bits called lazzi along with set speeches that always ended with rhetorical flourishes. The actors made use of these during their impromptu performances. The productions were performed in a presentational style, directly to the audience, and frequently lasted over three hours.

The two traits indicative to Commedia Dell' Arte are stock characters and improvisation.

Lazzi

Lazzis were physical comedy routines based on human needs such as hunger, bodily functions, and material and physical desires. Some lazzis were as simple as slipping on a banana peel or having a pie thrown in the face. Other lazzis were very physically challenging such as falling down into leg splits, then immediately going into a backward summersault and ending up flat on the back. The actors would add sound effects to enhance the lazzi, and one of the most important ingredients was the look of physical pain on the actors' faces at the end.

In order for a lazzi to be effective, it could not deviate so far from the basic story as to confuse the audience. It took a great deal of skill to execute

Lazzis were physical comedy routines that were typically based on basic human needs such as hunger, bodily functions, and material and physical desires.

a properly structured lazzi. It had to follow a logical order and was dependent on timing and pacing. The successful lazzi always took the audience by surprise.

Lazzis are still used in modern theatre and film. For example, *The Three Stooges* were popular twentieth century comedians that created entire comic scenes out of "slapstick" routines. These routines were similar to the Commedia lazzi. The modern term slapstick is derived from a prop—a wooden "slap-stick" that the commedia stock character, Harlequin, used during the productions.

Masks

All of the characters wore masks with the exceptions of the lovers and the servants. Masks required the actors to find expressive ways to use their bodies and voices so that they could be understood clearly by the audience.

Actresses

Women not only performed in the shows, but were also some of the first troupe managers.

Women not only performed in Commedia Troupes, but were also some of the first troupe managers. Isabella Andrieni was one of the most celebrated female troupe managers. She and her husband, Francisco, led the Gelois company. The manager was the most respected member of the company and usually owned it. He or she was responsible for the scenarios, collection of the props, and for explaining the relationships between the characters and the plot. The manager also selected the lazzi that would be performed.

Financial Rewards

Most of the senior members in the company shared the profits equally. The young members, if the troupe had any, were placed on a salary until they had proved themselves and were invited to become full members.

The Stock Characters

Arlecchino (Harlequin)

Harlequin was a zanni (comic servant) who, most often, was a shrewd, uneducated valet who served one of the lovers. He had a diverse personality but was usually a greedy and charismatic rogue. Harlequin had the reputation of being clumsy, lazy and impulsive clown. He constantly struck poses and then leaped, like a drunk, into a new pose. Originally, Harlequin wore a costume made from different animal skins patched together; but as time went on, his costume became a multi-colored suit. He also wore a black half mask and carried a wooden sword or a "slap-stick" which he would flourish.

Pulcinella

The Pulcinella character was probably created during the middle ages to act as a buffoon. His original appearance included a hunchback figure, a phallic-shaped nose, a long mustache and a pointed beard. He wore a white cloak which was drawn at the waist with a cord. Eventually, the character lost his beard and the mustache, and instead wore a dark-colored half mask etched with deep wrinkles, a prominent wart on the forehead and a large beak-shaped nose. Pulcinella played numerous roles in the scenarios including servant, peasant, dentist, physician, pirate, advocate, painter, and retired military general. He contributed great comedy to the productions with his mysterious intrigue, his inability to be silent or to sit still, and his musical talents—he played an instrument or sang. It was this character that inspired the English clown Punch.

Dottore (The Doctor)

The Doctor was an ostentatious fraud who talked too much. He used long gibberish words and was a pretentious man of learning who tried to impress everyone he met. He usually played a lawyer or professor in the scenario or was the father of one of the young lovers. Occasionally, he had a love interest himself. His costume included a black mask which covered only the upper part of the face and included a comic nose and a short pointed beard. He wore an all black outfit (often an academic robe) and a gigantic black hat.

El Capitano (The Captain)

The Captain was a braggart soldier who often referred to himself as a hero and believed himself to be the man for whom all the women swooned. In actuality, he was a coward, known to run and hide if anyone made the slightest aggressive move. His costume was a flamboyant outfit which included a plumed hat, a mask with a Cyrano-like nose, an exaggerated mustache, and a long cape.

Pantalone

This character was the elderly man in the scenario. He was frequently played as a bumbling idiot who complained about aches and pains and lusted for young women and money. One of his lazzis was to fall flat on his back when he heard bad news. He wore Turkish slippers turned up at the toes, a reddish brown mask with a hooked nose, a pointed beard, a black ankle-length coat over red breeches, red stockings, and a pair of spectacles.

The Maid/Servant

The maid or servant role was usually played without a mask. She wore a skirt, bonnet, and apron, all of which were composed of several colors. Maids/servants typically had numerous quick changes during the productions in order to create disguises. The character had an effervescent, sassy personality and was extremely sharp witted. Common names for the character included Franceschina, Oliva, and Colombine. They normally teamed with the Harlequin character to help the lovers get together.

The Young Lovers

As mentioned earlier, most of the scenarios revolved around love. The Young Lovers were the straight characters in dialogue, dress, and mannerisms. They never wore masks and spent a good deal of their off-stage time researching poetry and popular literature to use in the plays. The lovers were particularly important to the productions because of their juxtaposition to the outlandish characters.

Active Learning Assignment
"Bringing Theatre to Life"

I. **"World of the Lazzi"—Non-object/physical lazzi** (Inspired by John Dennis)

The following in-class activity is designed to allow students to experiment with physical lazzi. Divide the class into groups of approximately 20. In the front of the classroom, arrange two groups of 20 students into two lines (or bunches, the arrangement will depend on the space available) roughly on the same horizontal plane. Leave a five- to six-foot space between the two groups. Taking turns, first one group and then the other, one student will enter the center space ("the world of the lazzi") on his or her way to join the other group. Before the student begins the journey, he or she is told what "world of the lazzi" he or she will be entering. The "world of the lazzi" changes with each student. While the student is in the center area, he or she will become fully immersed in and interact with the environment. For example, the world might be made entirely of peanut butter, or cotton candy, or the planet Mars, or a civilization composed of robots, or a swamp, or an ocean, etc. Once the student has explored the "world of the lazzi" he or she may join the other group, at the end of the line. Repeat the exercise until all students have had an opportunity to explore the "world of the lazzi."

II. **"World of the Lazzi"—Prop lazzi with stock character traits** (Inspired by John Dennis)

The following in-class activity is designed to allow students to experiment with imaginary prop lazzi. Divide the class into groups of approximately 20. In the front of the classroom, arrange two groups into two lines (or bunches, the arrangement will depend on the space available) roughly on the same horizontal plane. Leave a five- to six-foot space between the two groups. Taking turns by alternating between the groups, one student (this exercise can also be done in pairs) will enter the center space ("the world of prop lazzi") on his or her way to join the other group. Before the student begins the journey, he or she is told what "world of prop lazzi" he or she will be entering. While the student is in the center area, he or she is to become fully immersed in and interact with their new environment. For example, the world might be one where he or she slips on a banana peel, or a world of never ending hunger, or a world of never ending lust, a world of a pie in a face, etc. This activity will be enhanced if the student first selects a stock character and takes on some of that character's personality traits before beginning the exercise. It will also be enhanced if the student or instructor provides some hand props to use during the activity. Repeat the exercise until all the students have an opportunity to participate.

Critical Thinking in Class Discussion

I. Satire, in one form or another, has been part of entertainment and literature since ancient Greek times. What is it about satire that makes it so popular?

II. What do we learn from satire?

III. What forms of modern day entertainment center around satiric themes?

England and the Theatre

When Queen Elizabeth I assumed the throne of England (1533-1603), she forbade the presentation of religious drama as a part of an effort to prevent civil war between Protestants and Catholics. One result of this was an influx of secular drama. This new form of drama was inspired by the Greek and Roman classics but retained some medieval theatrical traditions. The vast numbers of plays extant from the period show that this was one of the most prolific periods of drama in England's history.

During the Elizabethan era, the majority of the "playwrights" (the term had not been invented so individuals who wrote plays were referred to as "authors," "writers," or, if they were fortunate enough, "poets") were often university graduates. One group was known as the "University Wits." One member of this group was Christopher Marlowe who wrote *The Tragical History of Doctor Faustus*, seamlessly combining the medieval era with the Renaissance in a beautifully poetic fashion.

Other notable Elizabethan playwrights include Francis Beaumont, John Fletcher, and Ben Jonson. The last is best known today for his play *Volpone* (*The Fox*). Written in 1606, its structure is similar to that of classical dramas. Ben Jonson was the first Englishman to publish his plays, forever changing the public's perception of plays from sheer entertainment to respectable literature. The most notable playwright of this period was William Shakespeare, the best known and most respected playwright of all time.

During the Elizabethan era, the majority of the "playwrights" (the term playwright had not been invented so individuals who wrote plays were referred to as "authors," "writers" or if they were fortunate enough—"poets") were most often graduates of universities such as Oxford or Cambridge and they were referred to as the "University Wits."

Shakespeare's Plays and Sonnets

William Shakespeare was born and raised in Stratford-on-Avon and received a free education at the King's New School there. Although he did not study the full ten years necessary for a degree, he was more educated than most, attending school from age six to age thirteen. In 1582, Shakespeare married Anne Hathaway, eight years his senior and a member of a well-to-do farming family. Not quite a year later, the couple had a daughter, Susanna. How Shakespeare spent the following seven years is unknown, but he suddenly appears as an actor and playwright in London. Perhaps he became stage-struck by the touring companies that frequently played in Stratford. Certainly, his first employment in the theatre was probably that of an apprentice who acted in small roles and cleaned the stage. His first play was produced in 1589, probably either *The Comedy of Errors* or *Henry VI, Part One*.

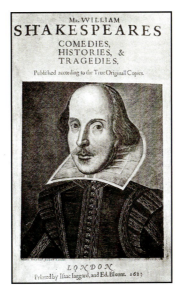

William Shakespeare

(April 23, 1564–April 23, 1616)

Shakespeare wrote, adapted, and co-wrote 38 plays, wrote two poems and over 100 sonnets. Shakespeare wrote three types of plays: comedies, history plays, and tragedies.

Shakespeare wrote, adapted, and co-wrote 38 plays, two long poems, and over 100 sonnets. Shakespeare plays are traditionally divided into three categories: comedies, histories, and tragedies. The exact dates of his plays are

unknown. The following is a list of his comedies and the approximate date of composition: *Love's Labor's Lost* (1590–92), *The Comedy of Errors* (1592–94), *The Two Gentlemen of Verona* (1592–94), *A Mid-Summer Night's Dream* (1594–96), *The Merchant of Venice* (1594–96), *The Taming of the Shrew* (1594–97), *The Merry Wives of Windsor* (1597–1600), *Much Ado About Nothing* (1598–1600), *As You Like It* (1599–1600), *Twelfth Night* (1599–1601), and *The Tempest* (1611–12). The majority of these plays include a clown character which he wrote for two real life clowns who performed with his company (The Lord Chamberlain's Men). The first comic actor to work with the company was Will Kempe, a farcical and boisterous clown, while the second, Robert Armin, was a court jester "white-faced" clown. The diverse comic styles of these performers affected the way Shakespeare structured his comedies.

Shakespeare wrote a number of history plays focusing on wars—those between England and France and the civil wars in England. Some of the best known include: *Henry VI, parts 1, 2, and 3* (1590–96); *Richard III* (1593–94); *Henry IV*, parts 1 and 2 (1597–98); *Henry V* (1598–99); *King John* (1594–96); and *Henry VIII* (1612–13). Shakespeare also penned great tragedies, notably *Hamlet* (1605–06); *Macbeth* (1605–1606); *Romeo and Juliet* (1594–97); and *Othello* (1604–05).

In 1613, Shakespeare retired to his home in Stratford after tragedy struck the Globe during a performance of *Henry VIII*. Wadding from a cannon fired as a sound effect during the performance set the thatched roof ablaze and the entire theater burned to the ground. It was rebuilt, but Shakespeare took the opportunity to retire from the theatre. His works remain the cornerstone of the English-speaking theatre and will always be a central part of our cultural heritage. Ben Johnson put it succinctly when he wrote, "He was not of an age, but for all time."

Permanent Theatres Are Built

Shakespeare was born into a world where actors were homeless and traveled around performing in crowded inn-yards or at the great noble estates. One reason permanent theatres were not built in London was because of the bubonic plague that swept Europe. The plague was highly contagious and large gatherings of people were not permitted. The second reason for the lack of theatres in London was the disapproval of the City Council (largely Puritans) who believed theatre going was morally wrong and also incited violence. If theatre in England was to have a permanent home, it had to be outside the jurisdiction of the City Council.

In 1567 John Brayne built the Red Lion Theatre less than a mile from London's city limits. It is known as the first permanent theatre "in" London. It is unknown how long that the theatre survived, but ten years later actor, manager, businessman, and brother-in-law of John Brayne, James Burbage, signed a twenty-one year lease on land just outside the city limits and built the second theatre in London, which he aptly named *The Theatre*. (Our word "theatre" comes from the Latin *theatrum* meaning 'viewing place.") *The Theatre*, still under construction, was opened the following summer so that the earnings could defer some of the building costs. While this first permanent theatre was being built, explorer Francis Drake began his epic journey, intending to become the first man to sail around the world. It is important to note that the concept that the earth was a sphere, termed "globe," was a relatively new concept—less than thirty years old.

After 21 years, Burbage's original lease expired and the owner of the land began making financial demands on Cuthbert Burbage, James Burbage's son, who had inherited responsibility for the theatre after his father died. (James Burbage's other son, Richard, was one of the best actors of the time and originated many of Shakespeare's great tragic roles including Hamlet, Richard III, and King Lear.) In order to begin anew without an unreasonable landowner causing the theatre further financial grief, Cuthbert and about 30 men dismantled the entire *The Theatre*, loaded it on boats and ferried it across the Thames. This secretive maneuver began at midnight on December 22, 1598.

The Globe Theatre
Image © Jupiterimages, inc.

Cuthbert and his crew reassembled the theatre on the south side of the Thames, but this time they used the wood to construct a circular shaped building, hoping that the shape would improve the acoustics. Cuthbert Burbage named this new theatre *The Globe*.

Perhaps the name was meant to capture the excitement of English explorers gathering and sharing great riches and novelties. The circular appearance (actually 20 sides covered in plaster) and height (over 30 feet) made it a sizable and distinctive landmark that London's visitors and residents could locate easily. To confirm that this was indeed the correct building, a large painting of a man holding a globe on his shoulders was affixed to the outer wall. Since most people were illiterate, the painting was meant to represent the theatre's name. For educated theatre goers, this Latin phrase appeared underneath the picture "Totus mundis agit historiem" or "here you see a whole world supported by our efforts."

Elizabethan Theatre Practitioners

By 1599, three permanent theatres were available in London—*The Globe, The Swan,* and *The Rose*. However, in order for actors, writers, and other members of a theatre company to have a respectable status in society, a nobleman was needed as a patron. Out of respect for his sponsorship, the theatre troupe would assume the name of the patron. Shakespeare's company requested that the Lord Chamberlain be their patron, and they assumed the name *The Lord Chamberlain's Men*. In time, they gained favor with Queen Elizabeth and were invited to give more court performances than any of the other professional companies. After Elizabeth's death, *The Lord Chamberlain's Men* became *The King's Men,* and were even invited to walk in Kings James's Coronation procession as "Gentlemen of the Chamber."

The Productions

There are numerous differences between the way in which Shakespeare's plays were produced and performed in his time and the way they are staged today. For example, women were not permitted to act on the stage during Shakespeare's time; therefore, boys played all of the female roles. Unlike a modern rehearsal period which is typically four to six weeks long, Shakespeare's plays received very little rehearsal time—perhaps only three or four days. The majority of this limited rehearsal time was focused on such technical elements as costume changes, sound (firing of cannons and music), lighting effects (fire pits and torches), sword fights and, if necessary, the choreographing of complicated movement. Actors in Shakespeare's theatre did not receive a copy of the entire script. They were given "sides" which consisted of cue lines and their own lines. For the most part, the actors were required to rehearse their roles on their own before the performance.

The Audience and the Viewing of the Production

Usually plays were performed in the afternoons during the work week, but this did not prevent hundreds of people from all walks of life, tradesmen, men and women of all ages, clerks, lawyers, and some nobility, from attending the productions. *The Globe* announced to the community that it was presenting a production by flying a large silk flag from the top of the theatre—black for tragedy, white for comedy. Audience members would make their way to *The Globe* at least an hour before the play was to begin in an effort to get the best possible seats (there was no reserved seating). An audience member had three areas from which to choose. He or she could pay a penny and stand in the yard (pit) pay two pennies and sit in the lower level of the gallery, or pay even more and sit in an upper level box. Wherever audience members chose to sit, they could move about during the production, eat fruits and nuts and drink ale. The performance took the entire afternoon and provided all the attendees with the opportunity to socialize and escape for awhile from the rigors of Elizabethan life.

Active Learning Assignment
"Bringing Theatre to Life"

I. **Write a Sonnet** (Inspired by Kelly Kiernan)

Small groups of four or five will write a story in the form of a sonnet that you would enjoy telling friends at a party. Then, take turns reading the sonnets aloud to the class. A sonnet is a short poem consisting of 14 lines—each line has ten syllables arranged using iambic pentameter. An iambic pentameter line is composed of five iambs. An iamb consists of two syllables, the first syllable is unstressed, the second is stressed. Some have compared it to the sound and feel of the human heartbeat (da, **DA**.)

A sonnet also has a rhyme scheme: AB, AB, CD, CD, EF, EF, GG. "A" rhymes with "A," "B" rhymes with "B," "C" rhymes with "C," etc. The thirteenth and fourteenth line constitute a rhyming couplet. (The rhyme has been marked in parentheses for clarity.)

Below is Shakespeare's Sonnet number 29:

(A) When, in disgrace with fortune and men's eyes,

(B) I all alone beweep my outcast state,

(A) And trouble deaf heaven with my bootless cries,

(B) And look upon myself, and curse my fate,

(C) Wishing me like to one more rich in hope,

(D) Featur'd like him, like him with friends possess'd

(C) Desiring this man's art, and that man's scope,

(D) With what I most enjoy contented least;

(E) Yet in these thoughts myself almost despising,

(F) Haply I think on thee,—and then my state,

(E) Like to the lark at break of day arising

(F) From sullen earth, sings hymns at heaven's gate;

(G) For they sweet love remember'd such wealth brings

(H) That then I scorn to change my state with kings.

Critical Thinking in Class Discussion

I. Was it difficult to write your story in the form of a sonnet? If so, why?

II. Were you surprised by the different themes of your classmates' sonnets?

III. When you read your sonnet, did it feel more natural then you expected it to feel?

Puritan Revolution 1640–1660

The English parliament rebelled against Charles I accusing him of abusing his power and ruling the people as a tyrant. The rebellion spurred the Puritans to support the Commonwealth (the government which was established by the Parliament in 1649) and encouraged it to make religious reforms—for example, ridding the Church of England of its Bishops. In 1653, Oliver Cromwell (1599–1658) became the first, and only, Lord Protector of England. He controlled the military, the Council of State, and

Parliament. During his rule, he enforced a strict moral code which included abolishing public theatre performances. Plays could be performed as part of education in school, but all public theatres were closed. However, toward the end of the Commonwealth, William Davenant (1606–1668) was permitted to stage the first English opera, *The Siege of Rhodes*, in his home at Rutland House. After Cromwell's death in 1658, the Commonwealth faltered and the restoration of the monarchy was inevitable.

The Restoration—Charles II (1630–1685) King of England, Scotland, and Ireland (1660–1685)

Three months after Charles II assumed the throne in 1660, he awarded patents to Thomas Killigrew (1612-83) and William Davenant so that each could organize a theatre company, build a playhouse, and present plays.

Killigrew was the first to organize his company, *The King's Players*; Davenant followed shortly after with *The Duke's Players*. One of the most significant innovations of the Restoration was the introduction, for the first time, of women on the English stage.

Surprisingly, Shakespeare's plays were not popular with the Restoration audiences. They were thought to be too complex, too poetic, and too old fashioned. Restoration audiences (largely the aristocracy) demanded plots that were uncomplicated and amusing with conversational dialogue. Thus developed a genre of plays referred to as *Comedy of Manners*. Comedies of Manners were written for and about the upper classes. They satirized the social customs of the well-to-do and frequently involved sexual intrigue and indiscretion. William Wycherley's (1640-1716) *The Country Wife* (1675) and *The Plain Dealer* (1676) examine a world where cuckolding and immoral values are virtually praised. Both plays are apt examples of Comedy of Manners, but perhaps William Congreve's (1670-1729) masterpiece, *The Way of the World* (1700) is the best example. Congreve's play features the typical battle of the sexes, boudoir intrigue, and the ridiculing of marriage, but at the same time it clearly delineates the foolish and the sensible characters.

Charles II's successor was Queen Anne (1665-1714) and her reign saw a "reformation of manners" which largely resulted from another Puritan outcry. Here *Sentimental Comedies* were preferred because most of the plays centered on characters that sought forgiveness for their flaws and shortcomings. Sir Richard Steel's (1672-1729) plays *Tatler* and *Spectator* make some attempt to reform the immoral behavior of his characters but his most noteworthy sentimental comedy is *The Conscious Lovers* (1722) in which the spouting of pious sentiments, repentance, and forgiveness overshadow comic situations.

Towards the end of the 18th century, the *Comedy of Manners* regained popularity. Richard Brinsley Sheridan's (1751-1816) *The Rivals* (1775) and *The School for Scandal* (1777) epitomize *Comedy of Manners* and are still performed today. Oliver Goldsmith (1730-1774) also harkens back to the comedies of the Restoration. During the 18th century, David Garrick (1717-1779), actor, director, manager, and playwright, made significant contributions to the theatre. He aided in the development of a technique of lighting the stage from the wings. Because the actors were more easily seen, they explored a more natural approach to acting rather than performing in a presentational manner. Previously, insufficient stage lighting was one of the reasons that actors delivered their lines directly to the audience. The naturalist style of acting would reach its height in the 19th century.

Summary

This chapter spans the Renaissance through the Restoration and the eighteenth century. The Italian Renaissance saw many theatrical innovations including perspective painting, intermezzis, operas, and the adoption of neo-classical ideals such as unities of place, action, and time. These affected theatrical development beyond Italy. Noteworthy French playwrights of the period include Pierre Corneille, Jean Racine, and Moliere (who was influenced by Commedia Del Arte' troupes from Italy). The Renaissance in England gave birth to the world's most influential playwright, William Shakespeare. Unfortunately, the Puritan Revolution resulted in the closing of the public theatres in England. When Charles II was restored to the throne, he legalized the theatre; however, Shakespeare's plays were not as popular as they once had been. The new aristocracy preferred plays that characterized their society. These plays were referred to as Comedies of Manner. The Restoration in England brought with it significant changes to the theatre including women performing on stage and, in the eighteenth century, lighting innovations that initiated a more natural style of acting.

Critical Thinking in Class Discussion

I. Fashion is an important part of contemporary culture. Who dictates fashion?

II. What impact does fashion have on a student's life?

III. Is an individual pressured to behave and dress a certain way? If so, why?

IV. There are several periodicals and television programs that focus on fashion and "modern-day royalty" (popular film, television, and music personalities). What messages do they send? Are the messages healthful?

Romanticism and the Battle of the "ism" (Naturalism/Realism vs. Symbolism, and Modern Experiments)

The Political Climate

The late eighteenth century was a period of political unrest in Europe, in part because of the French Revolution. In 1789, the French Revolution began with a fury and progressed so quickly that surrounding countries feared the violence might spread beyond the French borders and declared war on France. In 1793, Louis XVI was beheaded and by 1795 the rest of his family had been executed. With the revolution over, the country's political and economic affairs were in flux. Napoleon (1769–1821) took advantage of France's venerability and assumed power in 1799. He then placed his family members on the thrones in Spain, Holland, and several German and Italian states. In 1804, he appointed himself Emperor. While in power Napoleon abolished the Holy Roman Empire, minimized the number of German states, and ended serfdom in small areas in Eastern Europe. Napoleon had intended to create a democracy, but instead he built a new empire—his Empire.

One-time followers and supporters turned against Napoleon who, while fighting to save his Empire, was defeated at the Battle of Waterloo and permanently exiled. The results of the Napoleonic war were economic hardship and industrialization in France and other European countries. The once independent craftsmen were met with financial difficulties and moved to the cities, taking jobs as factory workers. Urban slum life proved to be intolerable and the factory workers began to demand social reform. Memories of the 1789 Revolution made governments uneasy and officials passed strict laws regulating the conduct of citizens. It was in this political and economic turmoil that Romanticism was born.

Romanticism

Romanticists were fed up with the rules and restrictions that made up the neoclassical ideal and sought out to create art that epitomized humans living in nature free from stifling governmental laws.

Romanticism dominated the theatre from 1800 until 1850. The Romanticists rebelled against the rules and restrictions of the neoclassical ideal and sought to create an art that epitomized humans living in nature free from stifling restraints and limitations. Romanticism began in Berlin when a group of writers used the term in the literary journal *Das Athenaeum* (1798–1800). The foundation of Romanticism encompasses these ideas:

I. Since the earth was created by a higher power, absolute truth exists only in the spiritual realm.

II. All nature is connected. Thus, if one has the ability to fully understand a small portion of nature, this knowledge will unleash the secrets of nature as a whole.

III. Human beings are composed of both body and soul, and the soul, trapped by physical boundaries, is desperate to transcend these earthly limitations.

IV. In order to see the unity which lies beyond superficial boundaries, one must have the capacity to fully use the imagination.

The Romantic Movement was based largely on a distrust of logic, a love of nature, an awakening of self, and a heightened consciousness. This was sometimes sought through the use of drugs and study of the occult. Most important, the movement was the protest against a strict structure of society. Artists involved in the movement believed that their art was not separate from themselves; thus, they dressed in an unconventional manner. Their cult-like dress mimicked their art. The Romantics also sought to inspire interest in mystery, the occult, beauty, and the absolute.

The ideals presented by the Romantics and the beginning of the Naturalist movement spawned the Symbolist Movement in the mid-nineteenth century. Naturalism strived to create "real life" onstage. The Naturalists intended to rid the theatre of stylized acting—actresses showing sorrow by dabbing pretend tears with their handkerchiefs. While the Symbolists valued a theatre that was spiritual, imaginative, and dreamlike.

Symbolism "Art for Art's Sake"

It may be said that Charles Baudelaire (1821–1867), author of *Les Fleurs du mal* (*The Flowers of Evil,* 1857), bridges the Romantics to the Symbolists and even to the later Surrealists. Baudelaire was inspired by the Romantics, but differed with them in that he redefined the meaning of beauty. His definition included suffering, horror, and sexual violence. He was the first to create poetry from evil and decadence. Although Baudelaire did not have much of an effect on his contemporary theatre, his avant-garde approach, including his use of juxtaposition and metaphor, coupled with his declaration that beauty cannot be separate from evil, inspired future playwrights such as Stephane Mallarme (1842–1898).

Mallarme attempted to create plays using physical gestures and images rather than traditional language. He felt that plays should be about dreams, ritual, and ceremony. His ideas inspired theatre artists so that his vision manifested itself in the nonrealistic theatre movements that followed.

Mallarme's visions were, in part, realized in the Symbolist Movement—a term coined in 1886. The Symbolists valued unconventional grammar, violent images, the use of bizarre sounds, and non-literal metaphors. They championed Mallarme's motto, "Art for arts sake," and attempted to strip away consciousness in order to reveal the true self. They believed the true self could be revealed only in dreams, nightmares, fantasies, and erotica. This new approach to the theatre was interpreted by many audiences as sheer madness.

Twenty-three-year-old Alfred Jarry (1873–1907), a French playwright, wrote and introduced *Ubu Roi* in Paris on December 11, 1896. This play greatly influenced the symbolist movement and shocked audiences. Before the play began, Jarry, dressed in worn-out street clothes, his face pale and drawn, stood in front of the stage curtain for ten minutes thanking people for helping him with the play. He then explained the set, hidden behind the curtain, in detail:

"In any case, we have a perfect *décor,* for just as one good way of setting a play in Eternity is to have revolvers shot off in the year 1000, you will see doors open on fields of snow under blue skies, fireplaces furnished with clocks and swinging wide to serve as doors, and palm trees growing at the foot of the bed so that little elephants standing on bookshelves can browse on them."

The Symbolists valued unconventional grammar, violent images, the use of bizarre sounds, and non-literal metaphors.

The first line of the play was "Merde (shit)," and it was the first time profanity had been used on stage. The audience responded with uproars. Some yelled at the actors and others got into fistfights. The following day the critics gave Jarry's production scathing reviews. Jarry's admirer, the Irish poet William Butler Yeats, defended *Ubu Roi*, by claiming the play was about power and resembled Shakespeare's *Macbeth*. At one point, Ubu is urged by his wife to kill the king and take the throne.

Although Jarry was a self-destructive rebel who never conformed to a particular ideology, he was an offshoot of the symbolists and paved the way for other non-realist movements such as Surrealism and Antonin Artaud's Theatre of Cruelty.

As the avant-garde artists were growing in numbers, touting "Art for art's sake," so were the Naturalists their "Slice of life" approach. The Naturalists based their approach on the scientific method—how heredity and environment create the individual's personality and subsequently affects behavior.

Naturalistic Theatre Movement

Proof

Directed by Matt Nesmith. *Photograph Courtesy of the University of South Dakota. Photograph by Dennis Chandler.*

Such diverse authors as Charles Dickens (1812–1870) best known for *A Christmas Carol*, Leo Nikolayevich Tolstoy (1828–1910), who wrote *War and Peace*, and Emile Zola (1840–1902), creator of the play *Therese Raquin*, were all considered naturalists. Theatre critic, novelist, and playwright Emile Zola, the leader of the Naturalist movement, wrote an essay called "Naturalism in Theatre" in which he declared that art should be approached as a science using acute observation and analyzing data. Zola believed that all literature ought to be socially oriented and reveal both the social and economic evils present in humanity. He wanted playwrights to create characters with complex inner lives, avoiding stereotypical characters.

In 1887, Andre Antoine and a group of amateur actors opened Theatre Libre, the first of the Independent Theatre movement. Antoine's theatre was dedicated to creating real life on-stage. The actors analyzed actual people in order to mimic their physical gestures and speech patterns. They used real hand properties and spoke to each other rather than simply delivering their lines to the audience. While Theatre Libre was in its infancy, additional naturalist theatre troupes were taking shape in other countries. For example, Germany's Freie Buhne used a realistic acting style as did The Independent Theatre in London.

The Naturalists sought to create drama based on objective observations of the world; the Symbolists revered beauty in the indescribable, and the Expressionists set out to "express" what was in the artist's mind rather than depict what the artist saw.

> The Naturalists sought to create drama founded on acute observations of an objective world, Symbolists revered beauty in the indescribable, and Expressionists set out to "express," rather than depict, what was ugly, bizarre, and decadent—whether or not what they were "expressing" was factual.

Expressionists

Art reflects politics, economics, culture, and individual tastes. Therefore, it is constantly evolving. For example, in the late nineteenth century, young adults who had been raised in stultifying, militaristic German families rebelled by becoming painters and writers. Many of these young artists, in protest against overbearing families, rejected the Symbolist and Naturalist methodologies. They wanted to create a completely free art, an art devoid of philosophy and rationality—Expressionism. Some early Expressionist dramatists wrote plays concerning German families that were ruled by cruel, overbearing parents, and sons who retaliated by killing their fathers and raping their mothers. Other Expressionists wrote plays that glorified suffering, self-sacrifice, and redemption. Regardless of their subject matter, Expressionist plays released all that had been repressed—all that was demonic, violent, and wild. Visual imagery took precedence over verbal language in the plays. The images were nightmarish and presented illogically with no frame of reference. This was an attempt to merge the character's inner and outer world. The limited verbal language was searing and the overall tone might be described as *Schrie*—the scream. Expressionist plays ignored conventional plot, and instead invented ways of evoking emotions through the use of music, dance, and exaggerated physicality.

Early expressionistic plays inspired Polish director Jerzy Grotowski's production of *Akropolis* (a play that is set in a German concentration camp) and Peter Brook's production of Marat/Sade.

Naturalism vs. Symbolism

At the end of the nineteenth century the struggle for dominance between the Naturalists and the Symbolists (realists versus non-realists) was still being fought, although the realistic style was winning in the popular mind. The naturalists focused on social and political evils, science, liberty, and social class. The Symbolists despised the confusion of art and politics and focused on the individual's vision. Sigmund Freud (1856–1939), an Austrian physician, began his famous study of dreams (published in a paper entitled *The Interpretation of Dreams,* in 1900). This gave encouragement to the

Symbolists; but Freud also developed a scientific approach to analyzing the personality and, thereby, seemed to support the Naturalists. The German political philosopher Karl Marx (1818–1883) wrote *Das Kapital,* an anti-capitalist manuscript that had an impact on many contemporary artists. Charles Darwin's (1809–1882) *On the Origin of Species* set forth the idea of natural selection. Thus the "ism" debate resulted in dramatists such as Strindberg and Ibsen writing both naturalist and symbolist plays. Even the great Konstantin Stanislavski, usually considered a naturalist/realist producer, explored Symbolism. He did not, however, change his psychologically-based approach to acting.

Anton Chekhov (1860–1904)

Anton Chekhov came from humble beginnings. Although his grandfather was a serf, Chekhov earned a medical degree from Moscow University in 1884. While in school, Chekhov supported himself by writing short stories that drew attention from Tolstoy and Gorky. These literary greats invited Chekhov to become a member of the Russian Academy, although Chekhov dropped his membership after the Tsar dismissed Gorky from the Academy.

Chekhov enjoyed the theatre, particularly the French farces that were popular at the time. His first plays reflected his tastes *The Bear* (1888) and *The Proposal* (1889) were one-act farces. His next one-act, *On the Road,* had a more serious tone but was banned by the censor. Chekhov's first three full length plays, *Ivanov* (1887), *The Wood-Demon* (1889), an early version of *Uncle Vanya,* and *The Seagull* (1896), were very different from his farces and contained delicate, subtle qualities. The use of subtlety was unfamiliar to Russian actors. They were used to performing in a presentational melodramatic style. Each of these full-length plays was produced, and each of the productions failed.

After the three failed productions, Chekhov was determined to end his playwriting career until Vladimir Nemirovich-Danchenko, who had recently co-founded the Moscow Art Theatre with Stanislavski, encouraged the playwright to let the MAT Company produce *The Seagull*. Chekhov agreed and the production was immensely successful.

The Moscow Art Theatre successfully produced all of Chekhov's major plays, including *Uncle Vanya* (1899), *The Three Sisters* (1901), and *The Cherry Orchard* (1904). Chekhov died not long after *The Cherry Orchard* was mounted. Today, his plays are produced worldwide in many languages and are regarded as some of the finest dramatic literature in the modern theatre. Chekhov is certainly one of the most influential realist Russian playwrights.

Vsevelod Meyerhold (1874–1940)

Stanislavski realized that his methodologies were unsuited to non-realistic theatre, but in order to explore this other realm, he opened The First Studio of the Moscow Art Theatre and appointed one of his former students, Vsevelod Meyerhold, to run it. Meyerhold admired Stanislavski, but felt that his teacher's approach led to passive acting and over-intellectualized emotions. Meyerhold believed that the inner life of a character could be communicated to the audience through what he called *plasticity*. *Plasticity* was the use of gestures, poses, and silent moments to express the *inner dialogue*—that which cannot be expressed by words alone. In order for actors to achieve *plasticity*, they had to be trained to respond physically to outside stimuli; and, to that end, Meyerhold created a system of training called *biomechanics*—labeled on intention, realization, and reaction. Essentially, it strived for total physical control.

Meyerhold envisioned unconventional settings in which to mount his productions. One such design was a tavern that enveloped the stage and the auditorium. As a result, the audience became a part of the production rather than simply spectators. Meyerhold frequently ignored the "fourth wall" in his productions because he wanted the audience to become a part of the play. In some productions, he used scaffolding rather than a traditional setting—a sort of "machine for acting" which become known as Constructivism.

Although their approaches were poles apart, Meyerhold and Stanislavski were both greatly influential. Before the Russian Revolution of 1917, new theatre movements were appreciated, but after the Bolshevik victory, only Stanislavski's approach was acceptable to the government.

Dada

The outbreak and aftermath of World War I spawned numerous artistic movements. One of the most interesting and influential was Dadaism. Dada was conceived by three artist's—Tristen Tzara, Hana Arp, and Richard Huelsenbeck—while meeting in a café in Zurich, Switzerland, in 1916. Unhappy with current artistic trends, they were determined to create their own movement and named it Dada because it was the first word that they saw when they opened a French dictionary. Dada was French for "hobby-horse" and Russian for "yes, yes," but for them, Dada meant anti-art, anti-reason, and anti-thought. In 1916, the three founding Dadaists performed in Zurich. The performance consisted of simultaneous banging of boxes, keys, and a drum, a poem shouted over this "music," while two of the three performers imitated bear cubs dancing and grunting around the stage. Afterwards, Tzara wrote the manifesto for Dadaism and was invited to be on the editorial board of a literary review called *Litterature*. The periodical promoted Dada, thus making it an official art movement.

The Dadaists did not confine their artistic efforts to theatre performances. For example, Tzara was invited to recite some poetry at a semi-formal gathering, but, instead of reading poetry, he opted to read the newspaper while ringing bells and shaking rattles. The Dadaists invited themselves to meetings and performances and created havoc by shouting and starting fist fights.

Dada was beginning to fade by 1922, but its performance techniques had a definite impact on avant-garde theatre. The Dadaists were responsible for the creation of "collage poetry" in which three or four people talk, sing, or whistle at the same time—a device since used by other experimental groups.

Surrealism

In the early twenty century, artists such as Pablo Picasso (1881–1973), Henri Matisse (1869–1954), and Guillaume Apollinaire (1880–1918) relaxed together in French cafés, sipping coffee, and discussing new art forms.

> *Freud's theories on dreams and self made up the foundation of Surrealism, a movement that can be described as "pure" thought.*

In 1917, Apollinaire was the first to use the term *Surrealism* in Jean Cocteau's play *Parade,* and by 1922, Surrealism was a full-fledged artistic movement.

Freud's theories on dreams and self make up the foundation of Surrealism, a movement that may be described as "pure" thought. Thought is deemed "pure" when it "is what it is," not because it is reasonable, esthetic, or moral. Surrealists valued the subconscious mind since it is composed of "pure" thought. Andre Breton (1896–1966), the leading Surrealist, fancied literature that was dream-like, nightmarish—stories that were written in a trancelike state. He developed a technique which he called *automatism*. It was designed to help the artist release his subconscious. In an *automatism* session, the author writes so rapidly that he does not consciously think about what he is writing. Breton believed that automatism was the key to unlocking the mysteries of the subconscious and dreams and bringing them into a tangible reality—a *surreality*.

The Surrealists conducted themselves much as the Dadaists had, attending public forums and instigating chaos. They viewed the world as a wasteland filled with tragedy and despair. The Surrealists personified anti-rationalism and self, and as a result their lives embodied their art.

In 1942, the Surrealists held an extensive exhibition in New York; a second exhibition was presented in Paris in 1947. After these presentations Surrealism as a movement began to decline, but their concepts continued to influence artists.

Antonin Artaud (1896–1948) and The Theatre of Cruelty

> *Artaud wanted to create theatre that would act as psychotherapy and allow for spiritual transformation. He created the Theatre of Cruelty.*

Antonin Artaud compared the theatre to the bubonic plague. He believed that the plays should emulate an epidemic and that the actors should attack and infect the audience so that when the audience leaves the theatre, they are cleansed. The epidemic would reveal those things present in the subconscious minds that infect and divide human beings. Once the subconscious was reached and the individual confronted himself a spiritual, re-birth would occur and the person would be cleansed. Essentially, Artaud wanted a theatre that acted as psychotherapy and would allow for spiritual transformation.

Artaud abandoned existing plays and called for the use of contemporary myths as subject matter. His ideal theatre would be based not on words but rather physical gesture, sounds, sight, and breathing. Speech would be used, not for its literal meaning, but for its sensuous and harmonious quality. He felt that effective theatrical productions would combine Oriental rituals, non-verbal sounds, grotesque masks, psychedelic lighting, and shocking costumes. These unconventional theatrical methods were intended to bypass the conscious mind, go directly to the subconscious, and cause a psychological catharsis.

Rather than the traditional theatre structure, Artaud wanted his plays performed in large open spaces such as barns or factory buildings. In an open space the actors could surround the audience and involve them in the performance, thus allowing more direct communication between the audience and the actors.

Artaud wrote numerous essays on his theories and included them in his book, *The Theatre and Its Double,* but he staged only one play—his adaptation of Shelley's *The Cenci*. The production was under-funded, under-rehearsed, and subsequently panned by the critics. Unfortunately, Artaud suffered from severe mental illness and was institutionalized. He never staged any other productions, but his theories inspired the radical theatre artists of the 1950s and 60s.

Absurdist Movement

The Holocaust and unprecedented destruction of World War II left many, especially intellectuals and artists, feeling empty and disconnected. These feelings inspired the Absurdist Movement. Playwrights such as Eugene Ionesco (1909-1994) and Samuel Beckett (1906–1989), influenced by the Dadaists and the Surrealists, used a "no-sense" approach when writing. The language in their plays was disconnected, filled with pauses and monosyllables and they used metaphors and symbols as a means of depicting an existential void.

From the 1950s through the early 1960s, Absurdist playwrights were the subject of inquiry and controversy.

The Holocaust and unprecedented destruction of World War II left people feeling empty and unconnected. These feelings inspired the Absurdist Movement.

Happenings

Action painter Allan Kaprow found two-dimensional arts to be limited and created a three-dimensional art form which he termed an *assemblage*. His first *assemblage* piece, *Mother's Boy* (18-1/2′ × 15-1/2′ × 12-1/2′) was composed of a large armoire, several mattresses, and a collage of fabrics and photographs. Another artist, George Segal, was inspired by Kaprow and created a three-dimensional work depicting a women's kitchen, complete with an actual kitchen table and hanging pots and pans. Segal's three-dimensional art form was termed as *environment*. The large scale of the *assemblage* and *environment* pieces made them difficult to display, so they were destroyed after their showings.

Kaprow found *assemblage* and *environment* pieces to have limitations and yearned to break through the barrier of space. He became interested in sound and enrolled in John Cage's avant-garde music course at the New School for Social Research. While Kaprow was enrolled in the course, he explored using everyday noises—car horns, trains, etc., as music.

Kaprow combined *assemblage* and *noisemusic* to create a new art form—happenings. He had originally created the assemblage because he wanted spectators to be a part of his art, and happenings, an extension of the assemblage, turned the spectators into actual participants. *Happenings* were based on the idea that humans are subjected to constant technological stimulation—radio, television, planes flying overhead, etc. *Happenings* formalize technological shapes, sounds, and people as objects, and redefine them as works of art.

Happenings as the term suggests, simply "happen"; they are made up of random: events, objects (which include people), and they take place in undefined spaces. Kaprow defined *Happenings* as having the following characteristics: real life and art should flow one into the other; any material should be used—except materials which are commonly associated with the

Happenings formalize technological shapes, sounds, and people as objects and redefined them as works of art.

arts; the location should be a wide space; and the location itself may change during the *Happening;* the duration of the *Happening* will be undetermined; a *Happening* will not be repeated; and there will be no audience members. *Happenings* were embraced by the rebellious art culture of the 1960s because they epitomized irrationality.

The Living Theatre

In 1947, husband and wife, Judith Malina and Julian Beck founded The Living Theatre, an experimental theatre ensemble, in New York City. Theatrically, The Living Theatre actualized Artaud's "cruelty" concepts.

In 1947, the husband and wife team of Julian Beck and Judith Malina founded The Living Theatre, an experimental theatre ensemble, in New York City. By 1964, they were under scrutiny from federal tax authorities and exiled themselves to Europe. The Dean of the Yale University School of Drama, Robert Brustein, invited the ensemble to return to the United States and to perform at Yale in 1968. While there, they staged four new works including Mary Shelly's *Frankenstein* and *Paradise Now*. During a performance of *Paradise Now*, the Beck's and some audience members were arrested for nudity but were released when the Dean Brustein spoke on their behalf. After a month's residence at Yale, The Living Theatre performed in New York City at the Brooklyn Academy of Music.

The Living Theatre company was comprised of some 40 men, women, and children and had a reputation for being political and theatrical anarchists. They used their productions to promote their own political agenda. For example, *Paradise Now* was intended to incite a non-violent revolution that would destroy the United States economy and replace it with cooperative living.

Theatrically, The Living Theatre actualized Artaud's Theatre of Cruelty concepts. The actors used their bodies to create physical symbols and abstract expressions, and they used ritualistic signals, groans, screams, and chants, instead of words. Similar to *Happenings,* The Living Theatre included the audience members in its productions and sought to make its art indistinguishable real life.

The audience members for The Living Theatre's productions were typically composed of people who supported the Beck's political agenda. This preordained political support tends to diminish the spontaneity of the performances, and spontaneity was an important aspect of The Living Theatre productions. Those who did not share the Beck's political views were not persuaded to join the revolution; instead they were offended by the production and left the theatre.

The Living Theatre's Judith Malina

Judith Malina

Judith Malina was born in 1926 in Kiel, Germany. In 1947, after studying acting and directing at the Dramatic Workshop at the New School with Erwin Piscator, she and Julian Beck founded The Living Theatre as an artistic challenge to the commercial theater, producing nearly 100 productions including *The Connection, The Brig, Frankenstein, Antigone, Paradise Now, Seven Meditations on Political Sado-Masochism, I and I,* and *Resistenza.*

FEATURE SECTION
An Interview with The Living Theatre Creator, Judith Malina

What was your inspiration for The Living Theatre?

Long Story! I was trained for the theatre by my mother—who gave up the theatre when she got married to a rabbi . . . she began to put her energy into training me. I was also trained by a director named Erwin Piscator who worked with Brecht (Piscator is known as the first major practitioner to the "Epic Theatre"). Piscator was my idol. He invented what I believed was the "modern political theatre" and it was because of my ambition and love for my mentor (Piscator) that I would carry on this tradition of political theatre—theatre for change.

At the age of seventeen, I met Julian Beck and we fell in love. We began working together to create a theatre that would be a part of the modern artistic movement, which was already going on in all aspects of art—painting, music, and dance . . . to expand on these advances to make politics more human . . . to humanize our political structure. There is a terrible lack of medical advances and many economic problems, aren't there? We fight against war, poverty—the lack of human services (health care, social services, economics), a march against capitalism—to use theatre as a vehicle to march against capitalism.

Judith Malina.
Photograph courtesy of Judith Malina

The Living Theatre's Mission Statement

To call into question
who we are to each other
in the social environment of the theater,

to undo the knots that lead to misery,

to spread ourselves across the public's table
like platters at a banquet,

to set ourselves in motion
like a vortex that pulls the spectator into action,

to fire the body's secret engines,

to pass through the prism
and come out a rainbow,

to insist that what happens in the jails matters,

to cry "Not in my name!"
at the hour of execution,

to move from the theater to the street
and from the street to the theater.

This is what The Living Theatre does today.
It is what it has always done.

Written by Hanon Reznikov

What do you enjoy most about your life in theatre?

The joy is creating with a company, living within a collective community, the work is happy. The struggle for economic existence is its flaw—but everyone has that struggle—economics is always the challenge whether you are a factory worker or farmer or an artist—everyone needs more. The fact is that even the rich say they need more (12 percent more). What is enough? That constant economic crisis takes away the artistic energy—sucks focus—however, we persist!

What is your favorite performance?

Last night's! I always say last night's, when asked that question, because it is true, the one you are working on at the time is. Wonderful cast, the young men (in this production of *The Brigg*) are a wonderful company of dedicated actors. (*The Brigg,* directed by Judith Malina won Obie Awards for directing and ensemble (2007).)

What advice do you have for a student wishing to create political theatre?

Clarify what it is you want to say. The more clear you are about what your purpose is will help you achieve your goal. (clarity = purpose = clear communication = goal.) If you have no burning statement—no passionate goal—don't do political theatre!

(If you do have a passion) get your people together—find out what you want to say—choose your play or invent an action to illustrate your statement—then do it! Get $100 or so together and if you want enough to rent a space . . . you can get a space for about $400. If you don't have any money, go out and perform it out on the street. Reverend Billy (Reverend Billy and the Church of Stop Shopping) has done a wonderful job of this. He fights consumerism so he performs in department stores. Anyway, clarify the idea, put on the play—that will carry your message.

We (The Living Theatre) do a lot of workshops. Our workshops are five days long. Our main goal is to create a work together. We begin by finding out what the group wants to say—what is important to them. Then we (as a collective) create a play around it, chose the words, and the actions. We (members of The Living Theatre) teach the group techniques (for expressing themselves) movement, sound, and tools to create the structure—in order to create a theatrical event around the subject. We explore how a theatrical event is created and how a collective work manifests itself. I participate with them. Afterwards a public performance is given.

It is very satisfying for people to realize they can do it themselves . . . even if they are not trained.

For more information about The Living Theatre visit their website: **livingtheatreorg@yahoo.com**.

Jerzy Grotowski (1933–1999)

Polish director Jerzy Grotowski was born into a Catholic family and was only six years old when Hitler's army invaded Poland. The Nazis seemed intent on annihilating the Polish people, whether they were Jews or not. In only a two-month period, September–October 1939, 700 Poles were murdered individually, 16,000 were mass murdered, tens of thousands were killed in aerial bombings, and others were shipped off to Nazi concentration camps. The mass destruction that Grotowski lived through made a permanent impression on him and was a catalyst for his work in the theatre. In 1959, Grotowski was only 26 years old when he and a small group of unknown actors formed the "laboratory theatre" in a small town about 80 miles from Auschwitz in Poland.

In 1959, Grotowski was only 26 years old when he lead a small group of unknown actors formed the "laboratory theatre."

Grotowski agreed with the symbolists that dramatic literature should be replaced with free flowing images and ideas. He felt that Greek and Roman myths could be transposed into meaningful, contemporary stories, and that the plays could include both dream- and reality-based scenes. Grotowski was also influenced by the Polish Romantics, in that his productions pose existential questions, are based on history and religion, and involve human suffering.

He believed that an actor's psychological behavior should be approached through biological, mythic roots. In *Lunatic, Lovers and Poets The Contemporary Experimental Theatre*, written by Margaret Croyden, Croyden quotes Grotowski as saying, "To be poor in the Biblical sense is to abandon all externals." To this end he created a "poor theatre" and published his theories in *Towards a Poor Theatre*.

Grotowski's productions did not use traditional makeup, hand props, costumes, or scenery. Instead, his actors used facial expressions to create the illusion of make-up, wore potato sacks as costumes—even a king's robe or a wedding gown—and wheelbarrows were used to represent set pieces—coffins, chairs, and/or tables. Additionally, Grotowski replaced traditional music with chants, songs, and whispers created by the actors.

Grotowski believed that the voice responds to physicality. First you stub your toe, and then you cry out. He rigorously trained his actors so that their voices and bodies were turned to optimum levels. He divided his physical exercises into two categories. The first category was *plastiques*, which involved fast rotations of joints—head, shoulders, etc. The second category was *corporeals*, which included strenuous acrobatics—high jumps, headstands, and flips, etc.—performed very rapidly.

Grotowski is considered to be one of the leading experimental theorists of the modern theatre. His productions involved the audience members as silent, but valued participants. His actors imbued language with emotional depth and great expression. His methodology continues to inspire other avant-garde theatre artists.

Bertolt Brecht

The German writer Bertolt Brecht grew up in an era when the style of German acting favored highly charged, emotional outbursts on stage. Brecht wanted the plays that he wrote to be performed in a more natural style. In

1922, he was directing a play and disagreed with the way the leading actress was approaching her role. His severe criticism drove her to tears and caused Brecht to determine that alienating his performers was not beneficial, so he vowed to take a more reasonable approach. In Munich in 1922 when he directed his own play, *Drums in the Night*, he began to formulate his unique approach to the theatre.

On the opening night of his second play, *In the Jungle*, Nationalist Party protestors released tear gas in the theatre. Political unrest was becoming fascism, and Brecht's plays were politically controversial. His communist sympathies were well known, and Brecht left Germany until after World War II. He wrote some of his best plays while in exile including *The Caucasian Chalk Circle* and *Mother Courage*.

Brechtian Acting

Brecht never wrote a specific manual detailing how he trained his actors. However, his goals for actors can be gleamed from his journals and theoretical writings, particularly *The Messingkauf Dialogues* (1937–1940), *A Short Organum for the Theatre* (1949), and *Theaterarbeit* (1952). The last is an impressive collection of notes and pictures from the first two years of his work with the *Berliner Ensemble*, a company formed for him by the East German government. *Theaterarbeit* includes hundreds of photographs of his productions. It showed that Brecht was very meticulous about his arrangement of the actors and scenery so that the stage pictures tell the story.

Brecht coached his actors to always be poised as if he or she might break into song at any moment. It was important to Brecht that his actors had a realistic quality, but he was not interested in emotional expression as were his predecessors. Brecht's actors were taught to speak matter-of-factly, but when they revealed an emotion, they were not permitted to unrealistically heighten it simply for dramatic value. Brecht admired his contemporary, Frank Wedekind, whose cabaret actors were emotionally cool and played in a presentational style. Brecht required his performers to research their roles in the hope that the information gained would surprise and intrigue them enough to keep their performances spontaneous. Brecht questioned humanity and society in his plays; and he wanted his audience to do the same, to be active participants who asked their own questions and contributed to society. Theatre for Brecht was not about "art for art's sake", but rather art that would have an effect on the audience and provoke change.

In an effort to encourage his actors, and in turn his audiences, to observe their world, question it, and make changes if they deemed their society to be wrong or unjust, Brecht would stimulate observation through a series of improvisations in rehearsal. These exercises focused especially on class and gender norms. One such exercise invited two female actors to perform a very simple task—folding linens. An audience would observe and, afterwards, Brecht asked the audience questions regarding the way in which

Theatre for Brecht was not about art for art's sake but rather art to have an effect on the audience and, if necessary, to provoke change.

women fold linen, if women approach folding in a different way than men do, and if so, why.

Additionally, Brecht devised ways for actors to gain different perspectives about his plays. He did this by asking his performers play tragic scenes as comic and comic scenes as tragic, during rehearsals. He also wanted to examine choice-making. When a person is consciously aware that a choice can be made and that each choice has a consequence, he or she knows that the individual has the power to change. Brecht wanted his audience to be constantly reminded that each individual has a choice, so he taught his actors to show the audience that their characters made choices. This was termed—"Not . . . But . . ." For example, a character in a scene is offered some fruit from a bowl. The character takes two pieces of fruit. After a moment, he or she decides *not* to take two pieces and returns one piece of fruit to the bowl. Thus, idea of choice is presented to the audience.

Other Experimental Theatre Companies

Numerous other individuals and experimental theatre companies have made an impact on the modern theatre. A few of the best known include Joseph Chaikin's Open Theatre, Peter Schmann's Bread and Butter Theatre, and John Vaccaro's and Charles Ludman's Theatre of the Ridiculous. Today, avant-garde theatre techniques continue to be explored. Performance Art has gained popularity in the last couple of decades. In some cases, what began as experimentation has become commercially viable, i.e., *The Blue Man Group*.

Performance Artist Cita Ricardo

Cita Ricardo

Cita was born in Northern Mexico in the city of Chihuahua, Chihuahua. In 1988, Cita received a BFA in Theatre from Eastern New Mexico University.

While in the United States, Cita's theatrical resume includes numerous genres such as musicals, operas, Shakespeare, and New York City's experimental underground theater. Her extensive dance resume includes both classics and modern expressions. Cita has also worked in television and film in both Mexico and the United States.

Actress, singer, director, choreographer, writer, and painter, Cita is currently working on her new record with producer, Ricardo Ochoa. She continues to perform throughout the United States with the band *Sus Muñecas Rotas*.

Cita Ricardo

Photograph courtesy of Cita Ricardo.

FEATURE SECTION
Cita Ricardo Comments on Performance Art

Performance art has changed immensely since the 1960s, art in all its different forms will constantly evolve as we, the artists of this world, reflect in our work the times we live in as independent mirrors of society.

What we do, as performance artists, is shock the audience into reevaluating who they are and their view of life, art, and its relation to their environment and their unique cultural taboos, at times including the spectator in our unexpected, unorthodox presentations of their community.

In this medium, you have the freedom to prepare a performance in a controlled environment with specific lighting, live or recorded sound, props, sets, costumes, crew and paying audience; or just use whatever environment is available with an unsuspecting audience, and no one but yourself.

That is the beauty of performance art, that all or nothing can be used in order to perform. This, of course, opens the door to everyone and anyone who wants to call themselves a performance artist.

I have seen wonderful performances by artists who have never had any formal training but they are very few and far between; and you can't help but wonder how amazing they could be if they were formally trained in the performing arts.

The more you experience, learn, and train with other artists and teachers, the more your body and mind find true freedom to create and explore beyond any boundaries created by others, and, as in most cases, yourself.

Performance art today has evolved; it is global and truly exiting. Nowadays, with cell phones having video capabilities, the audience can literally capture the performance and send it via the Internet in seconds, changing a street corner "happening" into a global performance where it can be viewed by millions. This is truly an amazing time to be a performance artist. So, seize the *mise en scene* and all control, command your media, mode, and method, determine your own representation. Be your own vehicle; you are your own medium.

For more information on Cita Ricardo see her website: www.citaysusmunecasrotas.com.

Melodrama

Although the definition of the word *melodrama* varies, it has been used for centuries. During the seventeenth century, in Germany, the term *melodrama* was used to describe the passages of spoken language which were accompanied by a musical underscore in operas. In the nineteenth century, the French writer, Jean-Jacques Rousseau called the musical interludes that underscored unspoken emotional moments *melodrame*. French playwright Guibert di Pixerecourt seems to have been the first to apply the term to a play.

In the early nineteenth century, melodramas were particularly popular in urban industrial areas such as New York City. Late in the century, electricity powered the moving special effects on-stage—for example, the famous shipwreck scene in the play *The Count of Monte Cristo*. Audience members worked in the nearby factories and frequently interacted with the production by booing, hissing, cheering the hero, and even throwing peanut shells at the villain.

Specific character types, suspenseful plots, musical interludes, and elaborate special effects are the elements that define melodrama. There are three specific types of characters that are characteristic of a melodrama. These include the vulnerable heroine, the evil villain, and the capable hero. The plot line of a melodrama follows a standard formula. The heroine is relentlessly pursued by an evil villain; during the villain's pursuit, the heroine will be put into situations that threaten her happiness, reputation, and/or life; each of the calamities typically requires elaborate special effects such as moving trains, explosions, and collapsing buildings; after the villain has subjected the heroine to numerous dangerous situations, the valiant hero rescues the frightened heroine. Melodramas typically have a simple moral—good prevails over evil; moments of high emotion are underscored with music; and, at times, the characters are inspired to sing and even dance.

Today, it is rare to see a play that contains all of the components of the classic melodrama; however, it is common to see elements of melodrama in nearly all forms of popular entertainment.

Summary

This chapter has given a brief overview of a rather eclectic group of theatre genres. These included Romanticism, Naturalism/Realism, and an assortment of non-realistic movements such as Symbolism, Absurdism, and Dadaism. It may seem as though these genres are unrelated, but in actuality many of the genres co-existed, in a historical timeline, and/or in the artists' mindset, and, as a result, influenced one another.

Active Learning Assignment
"Bringing Theatre to Life"

I. Reenacting History

1. Break the class into groups of 10 to 15 people.
2. Divide the key points of each of the genres equally among the groups.
3. Each group will select four important pieces of information from the section it has been assigned.
4. The groups will then devise a theatrical method of presenting the material to the class. For example, a talk show could be simulated with the host's special guest, Jerzy Grotowski. The two discuss Grotowski's theatre innovations.
5. These presentations should be between five to seven minutes in length.

Critical Thinking in Class Discussion

I. What were the four main points that each of the groups covered?

II. Were there important facts that were missed? If so, what were they?

III. What are the most surprising facts about romanticism, melodrama, realism, naturalism, and non-realistic theatre?

IV. If you could travel back in time, which one of these would you like to be a part of and why?

American Musical Theatre:
Storytelling through Song and Dance

by: Robin Carr

Assisted by: Adam Sechelski

The American musical has made a significant impact on the evolution of the modern theatre and continues to grow in popularity. Springing from opera and operetta and continuing to develop through minstrel shows and vaudeville, the American musical won the hearts of audiences who recognized that telling a story through song and dance can lift spirits and even transform lives. More than most other forms of theatre, the musical is capable of transporting its audiences to another time and place, somewhere "over the rainbow" where life is good even when disaster is imminent. It is said that any musical that has the audience humming a tune when they exit the theatre is almost sure to be a box office hit. Ranging from the book musical to musical reviews, Broadway shows are largely successful because of the variety they offer. To experience a musical is like no other theatrical experience: the lights dim, the overture begins, and a singing character strides on stage ready to tell the story. The following is a brief history of American musical theatre, including the most influential artists and musicals.

THE EVOLUTION OF MUSICAL THEATRE

Pre-Opera

Since the origins of theatre, music and dance have been an integral part of storytelling. They have been used theatrically in all major civilizations throughout history. For example, in ancient Greek theatre, the chorus would chant and dance as a way to communicate the story. In Renaissance productions, musical entertainments (called *intermezzi*) were presented in between acts of longer works. Later, music and dance became a more showcased form of entertainment. The American musical theatre not only began from these roots, but was also influenced by opera, operetta and vaudeville.

Opera and Operettas

Opera began in the Baroque period in Italy around 1600 and was influenced by Ancient Greek and Roman dramas. The musical elements of opera consist mainly of solos (*arias*), sung dialogue (*recitative*), duets, ensembles, large chorus numbers, and instrumental accompaniment. Other elements of opera include lavish costumes and elaborate staging and theatrical design. Opera influenced musical theatre because of its emphasis on storytelling through song, character, and use of chorus. The principal characters in most operas consist of a soprano (female) and a tenor (male), and the same archetypes can be found in almost all musicals. In addition, operas incorporate epic stories, ballet, and extravagant characters, and these same elements can be seen in musical theatre today.

Photograph courtesy of Luis Saldalgo.

During the eighteenth century, Italian serious opera (*opera seria*) and comic opera (*opera buffa*) became extremely popular throughout Europe and influenced the development of other French and German opera genres. Many types of opera have characteristics that can be identified in musical theatre. The German *Singspiel*, such as Mozart's *The Magic Flute* (1791), bears resemblance to musical theatre because of its use of spoken dialogue, comic elements, popular songs and special effects. Nineteenth century French Grand Operas, such as those by Giacomo Meyerbeer (1971–1864), often contain spectacular theatrical elements, such as a volcano erupting on stage, a building on fire, or the stage opening up to reveal a lake of water or ice below. In addition, many operas incorporate exotic locales, such as Georges Bizet's *Carmen* (1875), and Giacomo Puccini's *Madama Butterfly* (1904).

Although serious and comic operas continued to flourish and develop in Europe, the first fully staged opera performance in America did not take place until 1825 in New York. To many Americans, opera plots seemed contrived, and the foreign language lyrics were difficult to decipher. In general, American audiences preferred more down-to-earth musical entertainment sung in English, popular hymns, ballads, and folk tunes. In England, the poet John Gay (1685–1732) wrote the first ballad opera, *The Beggar's Opera* (1728), a libretto satirizing English society. In *The Beggar's Opera*, all of the songs were set to well known popular tunes but were given new lyrics. The ballad opera was an immediate success, due primarily to the style of its music.

Audiences' love of comedy and music led to the emergence of operettas. Operettas (meaning "little opera") became tremendously popular due in large part to their witty, satirical lyrics and rather absurd plots. Operettas have some spoken dialogue and include ballads, as well as fast-paced, language-driven patter songs. Some of the most popular operettas were written by librettist W. S. Gilbert (1836–1911) and composer Arthur Sullivan (1842–1900) who, although English, made a lasting impression on American musical theatre. Their operettas, such as *H.M.S. Pinafore* (1878), were immensely popular in America. *H.M.S. Pinafore* was given over 214 performances at the Boston Museum before it opened in New York, and it was followed in 1879 by an even greater success, *The Pirates of Penzance*. Gilbert and Sullivan operettas continue to be popular in today's theatre.

The Musical Theatre Movement

While opera and operettas heavily influenced the birth of musical theatre, there were other forms of entertainment that played equal parts in its evolution. Minstrel shows, beginning in the 1840's consisted of comedy sketches plus songs and dances, all filled with racially charged material. The characteristics of the minstrel shows paved the way for vaudeville's emergence in the late nineteenth century. During the transition from minstrel shows to vaudeville, *The Black Crook* (1866) appeared and is often referred to by theatre scholars as "America's first musical comedy." *The Black Crook* was the first long running musical production that featured elaborate costumes and scenic elements, a large cast of scantily-clad female dancers, and ballet as a part of the show. Following *The Black Crook*, vaudeville became one of the most popular forms of entertainment in America, taking the minstrel show structure of separate acts and performing them on a larger more extravagant scale. Vaudeville was filled with many diverse performances such as singing, dancing, burlesque, jugglers, magicians, and more.

During the height of vaudeville, Florenz Ziegfeld, Jr. (1867–1932) created a genre of entertainment that changed the world's stage performance and popular music. The Ziegfeld Follies (1907–1931) established one of the most successful forms of entertainment ever created. The Follies consisted of beautiful dancing girls with elaborate costumes combined with vaudeville acts. One of Ziegfeld's most famous actresses was comedian Fannie Brice (1891–1951). The popular composer Irving Berlin (1888–1989), who wrote such classics as *Annie Get Your Gun* (1946) and *Call Me Madam* (1950), began his career with the Follies. The Ziegfeld Follies was an important step in the maturity of the American musical because it showcased the performer not only as a singer but also an actor and entertainer. At the height of the Follies, George M. Cohan (1878–1942) took the musical comedy form a step farther by concentrating more on one plot than separate variety acts. Cohan's patriotic themes, memorable songs and linear story lines can be found among his many successful shows such as *Forty Five Minutes from Broadway* (1904), and *Little Johnny Jones* (1906). In 1968, the musical *George M.* was written as a tribute to the life and accomplishments of Cohan and featured well-known tunes such as "The Yankee Doodle Boy" and "Give My Regards to Broadway". Cohan opened a door to a new type of musical that combined song, plot, and dance more cohesively and set the stage for one of the most important events in musical theatre history.

On December 27, 1927 *Showboat* opened and changed the American musical theatre scene. Set on river boat in Mississippi, *Showboat*, written by Jerome Kern (1885–1945), tells the story of a young woman's rise to fortune and fame. This, however, was juxtaposed with a serious story of interracial marriage. *Showboat* paved the way for more serious plot lines and legitimized the American musical in a way that had never been done before. *Showboat* gave permission for future musicals to confront controversial subject matter and further establish the story as the primary focus of the production.

As the structure of musicals was solidifying, artists such as composer and lyricists Richard Rodgers (1872–1979) and Lorenz Hart (1895–1943), George (1898–1937) and Ira Gershwin (1896–1983), and Cole Porter (1861–1964) were making their marks. Rodgers and Hart were the first composer and lyricist to work together as a team. They began working together in 1919 and consistently wrote musicals that were loved by audiences. The Gershwin's composed music that combined jazz and classical styles, such as *Rhapsody in Blue* and *Someone to Watch over Me*. Some of the Gershwin's more popular works include *Girl Crazy* (1930) and the first musical to win the Pulitzer Prize, *Of Thee I Sing* (1931). Cole Porter, a contemporary of the Gershwin's, rose to fame when he composed the music and lyrics for *Anything Goes* (1934). Porter went on to become one of the best known composers with musicals such as *Red, Hot and Blue!* (1936) and *Kiss Me, Kate* (1948). Rodgers and Hart, George and Ira Gershwin and Cole Porter were important pioneers that helped transition musical comedy entertainment into what can be identified today as musical theatre.

TYPES OF MUSICAL THEATRE

Beginning in the 1920's, the musical started to establish itself as a recognizable form of theatrical entertainment. Throughout the decades, the musical has shaped itself into four major types. Although there are many variations, each type has distinct characteristics. In contemporary musicals, these forms are often combined.

Book Musicals

Richard Rodgers (1902–1979) and Oscar Hammerstein II (1895–1960) made significant contributions to American musical theatre with their first successful production, *Oklahoma!* (1943, winner of the Pulitzer Prize, 1944). The production's significance was that it was the first pure form of what we know of as a *book* musical. It was referred to in this way because the storyline was the focal point of the production. In addition to the dialogue, the songs and dance numbers were also integrated to further the dramatic action. *Oklahoma* was a milestone due to the complete integration of dance into the story and the introduction of modern choreography by Agnes de Mille (1905–1993) especially in the production's dream ballet. Rodgers and Hammerstein went on to write numerous successful musicals, including the Pulitzer Prize winning *South Pacific* (1949), *The King and I* (1951), and *The Sound of Music* (1959).

The Secret Garden

Directed by Matt Nesmith. *Photograph courtesy of The University of South Dakota. Photograph by Dennis Chandler.*

Book musicals became the cornerstone of the musical theatre art form and gave rise to other productions such as *Guys and Dolls* (1950), *The Music Man* (1957) and *The Secret Garden* (1991). Based on the novel by Frances Hodgson Burnett, *The Secret Garden* tells the story of Mary Lennox who, while living with her Aunt, discovers the healing power of nature through a forgotten rose garden. *The Secret Garden* has all of the classical elements of a book musical.

Concept Musicals

The concept musical tells a story based on an idea or theme. The stories are often told in a non-linear fashion by using vignettes or multiple plot lines. Probably the most famous creator of concept musicals is Stephen Sondheim (1930–). A student of Oscar Hammerstein II, Sondheim made a substantial impact on the style of American musicals. Similar to his mentor's style, the musical numbers in Sondheim productions are an

Into the Woods

Directed by Seth Panitch. *Courtesy of the University of Alabama. Photograph by Porfirio Solorzano.*

integral part of the dramatic action. However, unlike Hammerstein's works, Sondheim's productions do not center on a tightly woven story, but rather a theme. One of Sondheim's innovations occurred in *Sunday in the Park with George* (1984). At first perplexing to critics, it includes no dance numbers. Sondheim has composed the music and written the lyrics for a long line of successful musicals, including *A Funny Thing Happened on the Way to the Forum* (1962), *Company* (1970), and *Into the Woods* (1987).

Rock Musicals

The Rock Musical tells a story with little or no spoken dialogue and with music that is composed in the rock style. As opposed to the more classical orchestral accompaniment, rock musicals use electric guitar, bass and drums to accompany musical numbers. One of the first successful rock musicals was the anti-war off-Broadway hit, *Hair* (1967), written by Galt MacDermot (1928–), Gerome Ragni (1942–1991), and James Rado (1932–). Following on the heels of *Hair*, Andrew Lloyd Webber (1948–) and Tim Rice's (1944–) *Jesus Christ Superstar* (1971) sold over three million record albums before it opened on Broadway. Other popular rock musicals include Webber and Rice's *Evita* (1978), *Joseph and the Amazing Technicolor Dreamcoat* (1981) and Jonathan Larson's *Rent* (1996). *Little Shop of Horrors* (1982) by Howard Ashman (1950–1991) and Alan Menken (1949–) is considered a rock musical as well, due to its musical mixture of pop, rock and do-wop.

Little Shop of Horrors

Directed by Robin Carr. *Photograph courtesy of The University of Southern Mississippi. Photograph by Steve Rouse.*

Musical Reviews

Musical Reviews are selections of songs usually written by the same composer and lyricist. Reviews have little spoken dialogue, no discernable story line, and are used to showcase a composer and lyricist's work. *Closer Than Ever* (1989) by Richard Maltby, Jr. and David Shire, *Smokey Joe's Café* (1992) by Jerry Leiber and Mike Stoller, and *Songs for a New World* (1995) by Jason Robert Brown are examples of musical reviews. Another prominent example of the musical review is *Five Guys Named Moe* (1992), which showcases the jazz music of Louis Jordon. Musical reviews are fun, entertaining, and short, usually running around ninety minutes.

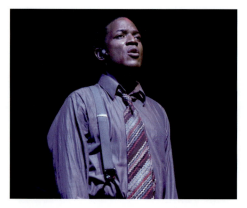

Five Guys Named Moe

Pictured: C. Mingo Long. *Photograph courtesy of Tim Fort.*

INFLUENCES ON MUSICAL THEATRE

Musicals have undergone many changes through the influences of history, popular culture, economics, and audience taste. These influences have brought about major transitions in the American Musical form. They have impacted musical theatre in ways that transcend time and push boundaries.

Culture and Diversity

African Americans have made a strong impression on the musical theatre movement. When musical theatre was in its earliest stages, African Americans performed in their own minstrel shows and introduced ragtime, jazz, and blues to the stage. Bert Williams (1875–1922) was the first African American performer in vaudeville. Williams, performing in blackface, was known for his self-deprecating comedy routine and melancholy tune "Nobody." Developed from a vaudeville sketch, *Shuffle Along* (1921) was the first musical written, directed and performed by African Americans and helped lead the way into the Harlem Renaissance. With the attempt to portray realistic characters in Gershwin's opera *Porgy and Bess* (1935), the excitement for telling the African American story of struggles and celebrations was heightened. This interest has continued with productions such as *Bring in 'da Noise, Bring in 'da Funk* (1996), *Caroline, or Change* (2004) and the musical adaptation of *The Color Purple* (2005).

Societal and political changes throughout history have also affected the creation of theatre in all of its forms. The need to express concerns and passionate beliefs has, of course, shaped musical theatre storylines. Plotlines can concern race, socio-economic status, sexual orientation, and political upheaval. *Kiss of the Spiderwoman*, based on the 1976 novel by the Argentine writer Manuel Puig, was adapted into a musical by John Kander (1927–) and Fred Ebb (1932–2004). It concerns a homosexual window dresser in a Latin American prison who falls in love with his cell mate. *In the Heights* (2008 Tony Award Winner), written by and starring Lin-Manuel Miranda (1980–), is about a diverse community that experiences the joys and struggles of surviving in Washington Heights, New York. *Once On This Island* (8 Tony nominations) was written by Stephen Flaherty and Lynn Ahrens and produced in 1990. Its tragic story, based on Hans Christian Andersen's *The Little Mermaid*, portrays a young woman, Ti Moune, who lives on an island in the Antilles and falls in love with Daniel Beauxhomme, the son of a rich land owner. Despite their love, Ti Moune and Daniel are from two different classes, and therefore, can never marry.

European Spectacle

Cameron Mackintosh, a British producer, ushered musical theatre into a new era in the 1980's by producing blockbusters such as Andrew Lloyd Webber's *Phantom of the Opera* (1988) and *Cats* (1982). These brought about a great popularity in America for the British Musical, along with Alain Boubil and Claude-Michel Schönberg's *Miss Saigon* (1981) and *Les Misèrables* (1987). The productions involved large budgets, epic storylines, and huge spectacle. These high cost productions were extremely successful and took musical theatre from an era of minimalism into one of extravagance. Thus, large production shows began a trend that continues today with large corporations dominating the Broadway theatre.

Disney

Over several decades, the New York borough of Manhattan changed as theatres became movie houses and clubs, and deteriorated into decadence. During 1980's, Time Square in Manhattan became the home of strip clubs

and pornography stores. The art of the theatre was becoming lost. Then, in the 1990's, The Disney Corporation gave Broadway a new face by redeveloping the former theatrical center, 42nd street, including the New Amsterdam Theatre. The New Amsterdam, after its complete renovation, opened in 1994 with the Tony Award Winner *The Lion King*, directed by Julie Taymor. *The Lion King* was a huge success and still runs today at the Minskoff Theatre. In addition to *The Lion King*, Disney produced numerous family oriented productions such as *Beauty and the Beast*, *Tarzan*, and *Mary Poppins*. Disney continues to dominate the Broadway stage with its crowd pleasing adaptations for all ages.

CONTEMPORARY TRENDS IN MUSICAL THEATRE

Musical theatre forms continue to evolve. Some reflect the past and others are blazing new paths. The musical structure of a story told through song, script and dance remains the foundation of musical theatre; however, *how* the story is told is ever changing. The following are some contemporary examples of these changes.

The revival of *Cabaret* in the roundabout theatre in Manhattan started a trend of featuring actors playing musical instruments. This convention was not so unusual for *Cabaret* since this story takes place in a jazzy cabaret club. John Doyle, a British director, continued this trend in his unique productions of *Sweeney Todd* and *Company* where actors would play their own instruments while performing their roles. For example, Bobby (played by Raúl Esparza), the lead character in *Company*, accompanied himself on the piano while singing the memorable song "Being Alive."

American audiences of today have been brought up on and are drawn to films and popular music. These have become a resource for the relatively new forms of the Juke Box musical and film adaptations. The Juke Box musical uses the music of today or of one particular musical artist and shapes a script around the songs. Examples of Juke Box musicals are *Mama Mia!* (2001), using the music of ABBA, *Movin' Out* (2002), with the music of Billy Joel, and *We Will Rock You* (London, 2002) based in the music of Queen. Film adaptations are also becoming extremely popular. *Legally Blonde*, *The Wedding Singer*, *9 to 5*, and *Shrek The Musical* are only a few among many that are popular today.

Darker, more controversial subjects are now seen more than ever in musical theatre. The rock musical, *Rent* (1996 Tony Award winner), based on the opera *La Bohème*, tells the story of individuals struggling to survive in New York City amidst poverty and disease. *Avenue Q* (2003) uses twisted humor and puppets

Urinetown The Musical (2002 Tony Award for Original Musical Score)

Directed by Robin Carr. *Photograph courtesy of The University of Southern Mississippi. Photograph by Steve Rouse.*

to tell the tale of generation y and its search for fulfillment. Songs such as "Every One's a Little Bit Racist" and "It Sucks to Be Me" reflect the musical's dark humor. Another dark musical, *Next To Normal* (2009), tells the story of a family struggling to stay together in the midst of dealing with a mother diagnosed as bi-polar.

To boost ticket sales, producers have been using television, film and music celebrities in starring roles of musicals. Tony Danza was featured in *The Producers* (2001), Brooke Shields and Rosie O'Donnell both performed in *Grease*, and Christina Applegate played the title role in *Sweet Charity* (2005). Even American Idol contestants have been seen in various roles. Clay Aiken sang and danced in *Monty Python's Spamalot* (Tony Award Winner, 2004) and Fantasia was in *The Color Purple* (2005). Whether their abilities lie in acting, singing, dancing, or are simply the result of personality, celebrities bring audiences to Broadway from all over the country.

THE MUSICAL THEATRE TEAM

A large group of artists is involved when a musical is created from its conception to the performance. Although each creative process is different, there is always a core group of collaborators involved. Below is a list and description of these individuals and their responsibilities.

The **Producer** is perhaps the most important and influential person on the musical theatre team. (There is even a musical called *The Producers* (2001), based on the script by Mel Brooks.) The producer's responsibilities, as in all forms of theatre, include finding donors and raising money, hiring the production team, and renting a theatre space. Many times the producer has the final say on all elements of the production from artistic to box office sales. In addition to Cameron Mackintosh, two of the most respected Broadway producers were Joseph Papp (1921–1991), associated with *A Chorus Line* and *Hair* and David Merrick (1911–2000), producer of *Hello, Dolly!* and *42nd Street*.

The **Composer** and **Lyricist** compose the music and write the lyrics, respectively. The composer and lyricist can be a team such as John Kander (1927–) and Fred Ebb (1928–2004), who created *Cabaret* and *Chicago*, or Alan Jay Lerner (1918–1986) and Frederick Loewe (1901–1988), who created *Camelot* and *Brigadoon*. Leonard Bernstein (1918–1990), who teamed up with various lyricists, was one of the most celebrated conductors and composers in America. He also created music for *West Side Story*, *Candide* and *On the Town*. The composer and lyricist can also be one person such as Frank Loesser (1910–1969), who wrote the music and lyrics for *Guys and Dolls* and *The Most Happy Fella*, or Stephen Schwartz (1948–), writer of *Godspell* and the box office hit, *Wicked*.

The **Librettist** writes the spoken words or script (also called the book) for a musical. Musicals can be taken from another source such as a book, theme, or film. Examples of

My Fair Lady

Courtesy of The Berkshire Theatre Festival. Director Eric Hill.

libretto sources would be *Big River* from Mark Twain's Adventures of Huckleberry Finn, *My Fair Lady,* based on Bernard Shaw's Pygmalion, and *Cats* (1982), based on poems written by T. S. Elliot.

The **Director** oversees the artistic vision of the production and works with all collaborators to tell the story. The director will stage the scenes with the actors and many times participate in choreographing the dances. Famous musical theatre directors include Hal Prince (1928–), who directed *Sweeney Todd* and *A Little Night Music,* and Jerome Robbins (1918–1998), director of *Fiddler on the Roof* and *Peter Pan.* In 1997, Julie Taymor won a Tony Award for her inventive concept and direction combining puppetry with live actors in the Broadway production of *The Lion King.*

The **Choreographer** creates all the dances for the production, making sure they are shaped to support the storyline. While some choreographers' style is technique based, others' are more character and movement driven. It should be noted that the choreographer is different from the *fight* choreographer who stages the combat. Susan Stroman (1954–) is one of today's most popular choreographers on Broadway. Her unique work can be seen in The *Producers, Contact,* and *Young Frankenstein.* Bob Fosse's (1927–1987) jazzy style of choreography in productions such as *The Pajama Game* and *Sweet Charity* has become iconic in musical theatre history.

The **Music Director** teaches the performers the music, usually serves as the conductor, and can even be the rehearsal or production pianist. The music director's primary objectives are to assist the actors in shaping the musical numbers, continuing the storyline through the song, and balancing the blend of voices and accompaniment.

The **Musicians** play the music the orchestrator has provided. They sometimes play more than one instrument. The number of instruments needed for a musical is determined by the producer, the director, or the orchestrator.

The **Performers** are the actors, dancers, and singers who perform the show. As in the ancient Greek theatre, many musicals require not only principal performers but also a chorus. The chorus is made up of singers and dancers that perform in large numbers, support the story by portraying supporting roles, and create a larger than life atmosphere. Some famous American musical theatre performers (in alphabetical order) include Joel Grey, Shirley Jones, Gene Kelly, Jerry Orbach, Angela Landsbury, Nathan Lane, Patti LuPone, Mandy Patinkin, Bernadette Peters, Audra McDonald, Brian Stokes Mitchell, Ethel Merman, Mary Martin, Idina Menzel, Alfred Molina, Zero Mostel, Ann Reinking, Chita Rivera, Ben Vereen, and Gwen Verdon. However, this list would not be complete, without mentioning British legends Julie Andrews and Michael Crawford.

TONY AWARDS FOR BEST MUSICAL

The Antoinette Perry Awards, better know as the "Tonys," are given by The American Theatre Wing every year for Broadway productions. The awards began in 1947, but the best musical category originated in 1949. Below is a list of the Tony award winners for best musical.

Year	Title	Composer and Lyricist
1949	*Kiss Me, Kate*	Porter
1950	*South Pacific*	Rodgers and Hammerstein
1951	*Guys and Dolls*	Loesser
1952	*The King and I*	Rodgers and Hammerstein
1953	*Wonderful Town*	Bernstein/Comden and Green
1954	*Kismet*	Borodin/Wright and Forrest
1955	*The Pajama Game*	Adler and Ross
1956	*Damn Yankees*	Adler and Ross
1957	*My Fair Lady*	Lerner and Loewe
1958	*The Music Man*	Wilson
1959	*Redhead*	Hague and Fields
1960	*The Sound of Music*	Rodgers and Hammerstein
1961	*Bye Bye Birdie*	Strouse and Adams
1962	*How to Succeed in Buisness Without Really Trying*	Loesser
1963	*A Funny Thing Happened on the Way to the Forum*	Sondheim
1964	*Hello, Dolly!*	Herman
1965	*Fiddler on the Roof*	Bock and Harnick
1966	*Man of La Mancha*	Leigh and Darion
1967	*Cabaret*	Kander and Ebb
1968	*Hallelujah, Baby!*	Styne/Comden and Green
1969	*1776*	Edwards
1970	*Applause*	Strouse and Adams
1971	*Company*	Sondheim
1972	*Two Gentlemen of Verona*	MacDermot and Guare
1973	*A Little Night Music*	Sondheim
1974	*Raisin*	Woldin and Brittan
1975	*The Wiz*	Smalls
1976	*A Chorus Line*	Hamlisch and Kleban
1977	*Annie*	Strouse and Charnin
1978	*Ain't Misbehavin'*	Waller
1979	*Sweeney Todd*	Sondheim
1980	*Evita*	Rice and Webber
1981	*42nd Street*	Warren and Dubin
1982	*Nine*	Yeston
1983	*Cats*	Webber and T.S. Elliot/Nunn
1984	*La Cage aux Follies*	Herman
1985	*Big River*	Miller
1986	*The Mystery of Edwin Drood*	Holmes
1987	*Les Misèrables*	Schönberg and Kretzmer
1988	*The Phantom of the Opera*	Webber and Hart
1989	*Jerome Robbins' Broadway*	Robbins
1990	*City of Angels*	Zippel and Coleman
1991	*The Will Rogers Follies*	Comden and Green/Coleman
1992	*Crazy for You*	Gershwin and Gershwin
1993	*Kiss of the Spiderwoman*	Kander and Ebb
1994	*Passion*	Sondheim
1995	*Sunset Boulevard*	Webber and Black
1996	*Rent*	Larson
1997	*Titanic*	Yeston
1998	*The Lion King*	John and Rice

1999	*Fosse*	Various composers
2000	*Contact*	Various composers
2001	*The Producers*	Brooks
2002	*Thoroughly Modern Millie*	Tesori and Scanlan
2003	*Hairspray*	Shaiman and Wittman
2004	*Avenue Q*	Lopez and Marx
2005	*Monty Python's Spamalot*	Prez and Idle
2006	*Jersey Boys*	Gaudio and Crewe
2007	*Spring Awakening*	Sheik and Sater
2008	*In the Heights*	Miranda
2009	*Billy Elliot*	John and Hall

FEATURE SECTION
An interview with Robert Dusold

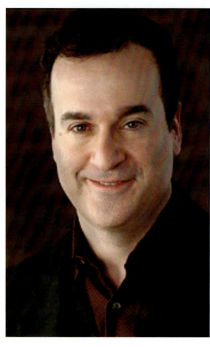

Robert DuSold

Photograph courtesy of Robert DuSold.

Robert DuSold recently played Harry Bright in the Las Vegas production of *Mamma Mia!* New York credits in the last year include *Mimi le Duck* opposite Eartha Kitt off Broadway, the title role in *Don Imbroglio* at the New York Music Theater Festival as well as Ned in the Drama Desk nominated *The Audience*. Broadway and National Tour credits include Jason Green in *The Producers*, Javert and Valjean in *Les Misèrables*, Monsieur Andre in *Phantom of the Opera*, Old Deuteronomy in *Cats*, Pete in Hal Prince's *Showboat*, assorted roles in *Jekyll and Hyde*, *Kiss of the Spiderwoman* and *Chicago*. Regional and Stock credits include Sweeney Todd in *Sweeney Todd*, at Connecticut Rep (Conn. Critics Circle Award Best Actor nomination), Jules/Bob Greenberg in *Sunday in the Park* at DC's Arena Stage, Benny Southstreet in *Guys and Dolls* at Papermill Playhouse, Father in *Chrysalis* at the Adirondack Theater Festival, Peron in *Evita* at California Music Theatre and various shows at the O'Neill Festival, Williamstown Theatre Festival and many others. Recordings include *A Gala for Harold Prince, Sondheim: An Evening in Celebration at Carnegie Hall*, the *Anastasia* soundtrack and others. Robert is also featured in the new book <u>Making It on Broadway: Actors' Tales of Climbing to the Top</u>, published by Allworth Press.

What is most enjoyable about your career?

The most enjoyable thing about my career is I love what I do. When it all comes together and creativity and commerce combine, it is a wonderful feeling. I have met some wonderful people. Each job is an adventure.

What is most difficult/challenging about your career?

There are many challenging things about a career as an actor. It is a constant process of putting yourself on the line: getting rejected, trying not to take it personally, working enough to support yourself, and reinventing yourself at every turn. I worked with Eartha Kitt a couple of years ago, and she said it was more challenging for her to reinvent herself at 80, but it was something she knew she had to do to stay viable and work.

If a student was interested in a career in musical theatre do you have any suggestions that might help them?

I went to the University of Cincinnati College Conservatory of Music, and I had 3 majors before I settled on vocal performance. I think it is essential to study classically—dance, voice, or acting, or all 3 to have a foundation to fall back on. My skills as a musician have served me very well in my career, especially for recordings. Everything is very fast and time is money, so a lot is expected quickly.

What are the steps in auditioning for a Broadway musical?

I went to open call after open call for Broadway and actually booked my first job on Broadway from an open call. You gotta keep going back. Once you have an agent you will get an appointment set up for you and go from there. I got my union card (Actor's Equity Association is the actor's union) before I moved to NYC; something I knew I would do before I started looking for work in New York.

Where do you see the future of Musical Theatre going?

I think the future of musical theater will rely more on corporate producers and will be more and more based on films and revivals-anything that is perceived as safe. I think New York will be less essential as the hub of theater. Musical theater will rely more on tours and regional productions.

Summary

Musical theatre, in one form or another, has been an important part of American culture since colonial times. It grew so much in popularity after 1900 that it is now the most prevalent theatre form on the Broadway stage and across the country. The roots of musical theatre began in opera and the form was influenced by minstrel shows, vaudeville, and the follies. In addition, numerous individual productions and artists have contributed to the development. The four types of musicals—book, concept, rock, and reviews—share the elements of song and dance; however, each has specific identifiable characteristics. The strong influence of the Disney Corporation and European spectacle along with savvy production companies and talented artistic teams have combined to make ticket sales soar across the country and around the world. The musical continues to evolve and change in an effort to meet the tastes and the needs of the American public. Contemporary approaches and trends are developed as theatre teams collaborate to create the storytelling through song and dance that is the hallmark of the American musical.

Active Learning Assignment
"Bringing Theatre to Life"

I. Create your own musical
1. Break the class into groups of 5–10.
2. Each group will invent an original musical with a synopsis.
3. The group will choose a genre or style of music for their production.
4. Have the groups create a list of song titles for their musical.
5. Each group will present their musical theatre title and lyrics for one song.

Critical Thinking in Class Discussion

I. What were the four main types of Musical Theatre explained in this chapter?

II. What are some aspects of culture and diversity, that weren't discussed in the chapter, which may have been influential to musical theatre?

III. If you could be a member of a musical theatre production, what position would you choose and why?

IV. What do you think would be the most challenging aspect of having a career in Musical Theatre?

*This chapter is dedicated to Matt Carr.

Special thanks to Don Bristow, Robert DuSold, Monica Hayes, Seth Panitch, Elizabeth Robertson, Rusty Tennant, and Daisy Nystul.

Theatre around the World

Manifesting itself in singing, dancing, and storytelling, theatrical ritual was an important part of nearly every ancient civilization. This chapter strives toward cultural understanding and inclusiveness as it unveils the origins, continued development, and contemporary realization of the theatre in the following: Africa, Arabic-language countries, Australia, Canada, China, India, Japan, and Mexico. It also reveals how, in some cases, the colonization of these counties by other nations and the dominance of the West has influenced the development of theatre in these areas.

Theatre on the Continent of Africa

There are more than 800 local languages that are spoken in thousands of villages across the African continent. In addition, Europeans and Arabs have, from time to time, seized control of various areas, begun colonies and imprinted foreign customs and languages such as English, French, Arabic, and Portuguese on groups of African natives. In order to achieve some clarity concerning the development of theatre in Africa, the following is divided into four sections: French-speaking Africa South of the Sahara; French-speaking North Africa; Nigeria; and Lusophone Portuguese-speaking Africa.

The Theatre of French Speaking Africa South of the Sahara

Originally, African natives believed that they were spiritually connected to their environment and to the universe. Their theatrical roots stem from the religious rituals that celebrated these beliefs. The focal person in religious ceremonies was the *"griot"* who sang, told stories, and was thought to have wisdom of the past while also being receptive to the community's immediate concerns. The role of the *"griot"* has remained an important part of modern theatrical productions in Africa. Dancing and singing also played an important part in native African religious ceremonies with each dance having its own specific meaning. Today, dance is still an integral part of modern African plays with each dance communicating a specific message. For example, generations of the Bambara natives of Mali have participated in *koteba*, a theatrical celebration which incorporates mime, gesture, comedy, and a dance mimicking the spiral shape of a snail. The dance represents human beings as they progress through life.

Village drama is usually performed in its vernacular, but the universal language of mime, song, and dance is used in many of the modern plays in order to facilitate communication with those speaking several languages. French is also used in many of these plays, but since not all in the audience have a firm grasp of French, playwrights frequently use a local variation of the language in their plays.

Modern African plays usually focus on one of three themes: historical, social, and political dishonesty or conflicts associated with traditional verses modern values. Historical plays depict courageous natives and their opposition to the European colonization. Social and political plays can vary from comedy, to serious drama, to satire.

G. Oyono-Mbia is one of the best known playwrights of social and politically themed plays. His plays are popular all over Africa, in part because he translates his French language plays into English, thus making them accessible to the English speaking peoples of Africa.

> *Modern plays in the theatre of French-speaking Africa usually focus on one of three themes: historical, social, and political dishonesty or conflicts associated with traditional versus modern values.*

French Speaking North Africa

The Arab conquest of North Africa during the seventh and eight centuries created the Muslim countries of Morocco, Algeria, and Tunisia. In 1830 the French seized Algeria; they conquered Tunisia in 1883; and then took most of Morocco in 1912. Resistance to the French occupation persisted for many years until Morocco and Tunisia finally gained their independence in 1956. Algeria earned its independence in 1962 after a bloody war lasting eight years. The combination of French censorship, war, and Muslim tradition discouraged the development of theatre in these countries. Virtually the only theatre during the early nineteenth century consisted of productions given by touring French companies and shadow theatre performances by visiting Turkish companies.

There was some admirable theatrical growth in North Africa, particularly after independence from France. National theatres were established in Algeria and Tunisia; and in 1969 at the Pan-African Festival in Algiers, all of the countries were well represented in the drama section. Rachid Ksentini, who wrote in Arabic, and French-speaking Kateb Yacine, are two of the best-known Algerian playwrights. Many of Kateb Yacine's plays attack the French government and colonial occupation. He writes in a poetic style but often uses violent language to unveil the coarseness of human behavior. Despite the works of these playwrights and a few other successful theatre ventures, religious and political restrictions continue to discourage theatre development.

National theatres were established in Algeria and Tunisia, and in 1969, at the Pan-African Festival in Algiers, all of the countries were well represented in the drama section.

Nigeria

Nigeria is home to over 250 ethic groups. Three of the most important are the Yoruba, Ibo, and the Fulani. Numerous theatrical celebrations are associated with each group. One example is the Yoruba's *egungen*. During this ancient festival, sacrifices are offered to bless and connect with the dead. A village member is chosen to be the "carrier" and this individual collects the evil that has gathered in the village and takes it away in a canoe. Portions of this theatrical ritual are still enacted today.

The Yoruba opera is one of the most beloved contemporary forms of Nigerian theatre. It was created by Hubert Ogunde who also began the first Nigerian opera company in 1946. The Yoruba opera, generally referred to as the Yoruba Traveling Theatre, begins and ends its theatrical productions with a *glee*, an uplifting musical number. The company's productions are highly entertaining but also communicate an important moral message.

When Nigeria gained independence in 1960, playwrights who wrote in English grew in popularity. Wole Soyinka, who wrote *The Strong Breed, Lion and the Jewel,* and *A Dance of the Forests,* among other plays, became the first African to win the Nobel Prize for Literature. He is devoted to the people of Nigeria and was not only imprisoned for attacking the government's policies but stopped writing plays in 1994 so he would have more time to devote to human rights.

There have been tremendous challenges in South Africa's theatre development.

There have been tremendous challenges in South Africa's theatre development, such as the policy of apartheid which separated white and black South Africans for over 40 years. Despite apartheid and other controversial challenges, South Africa has been home to several internationally renowned playwrights. The most celebrated is Athol Fugard (1932–) whose many plays include *No Good Friday* (1958), *Blood Knot* (1960), and *Master Harold and the Boys* (1982).

Lusophone (Portuguese-speaking) Africa

Angola, Cape Verde, Guinea-Bissau, Mozambique, and San Tome'e Principe were controlled by the Portuguese until 1975. During Portugal's rule, theatre consisted mostly of vaudeville acts that were designed simply to entertain the white settlers; but when Catholic missionaries arrived, they used theatre as a means of spreading their religious beliefs. In 1975, Portuguese speaking Africa gained independence, Angolan theatre, particularly, was used as a propaganda instrument to reinforce the ideology of whatever political party was in power.

Arabic Theatre

Early Arabic Theatre

As is true for most cultures, theatre performance has been an important part of Arabic culture for generations. The foundations of the traditional Arabic theatre include shadow puppetry, satiric monologues, and numerous styles of dances. In 1817, and again in 1855, European drama was brought to Syria, which at the time included Lebanon, by a businessman from Beirut named Marun al-Naqqash. The first play to be performed was Marun al-Naqqash's own play *al-Bakhi*, meaning *The Miser*, although it had no similarity to Moliere's play. Marun al-Naqqash and his family first performed the play in their home in 1847. After this experience, some of the family members went on to continue careers in the theatre in Alexandria, Egypt, and Damascus where they discovered that theatre was already being explored in the universities.

At Al Azhaz University in Cairo, Sheika Rifaa Rafe al Tahtawi had been translating classical French plays into Arabic, and Yacub Sannu, of Jewish descent, had founded the first national theatre in Cairo. He also translated and wrote some 30 plays. In 1865, a student of languages named Sheik Ahmad Abu Khalil al-Qabbaani began producing plays in Damascus, but the conservative religious leaders there had his theatre closed in 1881. He promptly moved to Egypt where he felt that the authorities were more accepting of theatre. Today, Egypt is a thriving location for Arabic drama.

The Language of the Arabic Theatre

The language in which Arabic plays are written has generated a great deal of controversy over the years. Marun Al-Naqqash wrote his plays in Fusha with only a few colloquialisms. Fusha is the language of the Koran; thus, it is the language used by Islamic scholars. Another playwright, Sunnu, composed his plays in an Arabic colloquial dialect, an approach which was severely criticized at the time. Toward the end of the nineteenth century, it became commonplace to write about serious topics such as historical events in Fusha and to use colloquial dialects when writing comedies and stories about local people.

The most recognized playwright of the Arab world, Tawfiq el Hakim wrote *Ahl al Kahf*, a play to commemorate the opening of the National Theatre of Egypt, in 1935. Because of his success, other playwrights, such as Yussuf Idris and Alfred Farag, were inspired and went on to enjoy international careers.

In 1975, when the Portuguese-speaking countries in Africa gained independence, Angolan theatre was used as a propaganda instrument to reinforce the ideology of whatever political party was in power.

The foundations of the traditional Arabic theatre include shadow puppetry, satiric monologues, and numerous styles of dances.

Although there were still many religious constraints in Syria, the Ministry of Culture (1958) and the National Theatre (1960) were created. As a result, many directors, actors, and critics had earned prestigious reputations by the 1970s. Playwright Sadallah Wannous became as influential a figure in Syria as Tawfiq el Hakim had been in Egypt. Lebanon and Iraq had prominent theatre movements, but these disappeared when civil wars broke out in the mid 1970s.

Contemporary Arabic Theatre

Today, when speaking of the Arabic world, three distinctive regions are identified. The first is the Middle East, including Egypt, Syria, and Lebanon. This region has developed its own dramatic literature and has the most interaction with theatre practitioners in the Western world. The second region encompasses Arabia, Bahrain, and Kuwait, more conservative states where government and religion have not encouraged the development of theatre. The third region covers the Arab states of Maghrib, Tunisia, Algeria, and Morocco. Their dramatic literature has been influenced mostly by their French colonial history.

Australian Theatre

Theatre Down-Under-Australian Theatrical Origins

The Aborigines have inhabited Australia for over 40,000 years and theatrical rituals have been a central part of their culture. Before a *corroboree* (dance drama) is performed, the male and female performers paint their faces and adorn themselves with feathers and plants. During the performance, some of the participants play traditional instruments such as clapsticks and didgeridoos (wooden trumpet-like instruments) while others sing and dance around a fire. The dancers intentionally shake their legs as they dance on their hands and feet in an effort to mimic animals. Traditionally, Aborigines believe that the spirits of their ancestors are present in these ritualistic, yet entertaining, ceremonies.

For over 40,000 years, Aborigines have inhabited Australia and theatrical rituals have been an important part of their culture.

In 1788 a British penal colony was created in Sydney, Australia, and in 1796, Robert Sidaway established a theatre there for the convicts. However, the prisoners' unruly behavior forced the theatre to close after only two years. Other convict theatres came and went but, between 1825 and 1830, even the free settlers frequented a convict theatre group located at Emu Plains. On Boxing Day in 1832, a production of Douglas Jerrold's *Black Ey'd Susan* inaugurated Australia's professional theatre in New South Wales at Barnett Levey's (1798–1837) Royal Hotel. (Mr. Levey had been granted a license by the colonial government.) Only one colonial theatre remains in operation today. It is the Hobart's Theatre Royal which opened in 1837 in Tasmania—also a penal colony.

Early Australian Playwrights

Convict David Burns wrote *Bushrangers*, a melodrama based on a Tasmanian convict named Matthew Brady. Burns went on to write several other plays in the 1840s, most of which tout an authentic colonial lifestyle. However, the

increasing population of free settlers was unnerved by the convicts and elected to impose the Lord Chamberlain's censorship guidelines on all theatre productions. These guidelines had the effect of diverting the subjects of the plays from convicts' lives and colonial living to subjects that had little or no contemporary relevance. Edward Geoghegan, a convict who had composed several plays on convict life, continued to write but only works such as *The Currency Lass* (1844), a light-hearted, romantic melodrama which met the censorship guidelines. Isaac Nathan's *Don John of Austria* (1844) was Australia's first opera and it embraced exotic local settings.

The Effect of European Touring Companies

In the 1850s, gold was discovered in New South Wales, Victoria, and Queensland. The result was a booming population that was thirsty for entertainment. George Coppin, the owner of four of the major theatres in Melbourne, began bringing in celebrities from Europe and America such as Edwin Booth, Sarah Bernhardt, and James Cassius Williamson to tour productions throughout the country. The popularity of these touring companies encouraged professional theatres to fashion their seasons to highlight European and American drama rather than that of Australian artists. In 1882, George Musgrove, Arthur Garner, and James Cassius Williamson began to establish themselves as a powerful management trio and brought in even more European stars to dominate the Australian theatre. The prestige of foreign stars made it exceedingly difficult for Australians to establish their own artistic theatrical tradition. From the 1890s to the 1920s, Australian farcical melodramas with stock characters such as bushrangers, gold-diggers, and feisty colonial heroines were the most successful native fare.

Between 1930 and 1950, serious Australian-themed plays were produced by several small amateur and semi-professional theatres. Interestingly, many of these theatres were operated by women, such as the Community Playhouse founded by Carrie Tennant (1907–1989) in 1930 and the Independent Theatre founded in 1932 by Doris Fittond (1897–1985). These theatres produced numerous serious dramas written by Australian playwrights such as Henrietta Drake-Brockman and George Landen Dann. These plays focused on various Australian topics, some of which examined cultural differences between urban and outback dwellers and the racial conflicts between Caucasians and Aborigines, while others depicted the realistic historical aspects of Australian life. Despite the success that these and other local theatres enjoyed, European touring companies such as the impressive Old Vic tour of 1948 with Laurence Olivier and Vivien Leigh, and the Old Vic tour of 1955 starring Katharine Hepburn still outshone the native talent.

Celebrating the Australian Artist

In an effort to give Australian artists some prominence, the Australian Elizabethan Theatre Trust was created in 1954. The trust was initially criticized for hiring an English director, Hugh Hunt, who in turn cast English actor Leo McKern in the title role of *Ned Kelly*, the most prominent bushranger in Australia's history. But during the 1950s and 1960s, theatres were created in which Australia's artists could strengthen their talents and develop their reputations. One of these was the Elizabethan Theatre Trust

Opera company opened, in 1956. In 1969 its name was changed to The Australian Opera. One of the most important discoveries the trust made in its first year was a play by Ray Lawler, originally named *The Seventeenth Doll* which became known as *The Doll's*. The play was well received in Australia, then in London, and then in New York. Other Australian playwrights rushed to adopt a style mimicking the structure of *The Doll's*.

In the 1960s the Australian Council of the Arts was established. In 1975 the name was changed to the Australian Council and it proceeded to open fully-funded theatres in each state capital, in many instances linking them with universities. These new theatre companies made it possible for native theatre artists to find local employment rather than having to travel to other counties, as their predecessors had.

Contemporary Theatre

Australia's contemporary theatre is wonderfully diverse and is a cherished part of the continent's culture. Australia is home to several notable theatre structures, the most renowned being the Sydney Opera House nestled in Sydney's Harbor. Sydney's Q Theatre and Ensemble Theatre-In-the-Round, La Boite in Brisbane, Playbox Theatre Company in Melbourne, and Troupe and Stage Company in Adelaide are some of the small, yet quite influential, theatre companies. All of these troupes showcase classical works but also produce original Australian plays. Many of them receive financial support from the central government and local arts councils, but support from corporations continues to increase.

Australians such as Jim Sharman, George Ogilive, and Rex Cramphorn have established themselves as respected directors. Numerous Australian playwrights have enjoyed international recognition—for example, Steve J. Spears, who won the New York Theatre Critic's Off-Broadway Award in 1980 for *The Elocution of Benjamin Franklin*.

Australia's contemporary theatre is wonderfully diverse and is a cherished part of the continent's culture.

Australian Youth Theatre

The youth theatre movement experienced substantial growth in the 1980s. One of the best known is the "Come Out" theatre national festival, a popular annual event. There are also several theatre-in-education programs such as Carclew Youth Performing Arts Center in Adelaide and the Australian Theatre for Young People. In 1985, Shopfront instigated the first international Young Playwrights' Conference in Sydney. There are also several puppet theatre companies, some of which perform at schools or produce holiday-themed plays. These include Handspan in Melbourne, Marionette Theater of Australia in Sydney, and Spare Parts in Perth.

Aboriginal Theatre

Betty Fisher began the first Aboriginal theatre group at the Nimrod Theatre in Redfern, a suburb of Sydney, after receiving accolades for her play *Basically Black* (1972). In 1982, Robert Merritts' production of *The Cake Man*, a drama which examines the supposed compassionate European influence on the Aborigines, had the distinction of being chosen Australia's entry at the World Theatre Festival in Denver, Colorado. *The Dreamers* was another extremely popular Aboriginal play. Written by poet Jack Davis, it toured

Australia in 1983. Today, Sydney is home to several theatre training schools with affiliated native performing companies such as the Aboriginal Islander Dance and Theatre and the Eora.

Australian Women's Theatre

In the early 1970s, the Carlton alternative theatre was instrumental in the development of the first "Women's Theatre Group." This gave women such as Jan Cornall, Kerry Dwyer, and Jenny Kemp the opportunity to write and direct. In 1981, the Women and Theatre Project was developed and funded by the Australian Council. Other Australian women's theatre groups include Brisbane Women's Theatre and the Canberra group Fool's Gallery directed by Carol Woodrow. Robyn Archer's feminist production of *The Pack of Women*, first produced in London in 1983, featured a cabaret-style evening of songs, poems, and sketches. Today, women are active participants in Australian theatre and their influence is felt at home and abroad.

English Speaking Canada

During the first half of the nineteenth century the theatre in North British America was performed mostly by military officers and amateur actors whose occupation was typically the law. They would perform in make-shift quarters until there was enough interest to warrant building a permanent theatre. It is interesting to note that, in 1842, Charles Dickens performed with a group of amateur actors while visiting Montreal.

Professional companies, composed of married couples, toured Canada at the time when access to the country was most formidable—by sleigh in the winter and water in the summer. In order to satisfy the growing demand for entertainment, resident theatre companies were created. However, most of the company members were from New York City, with the exception of visiting stars who were, most often, British.

One would think that these resident theatre companies would inspire native Canadians to write plays, but very few writers had an interest in the theatre. Many writers did create works of drama, but with the intention that the works be read rather than staged. Even if a Canadian did write a play for the stage, the visiting stars preferred to perform familiar works, such as Shakespeare. Nonetheless, by the end of the 1870s Canada's population had grown sufficiently to support several new theatres, each of which could accommodate up to two thousand playgoers.

Toward the end of the 1870's, there was a significant change in North American and Canadian theatre. Resident companies that had traditionally produced several plays during a season were being replaced by touring companies doing only one play. These companies were usually based in New York City, giving Canadians little opportunity to develop their own theatre. But there were some small local companies that featured Canadian performers such as the Marks Brothers who performed in both Canadian and American circuits. Additionally, several other Canadian performers such as Julia Arthur, Margaret Anglin, and Mary Pickford began their careers in small local theatres.

A Canadian journalist, Roy Mitchell, became the first director of the Hart House Theatre in Toronto (1908) and, during his tenure, more Canadian plays were produced than ever before. Most of the plays were one-acts such as Merrill Denison's *Brothers in Arms*, but unfortunately, just as Canadians were beginning to find their theatrical voice, audiences were turning to movies and vaudeville for their entertainment. The great depression in America had an effect on the Canadian theatre, and by the 1930s professional theatre in Canada was nearly dead although, fortunately, a handful of amateur theatres were still thriving.

The 1930s saw social theatre and agit-prop presentations produced by groups such as Toronto's Workers' Theatre. These theatres were mostly supported by leftist Progressive Arts Clubs. *Eight Men Speak* (1933) was one of the most notable plays of this period. It was about the arrest, trial, and attempted prison murder of a Communist Party leader. The play was controversial and similar presentations introduced Canadians to radical American playwrights such as Clifford Odets and Irwin Shaw.

Oddly, one of the most significant contributions to the Canadian theatre was the creation, in 1936, of the Canadian Broadcasting Corporation. Radio dramas were already an established form of entertainment, but when Tyrone Guthrie produced an historical series, *The Romance of Canada*, the radio drama became even more popular and subsequently provided steady employment for professional actors and playwrights.

Although the nation of Canada was formed in 1867, it did not become independent until 1931, and it wasn't until after World War II that the nation began to truly define itself. After the war, there was a good deal of interest in the arts and the government became very interested in promoting art and culture. To that end, it hired Vincent Massey to investigate the role of the arts in the lives of Canadians. His findings led to the creation of the Canadian Council (1957) whose mission was to support artists and arts organizations.

The end of World War II saw the beginning of several Canadian theatres such as Sydney Risk's *Everyman Theatre* which existed as a touring company until Mr. Risk established a studio in Vancouver. Lorne Green, later known to Americans for his role on the television series, *Bonanza*, founded the *Jupiter Theatre* (1951) in Toronto with other CBC artists and produced a number of Canadian plays such as Lister Sinclair's *Socrates* (1952) and *The Blood is Strong* (1953). Of course, one of the most successful theatre ventures was the Stratford Shakespearian Festival (1953). During its first season, the acting company included William Hutt, Douglas Rain, and Richard Easton; and in following seasons, actors such as Christopher Plummer and Lorne Green. It should be noted that the Stratford Shakespearian Festival is in its 56th year and has earned an international reputation for excellence. In 2008, Christopher Plummer returned to perform with the company and other well known actors such as Brian Dennehy and Adrienne Gould have performed on the Festival stage in recent years.

Another theatre that enjoys worldwide acclaim is the Shaw Festival in Niagara-on-the Lake which celebrates the plays of George Bernard Shaw, his contemporaries, and contemporary plays covering the years 1856–1959— Shaw's lifespan. The theatre was created in 1962 by Niagara-on-the-Lake lawyer and playwright Brian Doherty with a small group of Americans and Canadians composing the original company. In its first season, the group produced eight weekend performances of Shaw's *Don Juan in Hell* and *Candida*. They entitled this production "A Salute to Shaw." Today the Shaw Festival is one of the few theatres to have a permanent acting company and even more interesting is its dedication to a specific historical period.

French Speaking Canada

Marc Lescarbot's *The Theatre of Neptune in New France* (1606) is the first recorded play to have been written and performed in French Speaking Canada. Written in verse, this play celebrates the return of the colony's leaders from a dangerous mission. Only two other plays survive with themes that focus on political agendas such as strategies for colonization and encouraging the authorities to support church projects. The latter was to be an ongoing topic in French Canadian dramatic literature.

From approximately 1650 to 1700, the plays of Corneille were quite popular, particularly in upper-class circles. However, the Catholic Church was very critical of the theatre. For example, when Governor Frontenac (1622–1698) arranged to stage Moliere's *Tartuffe,* the Bishop Saint-Vallier bribed Frontenac not to mount the production. Frontenac accepted the bribe, but in the end he suffered because the Bishop went on to officially ban all public theatre performances.

Not long after New France's cession to the British and Spanish governments in 1763, the British garrison in Quebec began theatrical performances in French, mostly of Moliere's plays. Montreal followed suit and by 1764 drama was reinstated as part of the curriculum in both schools and colleges. This infuriated the Catholic Church which sought to end all theatrical activity by preaching its evils during sermons and shaming theatre lovers during confessionals. As a result, theatre left the stage and found a new home in literary journals. The plays had mostly political themes and would not be performed until the 1860s.

Pierre Petitclair was the first native French Canadian to publish a play, *Griphon, ou La Vengeance d'um Valet Griphon* or *A Valet's Revenge* (1837). Unfortunately, it was not staged; but a couple of his subsequent works were, including his melodrama *La Donation*, which is the first French Canadian play to be both published and performed.

In the mid-1800s the Catholic Church, unable to get rid of the theatre, decided to take advantage. The Catholic clergy set out to write and produce numerous plays on such subjects as the dangers of alcoholism and the ills of attacking an individual's enemies. Despite the Church's involvement with the theatre, French Canadians were not writing very many plays intended to actually be staged. Touring companies kept the theatre alive in Montreal and Quebec, featuring stars such as Sarah Bernhardt who began her tours in 1880. but the Church was opposed to Bernhardt's choice of plays. Numerous patriotic and historical plays were written in the late 1800s, such as Joseph-Louis Archambault's *Jacques Cartier, ou Canada Venge* (*Jacques Cartier: or Canada Avenged,* 1879).

The years 1898–1914 mark the "Golden Age of Theatre in Montreal," however, of the 500 plays staged, only 15 were written by French Canadians. Fortunately, the college and university stages were still producing excellent plays written by native dramatists. But, by 1914, the French Canadian stages had been infiltrated by American vaudeville, burlesque, and revues. The cinema struck another blow to the emerging French Canadian theatre when it was introduced in 1902 in Montreal. But when radio was introduced in the 1920s a kind of cultural solidarity came with it; and by the 1930s radio dramas and serials became extremely popular.

The National Theatre School of Canada, located in Montreal, was established in 1960. Its first Executive Director was Jean Gascon and legendary teacher and director Michel Saint-Denis was named Artistic Director. Today it is a bi-lingual school (English and French) and it is known internationally as a school of excellence with acceptance to the programs (Acting, Directing, Playwriting, Set and Costume Design, and Technical Production) only by audition. Even then, very few students are admitted each year to this rigorous course of study. French Canadian theatre is alive and well today. It will be interesting and exciting to see what the future brings.

Chinese Theatre

Origins of Chinese Theatre

Theatre-like performances have been a part of Chinese culture for thousands of years. Singing and dancing were integral to shamanistic rituals during both the Shang Dynasty (1600–1027 B.C.) and the Zhou Dynasty (1027–257 B.C.). The Han Dynasty (202 B.C. to 220) featured court entertainment which included singing and dancing in addition to horn-butting games, puppetry, costumes, and stories that were acted out. The Tang Dynasty (A.D. 681–907), a period of time that was free from wars, allowed for further cultural development including the initial productions of the "adjutant play" or *canjum xi* which combined acting, singing, and the playing of musical instruments with performers donning both costumes and make-up.

During the Yuan Dynasty (1279–1368) more theatrical elements were incorporated into the performances such as set design, larger casts, and more complexity in the stories themselves. These plays, or *zaju*, frequently began with introductions, were written in four acts, and used many of the theatrical elements commonly associated with opera. During the Ming Dynasty (1368–1644) over 500 *zaju's* were written but, ironically, one of the most notable contributions of the Ming Dynasty era was the *kunqu* (spoken drama).

Theatre-like performances have been a part of Chinese culture for many generations.

Traditional Chinese Drama-Opera

Chinese opera titles always represent the region of the country where they originated, for the simple reason that dialects differ from region to region. But regardless of the region, all Chinese operas share many of the same characteristics—for example, the use of very few hand properties. This is done to encourage the audience members to use their imaginations to recreate the historical events, myths, and well-known stories upon which the traditional operas are based. Performers gesture in a stylized manner and wear brightly colored costumes and make-up in order to create a production that is symbolic rather than realistic. During the Yang Dynasty, the drama included four stock characters—*sheng*: the male, *dan*: the female, *jing*: the man with a painted face, and *chou*: the comic. Contemporary Chinese operas use the same stock characters but, in some cases, they are given more specific attributes such as a definite age or social status.

Casting of the Operas

Traditionally, performers in Chinese opera began training at a very early age, and since gender is not a consideration, it is not uncommon to cast men in women's roles and women in men's roles. In 1949, when the People's Republic of China was formed and the homophobia of the Western world affected China, gender appropriate casting became commonplace. Today, there are only a few regional operas, such as the Taiwanese opera, in which the male leads are still played by females.

Chinese Opera Performance Spaces

Originally, opera was such an important part of ritual life that wealthy families kept their own private opera troupes to perform on special occasions. Families of lesser means would hire a puppeteer and musicians to perform during some ceremonies. Today, opera is enjoyed in proscenium-style theatres, parks, and opera clubs. The Chinese audiences are more outgoing than typical western audiences in that they cheer, eat, and talk while enjoying the performances.

China's International Theatre Exchange

China has been dedicated to cross-cultural international theatre since cultural exchanges with the West reopened in the 1970s. In October 2001, the Shanghi Theatre Academy hosted an international theatre festival with participants from North America, Europe, Australia, and Asia. Well-known American theatre artists such as Arthur Miller, Charlton Heston, George White, and Margaret Booker have directed productions in China. In the last few years, the Chinese Republic has invited foreigners to create new productions; but rather than turning the entire project over to these artists, the Chinese have maintained control of the productions.

Chinese artists have also directed Western plays. *A Doll's House* was staged by Wu Xiaojiang at Beijing's Center Experimental Theatre (1998 and 2000). The production starred Norwegian actress Agnette Haaland and Wu re-wrote Ibsen's play to emphasize the clash of cultures rather than equality between the sexes. In Wu's version, Nora, while living in Norway, marries Chinese banker Han Ermao (Torvald Helmer) who is studying in Norway. Wu's cultural alterations also included changing the Christmas Eve celebration to a Chinese New Year celebration and the Italian tarantella to a Beijing opera performance. Nora comes to feel that she is alienated in this environment and the couple's relationship becomes so fragile that they toy with the idea of having a transnational marriage. Currently, transnational marriages are popular in many Chinese cites, but Wu pictures this marriage option as being socially destructive.

The ironic beauty of Wu's socially charged production was that Ermao talked to Nora in Mandarin and she answered him in English. Subtitles in Mandarin were projected above the stage and the program also included notes in English to help the audience better understand the actors. Wu's production was critically well received and epitomized the challenges that exist in a world that is becoming more cross-culturally aware.

Indian Theatre

Indian Theatrical Origins

Sanskrit drama was one of the earliest forms of theatre in India. The *Natyasastra* (The Art of Theatre) by Bharata and other unknown writers provides the greatest information available on Sanskrit drama. Sanskrit drama focuses on *rasa*—mood, aesthetics, and blissful consciousness—unlike Western drama which is grounded in dramatic action and character development. Sanskrit plays always end with good defeating evil, thus creating a feeling of harmony for the audience. According to the *Natyasatra*, there are ten types of Sanskrit plays—the two most important being the heroic and the social. Bhasa (second or third century C.E.) wrote the oldest surviving Sanskrit plays, two of which are *The Vision of Vasavadatta* and *Carudatta*. During the twelfth and thirteenth centuries when the Muslims assumed power over most of the country, there was a significant decline in Sanskrit drama with the exception of those performed in the temples.

As early as the fifteenth century, Indian folk plays began to develop in several regions. Although the language of the folk play is specific to the region where it originates, nearly all folk plays share similar characteristics such as use of a narrator, a lack of scenery, stylized acting, music that accompanies the entire performance, and the use of a thrust stage. Indian folk plays were even allowed to be performed during the time the Muslim government was in power.

In the nineteenth century, Western-style plays began to be written in India by a number of playwrights. The best known is Rabindranath Tagore (1861–1941) who wrote *Chitra* (1861) and *King of the Dark Chamber* (1914), plays which combined both Western and Indian traditions. The *sangeet natak* (musical theatre) of Maharashtra was also a product of the nineteenth century. It spawned a number of very popular singer-actors such as the legendary female impersonator, Balgandharva, who many Indian women regarded as the ideal representation of femininity.

> Sanskrit drama was one of the earliest forms of theatre in India.

Languages and Drama Education

There are 17 major languages spoken in India but the National School of Drama has always educated its students in Hindi. Although many have criticized the school for not teaching the use of other languages, it has trained many very successful Hindi-speaking actors and directors. Well-known directors such as B. V. Karanth and Kavalam Narayana Pannikkar have worked very closely with the National School of Drama to revive the traditional Indian theatre. Karanth and Pannikkar create plays that combine traditional acting styles with narratives, folk music, and martial arts. Several schools do offer training in languages other than Hindi. Among them are The Ninasam Theatre Institute, located in the village of Heggodu in Karnataka, and the School of Drama in Trissar (Kerala). Once a student has completed training, in any of the schools, he or she faces the challenge of obtaining employment at a theatre. This is extremely difficult since India has very few professional repertory companies, and those companies that do exist are in such financial strife that many theatre artists have to maintain outside jobs in order to support themselves.

Indian Theatre's International Influence

One of the most internationally renowned Indian theatre artists is Ratan Thiyam. This is despite the fact that many of his countrymen feel his use of martial arts is overly exotic. Traditional Indian theatrical forms have influenced a number of European directors such as Jerzy Growtowski, Eugenio Barba, and Peter Brook, who used traditional narratives in his production *Mahabharata*. Peter Brooks' production was particularly important in that it initiated a series of discussions on the politics and ethics of intercultural exchange.

Contemporary Theatre

There are numerous contemporary Indian playwrights such as Utpal Dutt (1939–), Mohit Chattopadhyay (1934–), and Girish Karnad (1938–) and the popularity of these and other Indian playwrights has generated a great deal of interest in the modern Indian theatre. As a result, more than 16 theatre festivals have been held at the Prithvi Theatre in Bombay since its founding in 1978. In addition to contemporary drama, traditional plays such as Sanskrit, folk, and dance drama are widely produced across India.

> There are numerous contemporary Indian playwrights and the popularity of these has generated a great deal of interest in the modern Indian theatre.

Japanese Theatre

Noh Drama

Japan was ruled by *shogun* (military dictators) from 1192 until 1867 when the American government returned the power to the emperor. When ruled by the *shogunate*, the Japanese people were divided into strict social classes, each with its own dress code and model of behavior. For example, the Samurai or warriors were members of the highest class. Much the same as to European royalty, the *shogunates* were determined by heredity, and in 1338 the Ashikaga family found itself in power. In 1375, it granted Kiyotsugu Kan'ami and his son Zeami Motokiyo Samurai power to develop the formal structure of the Noh drama.

Noh plays are rooted in Zen Buddhism which was brought to Japan from India and China in the sixth century A.D. Fundamentally, Buddhism seeks to find inner peace by becoming one with all living things and thus understanding that nothing in the earthly world is permanent. As a result, the protagonists in Noh plays are most often ghosts, demons, or humans that are still obsessed with and tormented by the earthy desires of the living world.

Noh playscripts are even shorter than most Western one-act plays. Since the dialogue is composed of a combination of verse and prose, which is most often sung, Noh plays are essentially musical dance/dramas intended to evoke an emotional response from the audience. The dialogue in Noh dramas does not provide the audience with a detailed story, but, rather, gives the audience a general outline of the story and the circumstances surrounding each of the characters. The final scene in a Noh drama is always danced.

The three categories of performers in a Noh play are actors, chorus, and musicians. The actors receive their roles as children and spend at least 20 years perfecting their parts at schools created specifically to teach Noh

Media: A Noh Cycle Based on the Greek Myth

Southwestern Oklahoma State University. *Photograph courtesy of Steve P. Strickler.*

performance traditions. Depending on the play, there can be from six to ten chorus members, all of whom sit on one side of the stage and sing. There are three or four musicians and each play specifies the number of drummers needed—either two or three. The drummers have the added responsibility of making vocal sounds that punctuate the actors' dialogue. There is also one flute player.

The principal characters wear wooden masks which are traditional and passed down from one generation to the next. The main characters' costumes are fashioned from the official court dress of the fourteenth and fifteenth centuries and are constructed of colorful silks that have been intricately embroidered. The chorus members wear the traditional dress of the Samurai which includes stiff shoulder boards and divided skirts.

The stage used to perform the Noh drama was standardized almost 400 years ago. It includes a bridge located upstage center; a pine tree painted on the upstage wall and bamboo on the right side wall; a *waki-za*, the area used by the chorus; and a temple-style roof that is supported by four posts. Noh drama is the most traditional and structured form of Japanese theatre. Today, the artists who create Noh drama strive to preserve its original structure and appearance.

Bunraku (doll theatre)

During the seventeenth century, Bunraku, or doll theatre, gained popularity and, as the name suggests, all of the characters are represented by puppets. At first, the puppets were only heads with pieces of cloth to indicate the rest of their bodies. Now, the dolls are between three and four feet tall; have movable eyes, eyebrows, and fingers; and are dressed in elaborate costumes. Three puppeteers, in plain view of the audience, bring these expressive puppets to life. The scenic designs are as elaborate as the dolls and each new location is depicted as the story calls for it.

Kabuki

Kabuki, first developed in the seventeenth century, was originally performed on a stage similar to that of the Noh drama, but contemporary Kabuki theatre is presented on a stage with a proscenium opening. The scenic elements used in Kabuki productions are always symbolic rather than realistic. For example, different colored mats are used—white representing snow, blue indicating water, and gray depicting the earth. Stage attendants, which the audience members consider "invisible," change scenic elements and costume pieces in plain view of the audience.

The plays are composed of several emotionally charged incidents, each of which comes to a dramatic conclusion when one of the principle characters sustains a *mie* or stylized pose. Kabuki actors do not sing, so if a play requires singing, a chorus and orchestra are employed. The orchestra is composed of a variety of instruments including flutes, bells, drum, gongs, strings, cymbals, and a samisen.

Kabuki actors begin learning their craft in childhood, usually because their fathers or grandfathers were actors. They perform with elaborately patterned make-up and costumes that can weigh up to 50 pounds. From 1603 to 1629, female actors performed the women's characters in Kabuki theatre, but the *shogun* believed that their erotic performances were encouraging prostitution. Thus, the women characters were replaced by young boys who proved to be equally erotic and were subsequently removed. Finally, the shogun decided to allow men to perform the female characters if they agreed to make themselves less sensual by shaving the front portion of their heads.

The male actors trained to play women's roles are called *onnagata*, and in the early twentieth century, heated debates ensued about whether or not to allow women to perform these female characters. Novelist Tamura Toshiko was one of the major advocates of casting women. She argued that women's bodies are intrinsically more feminine and express a women's essence more effectively than an *onnagata*. She also believed that it is impossible for an *onnagata* to understand the intellectual complexities that a modern education gives women, and that this lack of comprehension would not allow *onnagata*s to effectively play female characters in modern Western plays.

On the opposing side of the issue, Minakuchi wrote that Japanese women are too short and soft-voiced, their noses too flat, their hips too large and unshapely, and their gestures not forceful enough. In short, Japanese women are physically unsuitable to play female roles. Morita Shoei, a novelist, agreed and argued that women are inferior to men both physically and mentality. In the Japanese version of Oscar Wilde's *Salome*, the female lead performs the "Dance of the Seven Veils" during which she undresses in front of her stepfather in order to win a treasured prize from him, the head of Jokanaan. Kawakami Sadayakko (1871–1946) and Matsui Sumako (1886–1919) each played Salome in two separate but groundbreaking productions. When the women undressed, it seemed clear to many that a woman's feminine qualities are epitomized in her body. In contemporary Kabuki theatre, *onnagata*s still perform female roles; however, women do perform female roles in other theatre productions.

Contemporary Japanese Theatre

Today, Japan is home to a variety of theatrical styles. There are Japanese adaptations of Western plays and musicals. There are also musicals and other types of plays written by Japanese playwrights. One notable Japanese playwright is Ota Shogo who in 1990 began writing and directing plays featuring an introspective look at contemporary Japanese life. He sets his plays in unusual settings such as garbage dumps, and many times his performers communicate non-verbally.

Today, Japan is home to a variety of theatrical styles including Noh, Bunraku, and Kabuki.

Mexican Theatre

The Aztec Natives

The Aztec Indians were the indigenous people of Latin America and their culture embraced theatre in the forms of music and dancing. But in 1519, Spanish conquistadors led by Hernan Cortez conquered the Aztec leader, Montezuma. Spanish missionaries soon arrived and used secular drama to covert the Aztecs to Catholicism. The Spanish government, which kept in close communication with the conquerors, began to influence the development of the theatre in Mexico.

The Aztec Indians were the indigenous people of Latin America and their culture embraced theatre in the forms of music and dancing.

After the Spanish Conquest

Playwright Juan Ruiz de Alarcon (1581–1639) was born in Mexico but his works made a substantial impact on the Spanish theatre. He wrote a number of plays, including *Las paredes oyen* (*The Walls Have Ears*, 1617), all of which were well received in both Spain and Mexico. He earned a reputation for being a moralist, but his plays were entertaining as well as educational. His characters had vices and serious personality flaws and he even influenced the French playwrights Corneille and Moliere. Another notable playwright of the period was the nun Sor Juana Ines de la Cruz (1651–95) who wrote *El divino Narciso* (*The Divine Narcissus*, c. 1680) and *Amore s mas laberinto* (*Love Is a Greater Labyrinth*, c. 1668). Her poetic and witty writing style gave her a reputation for excellence that critics of the time felt surpassed many European writers.

The eighteenth century in Mexico saw the end of secular plays. For the most part, the plays performed in Mexico were the same plays that had already been successfully produced in Spain. The most popular Mexican playwright of the century was Euebio Vela (1680–1737). He was a prolific playwright; however, only three of his plays have survived.

From September 16, 1810, known as Independence Day, until the fighting ended in 1821, Mexico was embroiled in a war with Spain for its independence. When the war ended, Mexican theatre artists were still very connected to Spanish culture, and their new works reflected Spanish artistic ideals. The most notable Mexican playwright of the period was Manuel Eduardo de Gorostiza (1789–1851) whose plays were produced in both Spain and Mexico. He was educated in Europe during the height of romanticism and wrote a number of plays, including *Contigo pan cebollo* (*Bread and Onion with Thee*, 1833), which satirized the sentimentality of the era. Another well-known playwright was Jose Rosa Moreno (1838–83) whose play *Sor Juana Ines de la Cruz* (1882) centered on the legendary love that a nun had for the Count of Mancera.

During the 1920s, traditional performance became the focus and theatres such as *Teatro Folklorico* (1921) and *Teatro del Murcielago* (1924)

produced native Mexican dances, songs, and ritual ceremonies. The *Sociedad de Autores Dramaticos* (Playwrights Society) which had been founded in 1902 to read and translate plays changed its name in 1923 to *Union de Autores Dramaticos* (Playwrights' Union). *The Union de Autores Dramaticos* modernized Mexican plays by ridding them of outmoded conventions and altered the dialogue from Madrid Spanish to Mexican Spanish. In 1927, the Union also adopted *Comedia Mexicana* (Mexican Comedy) as a new style of drama.

Experimental Theatres

In the early twentieth century there were very few professional theatres in Mexico, but in 1929, the first experimental theatre *Teatro de Ulises* (Ulysses Theatre) was opened only to close after two seasons. *Teatro de Orientacion* (Theatre of Orientation) was another small experimental theatre. It opened in 1932 with limited funding from the government. The theatre invited European luminaries such as Stanislavsky and Reinhardt to direct Spanish translations of plays by Shakespeare, Chekhov, Shaw, and Ibsen. These productions inspired Mexican artists to write and create their own productions. Playwright, diplomat, and theatre historian Rodolfo Usigli (1905–79) wrote numerous plays including *El gesticulador* (*The Imposter*, 1938) and *Corona de sombra* (*Crown of Shadow*, 1943).

Professional Theatre

In 1947, *Instituto Nacional de Bellas Artes* (National Institute of Fine Arts) was created to provide acting classes in addition to professional productions. It also began a series of annual drama festivals that awarded prizes for outstanding plays. Most Mexican plays written after World War II were structured as either realism or fantasy-driven expressionism. Emilio Carballido (b. 1925) was an innovative and flexible playwright who wrote effective plays in either style. His work paved the way for younger artists and he offered classes in playwriting and directing. Hector Azar (b. 1930) was also involved in training actors whom he allowed to perform in his original plays and translations.

Mexico's *Poetry Out Loud's* (1956–1963) goal was to inspire the most talented and imaginative artists to help reconstruct the Mexican theatre. During the eight years the group performed, it presented a wide variety of plays. Although the critics were less than impressed with the group's productions, many directors and actors gained valuable experience and their subsequent productions benefited from their artistic growth with *Poetry Out Loud*. In 1969, playwright and novelist Jose Agustin used modern technology closed-circuit television, audio recordings, and projections in his groundbreaking production of *Abolicion de la propiedad* (*Abolition of Property.*) This was an attempt to connect with a generation immersed in rock music. Another novelist who worked in the theatre was Vicente Lenero. His play *Orquideas a la luz de la luna* (*Orchids in the Moonlight*, 1982) was written to be performed both in English and Spanish and investigated the lives of two aging Mexican film stars.

Summary

Nearly every ancient civilization participated in religious rituals involving theatrical elements such as singing, dancing, and storytelling. Although it would be impossible to cover the specific theatrical origins of every civilization, the following were examined—Africa, the Arabic-language countries, Australia, Canada, China, India, Japan, and Mexico. It is important to note that theatrical practices in these and other countries continue to adapt in order to meet the ever-changing needs of their people.

Active Learning Assignment
"Bringing Theatre to Life"

I. Reenacting Theatre from a Variety of Nations

1. Break the class into groups of 10 to 15 people.

2. Divide the keynotes sections about theatre from Africa, the Arabic-speaking countries, Australia, Canada, China, India, Japan, and Mexico equally among the groups.

3. Each group will select four important pieces of information from the section that they have been assigned.

4. The groups will then devise a theatrical way to communicate this information to the class. For example, a talk show could be simulated and the host's special guest could be Tawfiqel Hakim, the most recognized playwright of the Arab world, who wrote *Ahl al Kahf*. Yussuf Idris and Alfred Farag could be special guests and talk about their new plays.

5. These presentations should be limited to between five and seven minutes in length.

Critical Thinking in Class Discussion

I. What were the four main points that each of the groups presented?

II. Were there important facts that were missed? If so, what were they?

III. What are the most surprising facts about theatre in Africa, the Arabic-speaking countries, Australia, Canada, China, India, Japan, and Mexico?

IV. If you could travel to one of the cultures discussed to see the theatre, which one would you choose? Why?

The Theatre in You

Humanity in the Theatre

Theatre gives us an opportunity to escape from our responsibilities and realities—temporarily transforming our lives into something that is fun and fanciful. But theatre can also be thought-provoking. It provides us with the opportunity to look deeply into the human condition, to examine it and, in some cases, change it. Shakespeare said "The purpose of playing . . . was and is, to hold, as 'twere, the mirror up to nature . . ." (Hamlet, Act III Scene ii). This reminds us of one of the most significant gifts that the theatre can contribute to humanity—the ability to depict life as it is. But this unpretentious goal is often met with criticism. Plays (and the way that they are produced) are sometimes accused of depicting inappropriate human behavior. It is true that some plays show people behaving in an unsavory fashion. Unfortunately, human beings do not always behave appropriately, ethically or morally. If the theatre is to do its job—". . . hold a mirror up to life," it must be allowed to reflect the whole of the human condition—the good, the bad, and the ugly. The theatre must be inclusive and honest in its portrayal of human life.

> The theatre must be inclusive and honest in its portrayal of human life.

Proof

Directed by Charles McNeely. *Courtesy of McNeese State University.*

Censorship

Theatre, in an effort to depict life as it is, has for decades revealed unsavory human behavior. For example, in the 1920s several plays were written about white slavery (poor innocent girls who were forced into prostitution). This form of slavery was (and still is) a real-life social tragedy and some playwrights chose to draw attention to the issue in their plays. One such play was entitled *House of Bondage,* based on a novel by Wright Kauffman, in which a young girl from a small town moves to New York to find work and is lured into a house of ill repute. Several religious groups were appalled by the subject matter deeming it immoral and vulgar. Others, such as Mrs. Emmeline Pankhurst (famous because of her vehement support of a woman's right to vote), upon seeing a play with a similar theme believed that the stage had finally began its mission—becoming a form of public education which informed audiences about life's foul truths. Despite support for these plays, pressure from a number of religious groups encouraged politicians to seek bans on productions thought to be immoral and indecent.

In the 1920s, the state of New York enacted penal code 1140, essentially stating that any person who participated in a play or any other form of entertainment which lead to the corruption of the morals of any other person is guilty of a misdemeanor. The New York City police force was sent to investigate suspicious productions and make arrests. Productions believed to be immoral were brought to trial and, more often than not, found guilty and forced to remove all indecent material or be shut down.

Although the first amendment of the Constitution protects citizens' rights of freedom of religion, speech, assembly, and petition, the amendment does not prevent townships and states from enacting statutes similar to penal code 1140. Many did.

Banned in Boston

The Massachusetts State Legislature gave local mayors the power to revoke theatre licenses for any reason (1904). In 1929, Boston's Mayor deemed Eugene O'Neill's Pulitzer Prize winning play *Strange Interlude* immoral and refused to license the production. *The Boston Globe* congratulated the mayor as being responsible for creating the most famous advertising in history, "Banned in Boston." The production was moved to the small township of Quincy, outside of Boston, and when a pastor in Quincy attempted to prevent the production from opening, the Theatre Guild, which had produced the play, defended O'Neill's play which was intended to illuminate social problems. In a private meeting between the Quincy Ministers' Association and the mayor, it was learned that not one of the clergymen had seen or read the play. A presentation of the production was given in order that they might evaluate its contents. The mayor was highly praised by the public for allowing the single performance and he granted the production permission to perform as long as the producers desired. It ran for one month.

Since that time numerous theatre productions have been threatened by local authorities. They were instructed to remove all immoral content or risk being closed, with all participating artists arrested for indecent behavior. For example, in the 1930s, a performance of *Lysistrata* was presented in Los Angeles and all 65 cast members were arrested.

By the 1970s, productions that included nudity, such as the Broadway musical *Hair*, encountered very little official opposition in New York City; but by the late 1980s, fundamentalist Christian groups and conservative politicians pressured the National Endowment for the Arts and several major theatres to reconsider financing any artistic project that did not support the ideals of these protestors. Since the money that the NEA was receiving was, in part, given by these protesters the NEA was forced, to some degree to compromise.

> Numerous theatre productions have been threatened to remove all immoral content or risk being closed—with all participating artists to be arrested for indecent behavior.

Today, many theatre artists find value in exposing audiences to new ideas, revealing social problems, and challenging traditional values, but there are also many who prefer to defend the status quo and traditional moral values. This is a conflict which has existed in the theatre since the Greeks and will, undoubtedly, continue.

Diversity in the Theatre

Today many theatre artists find value in exposing audiences to new ideas, revealing social problems and challenging traditional values, but there are also those who prefer to defend the status quo and the moral values.

Before the civil rights movement, white actors would frequently (particularly in minstrel shows) portray African Americans by painting their faces with black make-up or shoe polish—a practice called blackface. Blackface is taboo in the modern theatre, although it is occasionally used in some satirical works. It must be admitted, however, that there is a disparity in the number of Caucasians actors compared with actors of other races. In an effort to bridge this gap, *blind casting* (casting a non-Caucasian in a role that has been traditionally portrayed by a Caucasian) has been encouraged by both AEA and SAG. Another term for blind casting is non-traditional casting. In recent years, minorities (and also women) have become more visible in the theatre as playwrights, directors, and producers.

Theatres Created by Specific Groups

Blind casting has been encouraged by both AEA and SAG in an effort to bridge the gap between the number of Caucasian actors compared with actors of other races.

Some theatres are created by individuals who wish to feature race (Indian, African-American, Asian, etc.) gender (all women) or sexual orientation (gay and lesbian). The following is a partial list of some of these theatres:

Native American Theatres

Thunderbird Theatre
tbird@ross1.cc.haskell.edu

Red Eagle Soaring
Resoaring@earthlink.net

Some theatres are created by individuals who wish to feature race, gender, or sexual orientation.

Native Nations Dance Theatre
vaughnda@nativeweb.net

African-American Theatres

African-American Shakespeare Company
www.african-americanshakes.org

Jubilee Theatre
www.jubileetheatre.org

Peoples Theatre
www.peoplestheatre.org

Asian American Theatres

Asian American Theatre Company
info@asianamericantheater.org

Women's Theatres

Women's Theatre Company (A Professional Equity Theatre Company)
www.Womenstheatrecompany.org

Arizona Women's Theatre Company
www.azwtc.org

Yorkshire Women Theatre
www.stellarquines.com

Gay and Lesbian Theatres

Theatre Rhinoceros
http://www.therhino.org

Diversionary Theatre
www.diversionary.org

Working Together

Theatre is a collaborative art. It requires that actors, directors, designers, technicians, producers, and managers all work together effectively and efficiently. We will learn more about the specific responsibilities of each of these positions in following chapters. This chapter, however, focuses on the interpersonal skills that everyone, regardless of vocation, can benefit from using. There are several skills to examine. These include being flexible, working as a team player, and maintaining a positive sense of self.

Theatre is a collaborative art.

Flexibility

Theatre practitioners know that they must be flexible in order to mount a production. It is not atypical for a director, designer, or actor to alter his or her strategy to deal with unforeseen circumstances such as budget cuts or illnesses. Even when a production is in performance, problems occur that call for flexibility. For example, if the telephone on-stage does not ring when it is supposed to, the actor on-stage must add last minute stage business or ad lib so that the audience is unaware. Flexibility is a valuable trait and one that can serve everyone in real-life situations.

Theatre practitioners know that they must be flexible in order to mount a production.

It is always a good idea to be prepared to make last minute adjustments no matter what the project. This can be helped by trouble-shooting—brainstorming possible problems and solutions before the project is underway. For example, directors hire understudies who are ready to perform in case an actor is suddenly ill or has an emergency. Having a plan in place will not only makes things run smoother but also helps to keep morale up and stress levels down. This is advantageous for employees regardless of their business. People who are able to remain calm and upbeat during a crisis make better team players.

Teamwork

Theatre practitioners champion teamwork while working on a production. Each realizes that being a team player means knowing how to compromise,

Theatre practitioners champion teamwork while working on a production.

Theatre is a particularly public art form and can place the artist in a vulnerable position.

how to accept different viewpoints and how to actively listen, even to those who don't agree. The production team members know that because they are part of a collaborative group, no one will get his or her way all the time, but if all learn to compromise, the team will be stronger. Theatre artists also strive to develop and maintain open and productive relationships within their team. They do this by being straight forward and honest while also being conscientious and considerate of others' emotions so that effective communication is possible.

Self Esteem

Theatre is a particularly public art form and can place the artist in a vulnerable position. Viewing a work of theatre is subjective in that one person may love an artist's set design while another may dislike it. This subjectivity exposes artists and may fill them with either a feeling of great self worth or with shame. How we define ourselves as individuals impacts our level of self esteem. In order to improve self esteem, we must challenge our self-imposed limits and redefine ourselves.

Active Learning Assignment
"Bringing Theatre to Life"

I. The Final Group Project—Writing and Producing a Play

A. Each group of 10 to 15 students (you will remain in this group until the end of the semester) selects a period or genre such as Medieval, Symbolist, Musical Theatre, etc. The group will, throughout the remainder of the term, write, stage and perform a play (running time five to seven minutes) written in the style selected. At this point, the groups should agree on which period or genre each will use.

B. The following elements help to make the production complete: dramaturgy, stage management, playwriting, producing, directing, designing—costume, scenery, lighting, properties—promotion, and the creation of a program. Upcoming chapters cover each of these production elements and include in-class activities.

C. The culmination of the in-class activities will be the production of each group's play. The play itself will be performed and constitutes the final project. The script, program, research paper (dramaturgical work), the stage manager's prompt book, and the performance itself will all be used in assessing each group's grade on the project.

D. The group will want to appoint or elect one or two people to take on specific production roles. For example, there should be only one stage manager and only one director and these individuals should not double as actors. The other members of the production staff may be doubled. Several individuals might work on the program, the set, the lighting, and the properties while also acting in the production. The research paper (Dramaturg "Bringing Theatre to Life" In Class Activity) has been designed so that all members of the group can and should participate in its creation.

Lend Me a Tenor

Directed by Deb Kinghorn. *Courtesy of University of New Hampshire Photographic Services.*

Dramaturgs and Stage Managers

Researching and Running the Show

Dramaturgs and stage managers are crucial members to the artistic staff.

This chapter focuses on dramaturgs and stage managers, not because they are directly related, but because, like producers and directors, they hold special positions in a theatre organization. Their work dramatically affects the look, continuity, believability, and, ultimately, the success of the production. Dramaturgs and stage managers are leaders/managers and collaborators as well as valued artistic members of the production staff. In commercial and regional theatres, it is paramount that these positions are filled by consummate professionals, but in community theatres, these roles, because of financial constraints, often fall to less experienced individuals. In either situation, dramaturgs and stage managers are crucial members of the artistic staff. This chapter provides an overview of their duties and spotlights interviews with respected professionals.

The Dramaturg's Responsibilities

Dramaturgs specialize in all issues dealing with dramatic literature.

Dramaturgs have many responsibilities, including researching, developing, and advising.

Dramaturgs specialize in all issues dealing with dramatic literature. Major professional companies have full time dramaturgs on staff while other theatres hire them on a show-by-show basis. Dramaturgs have many responsibilities prior to a production including researching, developing, and advising. For instance, a dramaturg might work with a marketing director in conducting surveys to determine the types of plays a theatre's audience is interested is seeing. If the audience enjoys classical works, the dramaturg may search for a title that is rarely produced, in the hope that it will intrigue the audience. In some cases, a play might be so obscure that a modern audience will have difficulty understanding its nuances. In such a case, the dramaturg will edit all or part of the script and adapt it to modern sensibilities. It could also be that the play is written in another language and needs to be translated. The dramaturg, if able, may translate the script or arrange for a translation.

Perhaps the dramaturg has located an original play that he or she thinks the theatre's audience might enjoy. In this instance, the dramaturg can work with the playwright in developing the play for production. The dramaturg provides the playwright with another perspective and gives suggestions on how to improve various aspects of the play.

The dramaturg might provide the audience with educational information about a play.

If there is concern that the audience may be unfamiliar with the play's historical or literary merit, genre, or playwright, the dramaturg may provide the audience with educational information. Perhaps the theatre is interested in attracting a young audience. In this case, a dramaturg could develop workshops or mini-performances of an upcoming production and arrange for them to be presented at local schools. Finally, the dramaturg will write a short synopsis of pertinent information to be included in the program.

Production Dramaturg

During the pre-production and rehearsal stages of a play, a great deal of research needs to be done. Many directors prefer to do their own research, but some find collaborating with a dramaturg during the production process is even more effective. It is helpful to first look at reviews of past productions. It is also important to find background information on the playwright and his or her previous plays. Such information can provide important clues about the play being produced. If a play is set in a country or time period unfamiliar to the production team, substantial research needs to be done in order to create a truthful production. Certainly, information regarding the customs and political and religious beliefs of the characters will be of value to both the artistic staff and the cast. Additionally, if the play contains language that is unfamiliar and/or words that have varying pronunciations, then the dramaturg will address those issues.

There are many ways to approach the analysis of a play. A dramaturg will utilize library resources such as books and journal articles and will also conduct research via the Internet. A dramaturg may also conduct interviews with specialists in fields relating to the production.

Dramaturg Liz Engelman

Liz Engelman

Photograph courtesy of Liz Engelman

Ms. Engelman received a B.A. in theatre from Brown University and a M.F.A. in dramaturgy at Columbia University. She is Chair of the Board of the Literary Managers and Dramaturgs of America having recently served as the President. Ms. Engelman's positions have included Literary Director of the McCarter Theatre, the Director of New Play Development at ACT Theatre in Seattle, Literary Manager/Dramaturg at Seattle's Intiman Theatre and Assistant Literary Manager at the Actors Theatre of Louisville. Ms. Engelman has had the privilege of working to develop new plays at The Playwright's Center in Minneapolis, Bay Area Playwrights Festival, ASK Theatre Projects, New York Theatre Workshop, the O'Neill Playwrights Conference, and South Coast Rep.

Ms. Engelman has directed new plays at these theatres: The Illusion Theatre (with Michael Dixon), Mixed Blood Theatre, The Playwrights' Center in Minneapolis, and Carleton College. She has been a guest artist at Washington University in St. Louis, the University of Puget Sound, and Cornish College of the Arts. Additionally, she has taught playwriting at Freehold Studio Theatre Lab and The Playwrights Center.

Ms. Engelman is an accomplished writer and some of her credits include co-editing several collections of plays with Michael Bigelow Dixon and two volumes of monologues on which she collaborated with Tori Haring-Smith.

Feature Section
An Interview with Dramaturg Liz Engelman

What inspired you to become a dramaturg?

When I was a junior in high school, I took a class called "Madness in Literature." One day, my teacher said to me, "Liz, you should be a dramaturg." I answered, of course, with the obvious "drama-what?" And then, like a true dramaturg, asked, "Why?" Her answer has stuck with me ever since; "You have the ability to look at the big picture and discern how it relates to the small details, and you're able to look at something small and relate it to the whole." For me, that became dramaturgy in a nutshell; the ability to focus on things in relationship, in context, one piece in conversation with another.

So then I became a 16–17-year-old dramaturg—whatever that means—in high school. I wrote program notes for our production of *The Crucible*, that sort of thing. Then, in college, a professor said, "Liz, you should be a dramaturg." By then, I knew what it meant. So I took an independent concentration in it, and the rest is a small history.

What do you feel is most challenging about being a dramaturg?

There are a few, some external, some internal. Externally, the challenge is establishing trust amongst your collaborators, since so often the profession forces you onto a colleague like a blind date. So how do you negotiate a new relationship in a relatively short period of time? Therein lies the challenge, and therein lies the trust. Trust in your opinion, in your respect for the project and process, trust in your support.

Timing's another. For questions, observations, notes, conversations.

Internally, the challenge is how to remain fulfilled as a creative person when often you're supporting, advancing, nurturing, exploring other people's visions and passions and expressions. For me, the challenge has remained how to continue to be a participator in the process, not only an observer, to be a generator and true collaborator and not only a reactor and researcher. Patience, that good old virtue, is another challenge. How to feel useful and helpful when much of your time is indeed spent observing and reacting. How to translate those experiences into something that doesn't feel like it's what I call BFWOT: big f***ing waste of time.

What is the most rewarding aspect of dramaturgy?

The conversations. The passion. The innovation. The opportunities to make connections: between people and places and theatres and things. Knowing that a play has been brought into this world because you commissioned it. Or that a playwright's career has flourished because you helped introduce her or him to an institution that then becomes their home. Then there are those smaller, yet still rewarding moments when you watch a play and smile to yourself because you remember how the scene used to end before you had that great conversation that led to a change . . . and no one else will ever know.

Do you have a favorite project? If so, what?

Way too many to list. They range from being the dramaturg at a two-day reading to creating entirely new festivals.

If a student were interested in becoming a dramaturg, how might he or she begin?

I found that interning at a regional theatre that values and focuses on new plays taught me more than anything about collaboration, programming, and vision in relation to execution. It exposed and connected me to writers, directors, actors, designers, stage managers with whom I still work to this day. Your experience as an intern can bring you fully into the culture of a theatre—and you might just stay. I've known several dramaturgs who had their start by selecting a theatre they were interested in, asked to volunteer there, and then worked their way up in different departments before landing in the literary office.

Active Learning Assignment
"Bringing Theatre to Life"

I. Researching for the Final Group Project—Writing and Producing a Play

Using a combination of books, Internet search engines, and professional journals, each group will research the historical period or genre that they have selected for their final. The group will then select one or two members to write a draft of a four-page research paper on the subject. The rest of the group members take turns reading and editing the paper which will be submitted on the day of the performance.

The Theatre in Your Career

No matter what vocation you choose, in-depth research will help you secure employment and advance in your career. Before you go to a job interview, make sure you have adequately researched the company. Use the library, the Internet and, if possible, personal interviews with others in the profession as research tools. During a job interview, you need to demonstrate that you have a firm grasp of the company's mission and only extensive research will provide you with the necessary information. An interview is best conducted when the job seeker is able to communicate how his or her skills can provide a needed service for the company. To alter a well-known quotation, "Ask not what the company can do for you, but what you can do for the company." It doesn't matter whether it's a theatre company or a company that manufactures cars. The approach is basically the same.

Stage Management

As you read this section, keep in mind that stage managers are managers and managers are leaders. The leadership skills and personal attributes that transform mediocre stage managers into excellent stage managers can be used in any management/leadership position. The vocation doesn't matter. For example, an effective stage manager practices interpersonal communication

skills including active listening, patience, and constructive criticism. The stage manager maintains a positive attitude, remains calm during stressful situations, and delegates tasks to others in a manner that is both respectful and encouraging. Additionally, stage managers are most effective when their leadership skills include organization, time management, and problem solving.

The Stage Manager's Responsibilities

Pre-Production

Stage managers are most effective when they have developed strong leadership skills including organization, time management, and problem solving.

The stage manager is responsible for organizing and managing the entire production from pre-production through post production. Before the rehearsals begin, the stage manager arranges and chairs several production meetings with the director and the designers. During these meetings, the stage manager will keep complete and accurate notes. After the meeting, the notes are organized, typed, and distributed to the artistic staff. Other pre-production duties include, but are not limited to, evaluating the theatre and its equipment, locating safety equipment and fire exits, organizing all important information (safety/health concerns, rehearsal times and agenda, contact information, etc.) on an easy to read, centrally located "call board," creating and updating a to-do list, and drawing up a master schedule for the production.

Stage managers are responsible for organizing and managing the entire production from early production meetings through post production.

Auditions

During auditions, stage managers are responsible for signing the actors in, collecting headshots and resumes, passing out *sides* (sections of scripts), introducing the actors to the directors at the appropriate time, and, in some cases, reading the script with the actors. At a professional theatre open call, there may be hundreds of actors which means that the stage manager is also responsible for crowd control.

Rehearsals

Before a rehearsal begins, it is absolutely imperative that the stage manager check the entire area for possible hazards. Accidents do happen, but many can be avoided by a complete examination of the rehearsal space, set pieces, and hand properties before the actors arrive. If an accident does occur, the stage manager should be ready to address the issue calmly and efficiently.

During rehearsals, stage managers take blocking (movement) notes for the director in a prompt book. This means that before the rehearsals begin, the stage manager makes his or her own prompt book. Usually this book is composed of loose leaf 8-1/2" x 11-1/2" pages containing a copy of the script which are placed into a three-ring binder. All the other information regarding the production is also kept in the binder. It is important to divide the prompt book into clearly marked sections that include contact and scheduling information, a properties list, sound and lighting cues, scenic design and *ground plan* (a scale drawing of the location of the set pieces in relation to the scenery), and the running time of the production.

One of the most important sections of the prompt book is the script itself which is, due to copyright laws, best made from the actual printed scripts. If the stage manager has two scripts available, he or she will unbind the script and adhere (using rubber cement or a glue stick) each page to its own sheet of blank, loose-leaf 8-1/2" x 11-1/2" paper. The reason for this is to create a large blank boarder around each page of script. This is where the director's blocking will be noted.

In addition to a prompt book, the stage manager maintains a kit holding a variety of items that may be needed during the rehearsal. Some of these items include, but are certainly not limited to, aspirin, acetaminophen, honey, sugar, powdered cream, individual bags of tea, paper cups, safety pins, pencils, hair pins, toothpaste, toothbrushes, hair spray, nail files, cough drops, candles, flashlights, towelettes, facial tissue, stop watch, chalk, one-inch brads, black ballpoint pens, electric extension cords, measuring tape, tailor's measuring tape, ruler, tacks, spike tape, masking tape, and a well-stocked first aid kit. It may seem like a great deal of equipment, but having these and other items nearby can save a great deal of time and frustration during rehearsals. Remember the old adage, "Whatever can go wrong will go wrong." A stage manager must be prepared for any situation; in fact, most professional stage managers are trained in C.P.R. and basic first aid.

In addition to making blocking notations and providing needed items for emergency situations, the stage manager is responsible for running the rehearsal. This basically means that the stage manager announces to the group that the rehearsal is beginning and informs them when it is over. The stage manager will time every scene during the rehearsal in order to calculate the total running time of the production. He or she calls breaks at appropriate times (Actors Equity Association, the professional stage actors' union, requires regular breaks for actors). The stage manager is also responsible for telephoning actors that are late to the rehearsal, although professionals are never late unless there is an emergency. The stage manager might also prompt actors when they forget lines, but this duty is frequently given to an assistant stage manager.

In addition to taking down blocking, providing needed items in emergency situations, the stage manager is responsible for running the rehearsal.

When the rehearsal is finished, the stage manager returns the set pieces and hand props to a storage area and writes a rehearsal report. Rehearsal reports might indicate to the costumer that an outer coat is now needed in a particular scene; the sound designer may learn that a special song is needed for a scene, etc. This rehearsal report is copied and distributed to the entire artistic staff.

Running the Production

While the production is in performance, the stage manager checks to make sure that the actors and running crew arrive at the scheduled times, synchronizes the opening of the theatre with the house manager, and calls actors to places. During the performance, the stage manager supervises the *running crew* (stage hands who move the scenery and the props). It is very important that the set changes occur quickly and smoothly—rough scene changes make a production sloppy and badly paced.

While the production is in progress, a stage manager checks to make sure that the actors and running crew arrive at the appropriate time, synchronize the opening of the curtain with the house manager, and calls actors to places.

The stage manager also calls the show during a performance. When a stage manager is calling the show, he or she is sitting at a desk, usually in the wings, informing the sound and light board operators (via headset) when to run each of the cues. For example, a light cue might be blackout (all stage lights off). A sound cue might be gunfire and is called when a character is supposed to be shot.

Another responsibility of a stage manager is to insure the integrity of the production.

A major responsibility of the stage manager is to insure the integrity of the production. Some Broadway productions can run for several years and the show needs to be played the same way every night. The director does not attend every performance and, thus, cannot give notes to the actors. The stage manager gives notes and may even call rehearsals when the show is not up to its original standard.

The production needs to be archived and the stage manager is responsible for organizing and running the photo call. Sometimes, the director and designers select pictures; at other times, selection is left to the stage manager. During the actual shooting, the stage manager needs to call actors to places and then call the needed light cues.

Post Production

There are several post-production duties that a stage manager must complete.

There are several post-production duties that a stage manager must complete. Some of these might include returning the rented scripts and/or scores, devising a strike schedule, and, if desired, writing thank you notes.

This section has provided a brief overview of the duties of stage managers. There are many other responsibilities which can differ depending on the theatre and the production itself. For example, a touring show will be handled differently than one staged in a permanent location, and a musical has responsibilities that exceed straight plays. Professional stage managers receive excellent salaries and good stage managers are always in demand.

Stage Manager Rick Cunningham

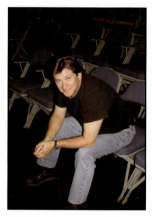

Rick Cunningham

Photo Courtesy of Nadine Howatt

An Actors' Equity Association stage manager since 1980, Rick Cunningham has nearly one hundred professional stage management credits. Some of these include Bulgarian Theatre Festival (Sopia); Roy Hart, The Roy Hart Theatre of France; German Theater Festival (Bremen); *Shakespeare for My Father* (Lynn Redgrave); *All The King's Men* (Adrian Hall); *Constant Star* (Tazewell Thompson); Contemporary American Theater Festival; Trump Plaza Casino, Atlantic City; and the Rosebud Theatre Company of New York City. He has also managed high profile events at and for the Gubernatorial Inaugurations in Massachusetts and Delaware, the National Football League, the Points of Light Foundation, the Kennedy Center, the AstroDome, the SuperDome, the FedEx Field, and the *First Night Wilmington '97–'02*.

Cunningham received an M.F.A. in Directing from Tulane University. Currently, he heads the M.F.A. Stage Management program at the University of Delaware—Professional Theatre Training Program and has served as the Coordinator of the Stage Management Mentoring Project for the United States Institute for Theatre Technology, 2003–2006.

FEATURE SECTION
An Interview with Stage Manager Rick Cunningham

What inspired you to become a stage manager?

I came in through the back door. All my training was in directing. During graduate school, I had an opportunity to be a rehearsal assistant and to be on the running crew and I really enjoyed it. I found my calling. Stage management has evolved from a technical position to part of the artistic production staff. The stage manager is the thread of the production that ties all of the departments working on the production together. Theatre has become so compartmentalized over the years. Directors and stage managers have become more collaborative.

What is the most challenging aspect of being a stage manager?

Perhaps the most challenging is to make every show your first show. This theory about stage managers leaving the profession because they are burned out, I challenge. Have they actually been bored out? I am relearning—I will continue to learn and I enjoy learning from everyone, from production assistants, assistant stage managers . . . everyone.

What do you enjoy most about being a stage manager?

I love rehearsals, seeing how a show grows. I particularly enjoy working on premieres; I have worked on between 50 and 60. (He has worked on premieres with numerous playwrights including Jane Martin, Adrian Hall, Sheri Wilner, Tazewell Thompson, Robert Schenkkan, Lee Blessing, Richard Dresser, and Romulus Linney.) I think stage management is the greatest job. I love to be involved in every facet of the production. I really love actors; I can't do what they do. Some people are jaded against actors. I am not. I have fun constantly seeking a way to make the actor's job easier. I have worked as a stage manager for 25 years now. I can't imagine doing anything else but stage management. The eye of the rehearsal room is at the stage management table. You must always be aware that everyone is watching you and not wear a spectator's face (look displeased if the scene is going badly). Of course, I can tell if the scene is going badly, so I try to think of a way to help improve it. I can offer to run lines with the actor or bring in a costume piece, music, or piece of furniture that may inspire the actor.

I see the role of a stage manager as an artist. Many directors ask for my artistic opinion regarding a scene and I am ready to respond.

I have one goal—to be great.

If a student were interested in becoming a professional stage manager, how would you recommend they get into the profession?

Do it wherever. Manage anywhere you can and the better you will become. Nearly all stage managers are hired as event managers. (Cunningham has managed Gubernatorial Inaugurations in Massachusetts and Delaware, among others.) When you manage a political event, the politician him/herself never goes to the rehearsal. They send

a shadow (stand in) that learns the blocking for the politician who then learns it from the shadow on the day of the event. Of course, the politician ends up making blocking mistakes during the event—stepping out of the light, etc., which makes for a lot of interesting stories.

When an educational or community theatre production begins, the stage manager is frequently the last person to be hired. The job is offered to an actor who is not cast in the show. But if a production is to go well, the stage manager should be picked first. The stage manager must be involved with the entire production process from auditions to closing night, so it is crucial to have excellent interpersonal skills. One way to develop a good and respectful relationship between the cast and the stage manager is for the director to allow the stage manager to have the first and the last words during rehearsals. For example, after notes at the end of rehearsal, the director might say to the stage manager "It's all yours." This is important because when the show opens, the stage manager is in charge. He or she will call the actors to the stage, make sure that the props are set, call the cues, and run any pick-up rehearsals.

Summary

The responsibilities of the dramaturg are all related to dramatic literature. These duties include—but are not limited to—researching and evaluating the literature and communicating what is found to the artistic staff. Production dramaturgs work closely with the director, analyzing past productions and historical information, and even providing appropriate pronunciations of words and phrases. Stage managers are responsible for the smooth operation of a production from beginning to end. They collaborate with the entire artistic staff and the administrative staff at the theatre. Their duties are many and varied and can include taking blocking notes, arranging meetings and photo calls, and supervising running crews. Although the responsibilities of dramaturgs and stage managers are very different, they are similar in value. Proper completion of their duties gives a production a greater chance of being fully realized.

Theatre in Your Career

As outlined in this chapter, the skills and personal attributes of an effective stage manager promote success in any vocation. As an example, it may be useful for an employee to organize and maintain a career (prompt) book. This three-ring binder can include evidence of training, successful completion of projects, unsolicited letters of appreciation, goals for the future, etc. The book can be taken to administrative meetings and used as an evaluation tool. If the binder is thoughtfully organized, most administrators will note the employee's attention to detail—a positive trait in any organization. In a competitive world, the theatre or business, it is essential to make a good impression at all times.

Active Learning Assignment
"Bringing Theatre to Life"

I. **Creating a Prompt Book for the Final Group Project—Writing and Producing a Play** (Inspired by Rick Cunningham)

Although only one person will act as the stage manager of the final performance, the entire group will have a production meeting to discuss the specific needs of the performance. For example, will any set pieces need to be pre-set? If so, where on stage should the spike tape (masking tape to indicate the position) be placed? What types of lighting, music, and/or special effects (PowerPoint, for example) will be a part of the production? At what points in the script will the cues be placed?

The stage manager will note the cues in a prompt book. For the actual performance, the prompt book need only contain the script with the blocking notes and the floor plan (the floor plan need not be to scale, a general sketch of the location of the set pieces will suffice). The stage manager will organize the scene changes, if any are needed. Because the final production will most likely take place in the classroom, the use of a headset to call the show will probably be impossible. It may be that the only lighting opportunities will be the overhead lights (on and off) portable lamps, or flashlights, and these will not be run through a central lighting board. Perhaps the stage manager could organize the people who will execute these cues. The stage manager will also organize the students who operate any PowerPoint and/or music cues.

The Art of Playwriting

The Playwright in You

It may be that you have never thought of writing plays, but many of the elements that constitute a well-written play can also be used to create effective political speeches, sales pitches, lectures, or the opening and closing statements of a trial. For example, pretend you are a lawyer writing your closing statement. Your mini-play (closing statement) includes: a **central character** (your client) who wants an **objective** (to be acquitted), there is **conflict**/obstacle (evidence against him/her), and a **resolution** ("Because of all of the reasons I have shown you today, it is obvious that my client is innocent of all charges brought against him."). The terms in bold type are four of the major ingredients that make up a well-written play. With so many revivals of older plays, it is sometimes said, "a good playwright is hard to find." If you are one who has a bent for writing, playwriting may be an avenue for you to explore. You don't have to quit your day job to write a play; it does not cost any money—all you need are an imagination, time, paper, and ink. Who knows? You may be able to make an artistic contribution to your community. This chapter examines playwriting techniques, how to market yourself as a playwright, and a brief overview of several well-known playwrights.

Crucial Ingredients in a Play

Exposition, central character, objective, obstacles/conflicts, crisis/climax, and resolution are the crucial ingredients for a well-written play.

Exposition leads the audience to empathize with the characters. It tells the audience who the characters are, how they relate to one another, what their desires and dislikes are, and what happened in the past that has landed them in the present situation. Although there are usually two or more characters in a play, the plot usually revolves around a **central character**. The central character will always have an **objective**—something he or she is desperate to obtain—but **obstacles/conflicts** make the goal very difficult or seemingly impossible for him or her to achieve. These small conflicts mount one on top of another (dramatic action) throughout the play; when one conflict appears to be resolved, an even more challenging conflict arises, thereby creating suspense. The audience is worried—will the hero (central character) win? These conflicts culminate in a major **crisis/climax;** and the audience members, as if sitting on the highest point of a giant rollercoaster, are filled with fear and anticipation. After the climax, there is a **resolution** involving the central character. Positive or negative, it will result in a physical and/or emotional change in the character.

Coming up with an Idea for a Play

Professional playwrights such as Athol Fugard and David Ives keep personal journals that include brief notes, daily observations, thoughts, etc., which they can later review for possible subjects. Brainstorming is another method for coming up with ideas for plays. Write down anything that comes to mind and then narrow down the topics; or your brainstorming session can be more specific, as Buzz McLaughlin in *The Playwright's Process: Learning the Craft from Today's Leading Dramatists* suggests, by setting a timer for three minutes and writing down any person or occasion that is important to your life. Remember, during any brainstorm activity, do not censor—just write. After brainstorming, you can review the list and select a topic. Since well-defined characters constitute one of the most important ingredients of a play, it is useful to consider basing central characters on close friends or family members. You will be more familiar with the individual and this will make it easier for you to create a believable and complex character.

In most cases, you do not need to be concerned that your real life characters will be recognizable because, as you write, their personalities will become altered—unless of course, you choose to write an autobiographical play that follows your own life, i.e., Eugene O'Neill's *Long Day's Journey Into Night*. Most playwrights believe that it is a good idea to allow six to ten years after an emotionally traumatic experience before writing about it. The time helps the writer to become more objective and allows one to structure the dramatic action rather than becoming bogged down in an emotional quagmire.

The first time playwright is advised to write a short play (10–15 minutes) about people, places, and situations with which he or she is familiar. Good playwrights begin by organizing and evaluating their ideas before writing. McLaughlin recommends answering the following questions: Who is the central character? What does the central character want? Who are the other major characters? Where does the story take place? What is the occasion? What is the major conflict? How does the story end? How does the central character change? What is the theme? What does the story mean? If you were considering writing a play based on *Little Red Riding Hood*, McLaughlin's questions would be answered this way:

All playwrights begin by organizing and evaluating their ideas before writing.

> **Who is the central character?** Red Riding Hood is the central character.
> **What does Red Riding Hood want?** She wants to go to see her grandmother.
> **Who are the other major characters?** The other characters are the Big Bad Wolf, Grandmother, and the Woodcutter.
> **Where does the story take place?** The story takes place in the woods and in Grandmother's house.
> **What is the occasion?** The occasion is a sunny afternoon—a lovely day to visit relatives.
> **What is the major conflict?** The wolf is hungry and wants to eat someone.
> **What is the climax?** The wolf eats Grandmother.
> **How does the story end?** The woodcutter kills the wolf and saves Grandmother.
> **What is the dramatic theme?** Don't trust wolves even if, at first, they seem friendly.

Writing Exposition

Playwrights have introduced expositional information in numerous ways.

Playwrights introduce expositional information in numerous ways. The opening scene in ancient Greek tragedy began with a choral ode that relayed all of the necessary exposition. Shakespeare used a similar approach by sometimes opening his play with a prologue. For example, the opening speech in *Romeo and Juliet*:

> The Prologue
> (Enter Chorus.)
>
> Chorus. Two households both alike in dignity
> (In fair Verona where we lay our scene)
> From ancient grudge break to new mutiny,
> Where civil blood makes civil hands unclean.
> From forth the fatal loins of these two foes
> A pair of star-cross'd lovers take their life,
> Whose misadventur'd piteous overthrows
> Doth with their death bury their parents' strife.
> The fearful passage of their death-mark'd love
> And the continuance of their parents' rage
> (Which but their children's end nought could remove)
> Is now the two hours' traffic of our stage,
> The which if you with patient ears attend
> What here shall miss our toil shall strive to mend.
>
> (Exit.)

Another popular approach to exposition is to create an occasion during which the characters will have an opportunity to "catch up"—perhaps at a dinner party or a dance. The most effective method to unveil the world of the characters is during the opening moments when dramatic action moves the story along. Ibsen explored several possibilities before discovering an intriguing way to deliver exposition in the opening moments of his play, *Rosmersholm*. *Rosmersholm* is a play focusing on the suicide of Pastor Rosmer's wife—she threw herself into the pond next to the mill. Kenneth Macgowan compares an early draft found in *From Isben's Workshop* with the final version:

In the first version Rosmer (then called Boldt-Romer) asks Rebecca West (then Miss Radeck) where his daughters are, and learns they are skating on the mill pond.

> Rebecca: Oh, there's no danger at all. It's not so deep, and besides, the ice is perfectly safe.
> Rosmer: I know that; it isn't *that* I was thinking of.
> Rebecca: I see, it's on account of—the other thing?
> Rosmer: Yes. I think there is something uncanny in the children skating and playing and making a noise just over the spot that was their mother's death-bed. . . .

In the final draft Ibsen handles the matter (exposition) perfectly:

> Madame Helseth: I suppose I had better begin to lay the table, Miss?
> Rebecca West: Yes, please do. The Pastor must soon be in now.
> Madame Helseth: Don't you feel the draft, Miss, where you're sitting?

Rebecca: Yes, there is a little draught. Perhaps you had better shut the window.
Madame Helseth: (about to shut the window, looks out) Why, isn't that the Pastor over there?
Rebecca: Where? (Rises) Yes, it is he. (Behind the curtain) Stand aside—don't let him see us.
Madame Helseth: Only think, Miss—he's beginning to use the path by the mill again.
Rebecca: He went that way day before yesterday, too. But let us see whether . . .
Madame Helseth: Will he venture across the footbridge?
Rebecca: That is what I want to see. No, he is turning. He is going by the upper road again. A long way round.
Madame Helseth: Dear Lord, yes. No wonder the Pastor thinks twice about setting foot on that bridge. A place where a thing like that happened . . .

According to Macgowan, the final version relays exposition through natural and plausible conversation and avoids directly stating the information. Playwrights usually write several drafts of these plays, often taking several years to complete the work. In re-writing, the playwright removes any line or section that does not move the plot along. In some cases, consummate playwrights begin writing a play, get to a certain point, and find they are at a loss on how to continue. Most playwrights keep all unfinished drafts with the intent of re-examining them later.

Naming the Characters

In comparing Ibsen's first draft of *Rosmersholm* to his final version, the playwright reconsidered using Boldt-Romer as the Pastor's name and chose Rosmer. He perhaps felt it more appropriately reflected the personality and stature of the character. Rosmer has a gentler sound than Boldt-Romer; perhaps Ibsen wanted the character to seem warmer and more approachable.

Foreshadowing

Foreshadowing indicates to the audience something unfortunate is soon to occur. Thus, information is planted early in the play. Foreshadowing creates and maintains suspense and believability. Here is an example of foreshadowing:

Foreshadowing creates and maintains suspense and believability in a play.

Scene One: A window washer is cleaning a bay window on the second floor of a two-story house. The house belongs to a husband and wife.
Scene Two: Upon returning home, later that evening, the husband and wife argue in front of the window. The husband leans on the window and nearly falls through; the window washer did not close it properly. After struggling with the latch, the wife manages to close the window and the couple continues to argue as they go into the bedroom.

Scene Three: The next morning the wife is re-hanging the drapes on the bay window; she leans on the glass; the window is pushed open; and she falls to her death.

The Plot

The audience wants to be compelled to worry about one particular character all of the scenes ought to focus on the central character.

The audience wants to be compelled to be concerned about one particular character. Thus, all of the scenes should focus, directly or indirectly, on the central character. Everything must drive the play forward; in other words, remove all unnecessary information from the play. If the information is of vital importance, it should be repeated a total of three times during the course of the play. If physical violence is needed to drive the plot, it might be a good idea to set the scenes off-stage, as the ancient Geeks did. In spite of Hollywood action films, violence is frequently more effective if it is imagined rather than seen on stage.

Locations—Where to Set the Scene

As a novice playwright it is best not to have too many locations in your play.

It is best for the novice playwright not to have too many locations in a play. Yes, new scenery adds interest, but a producer will be more apt to back the play if there are only one or two scene changes. It is considerably less expensive.

Staged Readings

A staged-reading is a public performance, in which the actors, although familiar with the characters and the dialogue, read from the script.

A staged-reading is a public performance in which the actors, although familiar with the characters and the dialogue, read from the script. Typically, a director rehearses with the actors beforehand, and gives them a few stage directions; a narrator is employed to read the bulk of the stage directions. Staged readings give playwrights the opportunity to learn how an audience responds to the play—laughing in appropriate places, empathizing with the central character, etc. Audience response will probably inspire the playwright to make revisions.

Influential Playwrights

There are a great many playwrights who have made valuable contributions to the modern theatre. A list of these would certainly include Thornton Wilder (1897–1975), Tom Stoppard (1937–), Sam Shepard (1943–), Tony Kushner (1956–), August Wilson (1945–2005), and Tina Howe (1937–). This book will closely examine the following significant individuals: Henrik Ibsen, Eugene O'Neill, Lillian Florence Hellman, Tennessee Williams, Arthur Miller, Neil Simon, Edward Albee, Wendy Wasserstein, and Nicky Silver.

Henrik Ibsen (1828–1906)

Henrik Johan Ibsen was born into a wealthy family in Skien, Norway, on March 20, 1828. Not long after his birth, the family suffered financial ruin and was forced to move to Venstop, located a few miles from Skien. Ibsen grew up in an era when there were no permanent theatres in Norway. There were a few small theatres in townships scattered throughout the country, but most of these featured vaudeville acts. In 1843, the 15-year-old Ibsen left his modest home and became an apprentice to an apothecary. Unlike the young Shakespeare, Ibsen was not exposed to traveling troupes of actors. Never having had an opportunity to experience live theatre, Ibsen spent much of his time reading Shakespeare's plays. He loved them and yearned to write his own plays, but those desires were shared only with his closest friends. He dedicated himself to studying for the entrance examination to the University of Christiania where he wanted to study medicine. Fortunately for the theatre, he failed the examination.

There are a great many playwrights that have made significant contributions to the theatre. Some of these include Henrik Ibsen, Eugene O'Neil, Lillian Florence Hellman, Tennessee Williams, Arthur Miller, Neil Simon, Edward Albee, Wendy Wasserstein, and Nicky Silver.

During the winter of 1848–49, Ibsen wrote his first play, a melodrama entitled *Catilina*, and submitted it to the Cristiania Theatre. Unfortunately, they were not interested in producing the work, however, his second submission, *The Burial Mound*, was staged. (Ibsen used the pen-name Brynjolf Bjarme when he submitted both of the plays.)

In 1851, he became Ole Bull's assistant at the theatre in Bergen. Ole Bull was a world famous violinist and advocate for Norwegian arts. During Isben's time at Bergen, he traveled to Denmark and Germany to study theatre techniques. His first successful play was the medieval drama *Gildet paa Solhaug*. It was poetic and romantic and celebrated Norway's history. When the theatre at Bergen closed in 1863, Ibsen became the artistic director of the Norwegian theatre, located in Christiania.

Ibsen earned a traveling fellowship in 1863 which gave him financial security and provided him the opportunity to visit Italy and Germany. In 1865, he was awarded a pension from the state, making it possible for him to dedicate all of his time to writing. Isben wrote his first major work, *Brand*, while living in Rome. This poetic drama was so successful that he gained a reputation throughout Europe as a playwright to watch.

Ibsen went on to write a number of influential plays, including *Hedda Gabler, An Enemy of the People, The Master Builder* and *Ghosts*, but he is probably best known for *A Doll's House*. This play revolves around a young wife, Nora, and her subservient relationship to her husband, Torvald. At the end of the play, Nora leaves her husband and children in an effort to become her own person. It was a very shocking play for the time. In 1882, an amateur company in America produced *A Doll's House* but renamed it *The Child Wife*. It was the first time *A Doll's House* was produced in America, but the producers altered the ending of the play, allowing Nora to stay with her children.

The controversy over Ibsen's plays began in 1880 when, after reading *A Doll's House*, critic P. P. Iverslie wrote a review for the Norden newspaper. Condemning the play and calling it "un-Christian," he wrote, "Partners in a Christian marriage were expected to endure each other's faults."

The play was again met with controversy when it was produced in London in 1889. Well-respected critic Clement Scott's review took to task a woman "who leaves her home and deserts her friendless children because she has *herself* to look after." Other critics praised the play for its honesty, as

did R. H. Hervey who observed "that many women are dissatisfied with their social position . . . and of their dissatisfaction Ibsen has made himself the mouthpiece."

A groundbreaking play, *A Doll's House* is timeless, still evoking controversy, praise, and rejection.

Eugene O'Neill (1888–1953)

Eugene O'Neill was born in the Barrett House Hotel, located at the corner of Broadway and Forty-Third Street (now known as Times Square). Ironically, he died in another hotel, The Shelton Hotel, in Boston, Massachusetts. His father, James O'Neill, was an actor and was portraying the role of Edmond Dante in *The Count of Monte Cristo* the night before Eugene was born. It is unknown if he made it to the hotel in time to witness the birth of his son. Once a promising actor, James was accused of selling out by agreeing to revive his role in *The Count of Monte Cristo* over and over some 3,000 times by the time he was in his mid-60s. Perhaps it was the repetition of the role that drove the actor to drink and carouse.

James' behavior may have contributed to his wife Ella's morphine addiction. Ella suffered from depression plus some other minor illnesses and a doctor introduced her to morphine. At the time, the drug was available in over-the-counter cough syrups and by mail order. After World War I, the sale of morphine was restricted. It took months before Ella realized she was addicted to the drug and even longer before James became aware of his wife's problem.

Eugene was raised by a detached mother and an overbearing father. He first learned about the theatre and playwriting by being backstage and watching from the wings during many of his father's performances. As a child, Eugene was plagued by frequent colds and respiratory infections which gave him a reputation of being "delicate." Touring the country with his family made it difficult for Eugene to make friends so he filled his days with reading and his imagination.

At the age of seven, Eugene was unhappily enrolled into St. Aloysius Academy for Boys. The school was located in the wilderness that then surrounded the Bronx, and the isolation filled the boy with loneliness and despair. However, Eugene completed his time at the school and continued his studies at De La Salle Institute in Manhattan—this time living at home. One day, upon returning home from school, he discovered his mother giving herself a morphine injection (his father was away acting in a play). The isolation Eugene had experienced in school now haunted him at home.

As a young man, O'Neill studied one year at Princeton University, dropped out, and then went to sea, traveling to South America and South Africa. When he was 24, his father secured him a job as a newspaper reporter for the *Liberty* paper. Eugene was perhaps not the best journalist; in fact, it was rumored that his father paid his salary. Eugene O'Neill wrote several one-act plays before his first full-length play, *Beyond the Horizon*, was professionally produced in 1920. He then went on to write many great plays including such important works as *The Hairy Ape* (1922), *Mourning Becomes Electra* (first seen in 1931) and *Long Day's Journey into Night* (1941).

Eugene O'Neill received the Nobel Prize for literature in 1936.

Lillian Florence Hellman (1905–1984)

Lillian Hellman was born in New Orleans and spent her childhood in New York City. She married at an early age and moved to Paris. After a divorce, she moved to Hollywood and began working as a script reader.

Lillian Hellman's first play, *The Children's Hour* (1934) concerns two female teachers whose careers are ruined because some students accuse them of being lesbians. The production proved successful despite its subtle homosexual overtones. The popularity of *The Children's Hour*, coupled with other financially profitable Hollywood projects, gave Hellman "staying power" when her second Broadway play, *Days to Come*, closed in a week. In 1939, *The Little Foxes* became a Broadway triumph and, in 1941, she won the New York Drama Critics Award for *Watch on the Rhine*.

Hellman did not view herself as a political person; she did not strive to write plays with strong political statements. She simply wrote about the people she knew and the world in which they lived, a time when Hitler was in power and the communist party was under scrutiny in the United States. Her anti-Hitler views, although subtle, were apparent in *Watch on the Rhine*, and *The Searching Wind* (1944) had a more obvious political slant.

Hellman was subpoenaed to appear at the Senator Joseph McCarthy hearings on May 21, 1952. On May 19 she wrote a letter to John S. Wood, Chairman of the House Committee on Un-American Activities. The letter essentially said that she was willing to talk about her own political views and accept the consequences, but she was unwilling to share information about her friends and their political views. She was advised by her attorney not to divulge personal information, because individuals that give up their right to Fifth Amendment protection are required to answer any and all questions posed to them. Instead of naming names, she delivered a well-rehearsed statement. As a result, Hellman was blacklisted in Hollywood from the late 1940s until 1960.

Toys in the Attic opened in 1960 and earned Hellman her second Drama Critics' Circle Award. In 1969, she won a National Book Award for her memoir trilogy, *An Unfinished Woman* and also wrote a bestselling novel, *Scoundrel Time* (1976).

One of the most respected American writers, Hellman died of a heart failure in 1984.

Tennessee Williams (1914–1983)

Thomas Lanier Williams III was born in Columbus, Mississippi. As a small child, he had an affinity for theatre, telling elaborate stories and acting out the comics from the newspaper. His father, Cornelius ("C.C."), was a traveling salesman and his mother, Edwina, was the daughter of an Episcopalian minister. The parents were emotionally distant from one other, thus creating tension in the home. Williams' sister, Rose, was his best friend and confidant. The two were inseparable and were called "the couple" by friends and family members. Despite spending two years of his childhood as an invalid suffering from diphtheria and other ailments, Williams cherished his boyhood in the small town in Mississippi.

When Tom was seven years old, his father acquired a managerial position in St. Louis and moved his family to the factory-filled city. The large city and C.C.'s late night carousing contributed to Tom and Edwina's

loneliness. Also, Rose was maturing into a young lady and developing new friendships—which further alienated Tom. In an effort to cheer the boy up, his mother bought him a second-hand typewriter when he was 12 years old. Tom wrote a short story, *Isolated*, which was published in the school newspaper. At 16 years of age, he won a contest run by *Smart Set* magazine with a piece entitled *Can a Wife Be a Good Sport?* The following year he sold a horror story to *Weird Tales* for which he was paid 35 cents. It was a violent story featuring women with strong personalities and a brother–sister relationship. Both of these would be subjects in the majority of his future plays.

In 1929, Tom entered the University of Missouri because it had an excellent journalism program. His first assignment was reporting the current prices of eggs and chickens, an assignment which bored the young Williams. Finally, he was given the opportunity to report on the death of a dean's wife, but he handled the delicate situation inappropriately, thereby ending his journalist career.

When Tom found out that the university had contests for plays, poetry, and other forms of writing, he began studying playwrights such as O'Neill and Strindberg, intending to improve his writing style, and entered each category in the contest. He also began studying with a playwriting professor, Robert Ramsay, who used the *ouroboros* symbol (the snake with his tail in his mouth) as a metaphor to describe the most effective plots—the beginning of the story foreshadows the end of the story.

Tom continued to read plays by a variety of authors, while making keen observations of people he knew and using these perceptions as research for his writing. His first play, *Beauty and the Word*, gave him the distinction of being the first freshman to receive honorable mention in the university's playwriting contest.

Tom's father encouraged him to join a fraternity, hoping that it would make him more of a man; but after joining the fraternity, Tom found he preferred writing and isolation to brotherhood. However, fraternity life was not a total waste of time. Williams future plays would be peopled by characters based on his fraternity brothers—specifically Mitch in *A Streetcar Named Desire* and Jim in *The Glass Menagerie*.

The young Williams failed military training in his junior year and his father, disappointed, withdrew him from the school. In 1932, St. Louis, along with the rest of the country, was mired in the Great Depression; but Tom's father found him a job in a shoe factory. The salary was equitable, but the work was monotonous. To relive the monotony, the young writer spent his workdays observing the personalities and habits of his co-workers, one of whom became the inspiration for the best-known character in American dramatic literature, Stanley Kowalski (*A Streetcar Named Desire*). On Tom's twenty-fourth birthday, he suffered a nervous breakdown and was fired from his position at the factory. Tom stayed in his Grandmother's home while recovering from his illness and read Chekhov—destined to be his greatest influence.

His health restored, Tom entered Washington University in St. Louis. It was during his stay at the university that his career as a playwright really began. Under the mentorship of Willard Hollard, artistic director of an amateur theatre company, Tom wrote several plays that were produced by the company. However, when Tom lost the university playwriting contest to a play he felt to be of lesser quality, he left school.

In 1937, Williams' sister Rose was committed to a state hospital for the insane. Mental illness seemed to run in the family and Tom suffered from periods of deep depression. In an attempt to maintain his mental stability, he enrolled in the University of Iowa's playwriting program. It was a rigorous program in which students submitted a short play every two weeks while also studying acting and stagecraft. This taught Williams to meet deadlines and to write commanding monologues and dialogue. The program also provided him a foundation in dramatic literature. It was while studying in Iowa that Tom Williams took the name Tennessee Williams. It is said to have been given to him by his classmates because of his southern accent.

The first time he signed his name as Tennessee Williams was when he submitted several of his plays to an under-25 five playwriting contest (he was actually 27) sponsored by The Group Theatre. He won a prize of $100 for *American Blues* and received an invitation for representation by a literary agent. Unaware of The Group Theatre's prestige, Williams did not take advantage of the opportunity; instead, he spent the summer on the beach reading D. H. Lawrence.

Williams graduated from the University of Iowa in 1938 with a B.A. in English. He went on to write numerous plays which are now considered American classics. These include *Summer and Smoke, The Rose Tattoo, Camino Real, You Touched Me!, Battle of Angels,* and *The Glass Menagerie,* which won the New York Drama Critic's Circle, Donaldson, and Sidney Howard Memorial awards. *A Streetcar Named Desire* opened on Broadway in December of 1947 with an outstanding cast including Jessica Tandy and Marlon Brando. *A Streetcar Named Desire* was the first play to win all three prestigious awards—the Pulitzer Prize for drama, the Donaldson, and the New York Drama Critic's Circle award.

Arthur Miller (1915–2005)

Arthur Miller was born on October 17, 1915, in New York City to Isidore and Augusta Miller. Although Isidore was illiterate, he was a successful coat manufacturer, enabling him to provide his family with many luxuries. Arthur was the younger of two sons and, as a youth, enjoyed playing sports more than school work. The family's financial stability ended in 1929 when the stock market crashed. His older brother, Kermit, left school to assist his father with the family business but Arthur continued to study at Michigan University. In order to pay for school, Arthur turned to playwriting. He entered the university play contest and won the Avery Hopwood Award and $250. The following year, his play entry at the university was awarded the Theatre Guild National Award, which included $1,200, and a second Avery Hopwood Award.

Miller's first Broadway production, *The Man Who Had All the Luck,* failed, closing after only five days; but in 1947, his second Broadway production, *All My Sons,* was a huge success, winning him the Drama Critics Award. The following year *All My Sons* opened in London, and *Death of a Salesman* premiered on Broadway. *Death of a Salesman* earned Miller a second Drama Critics Award and a Pulitzer Prize.

He went on to write a total of 25 plays, among them *The Crucible* (1952) and *A View From the Bridge* (1955). The critical success and popularity of these plays solidified his position as one of the great American dramatists. Miller also wrote several screenplays, novels, and an autobiography. During

his lifetime, he was honored with three Tony awards, the Pulitzer Prize, a John F. Kennedy Award for Lifetime Achievement, and an Emmy Award.

Miller's personal life was as eventful as his career. In 1956, he married international motion picture star Marilyn Monroe. Unfortunately, their marriage was not successful and ended in 1961. Arthur Miller was dedicated to protecting and defending human rights. For example, during the communist scare of the 1950s when many artists were accused of being communist sympathizers and, as a result, blacklisted, Miller continued to work with them. He stated that he would not be a party to blacklisting of any kind.

Arthur Miller's plays reveal his consummate theatrical craftsmanship and his uncanny ability to accurately portray and examine serious social issues. His characters are plunged into situations that test their ethical codes and levels of commitment. These characters continue to resonate with modern audiences that are still searching to define and maintain morality and responsibility.

Neil Simon (1927–)

Neil Simon was born on July 4, 1927, in the Bronx, New York City. He grew up in Washington Heights and attended De-Witt Clinton High School, an all-boys school. After graduation, Simon enrolled in New York University as an engineering major. Not long after entering NYU, Simon left school and joined the Army Air Force Reserve in order to serve his country during the Second World War. The war ended one week after Simon joined.

Discharged from the Reserve, Simon began working as a mail clerk for Warner Brothers in New York. His career as a mail clerk was brief; he and his brother were offered a job writing comedy for Sid Caesar's *Your Show of Shows*. Working with the likes of Mel Brooks and Woody Allen, Simon was a staff writer on several network television programs, including *The Tallulah Bankhead Show*. Unhappy with the restrictions that governed the television networks, Simon decided to write a play and the result was *Come Blow Your Horn*. The production was successful and ran 84 weeks on Broadway.

Simon's *Barefoot in the Park* opened on Broadway in 1965 and ran for over 1,500 performances. Between 1966 and 1988 Simon averaged one new Broadway play per year. Critics took a special interest in his autobiographical trilogy—*Brighton Beach Memoirs*, *Biloxi Blues*, and *Broadway Bound*. *Brighton Beach Memoirs* concerns a young boy growing up in a small dilapidated home in Brighton Beach during the Depression; *Biloxi Blues* focuses on army life during World War II; and *Broadway Bound* shows two brothers who set out to write plays together.

In 1985, Simon won a Tony Award for *Biloxi Blues*, and in 1991, he was awarded a Tony, the Drama Desk Award, and the Pulitzer Prize for *Lost in Yorkers*. To date, Neil Simon has written over 30 stage plays and an equal number of screenplays.

Playwright Edward Albee (1928–)

Born in Washington, DC, Edward Albee was adopted by Reed and Frances Albee—heirs to the prosperous, well-respected Keith-Albee vaudeville chain. The newborn came to the Albee mansion at two weeks of age and was immediately greeted by nurses, servants, and, when he came of age, tutors. By age five, his family began sending him to Broadway productions—in a chauffeured Rolls Royce. Albee was somewhat rebellious and at the age of 11 was sent to Lawrenceville Boarding School. After a year and a half of tolerating Albee's bad attitude and inappropriate behavior—cutting classes, not doing homework, not participating in sports—the boarding school administrators expelled him. When Albee returned home, it quickly became evident that his attitude

Edward Albee

Jerry Speier is the photographer. *Courtesy of Edward Albee.*

had not improved. His mother attempted to correct his behavior by enrolling him in one preparatory school after another. Albee finally ended his formal education after attending Trinity College in Hartford, Connecticut, for a little over a year. He returned home and stayed there for a year, working as a writer for a radio station and enjoying the country club.

At the age of 20, still unable to peacefully coexist with his family, Albee moved to an apartment in Manhattan which he shared with a childhood friend. He used a portion of an allowance ($250 a month) given him by his paternal grandmother, to pay his share of the rent. After a year, the generous allowance came to an end. Albee was forced to move to a less expensive apartment and get a job. Unable to keep any one job for an extended period, he worked variously as a waiter, a salesman, a copy boy, and as a messenger for Western Union.

Rather than waste his time working at odd jobs, Albee wanted to devote his time to his one passion—writing. He shared an inexpensive cold-water flat with composer William Flanagan, but the cold and dilapidated apartment depressed the young writer so much that he began spending long hours in coffee houses until it occurred to him that he was not focused on his writing.

To fight his despair and frustration, Albee sat down and began to write a play concerning a depressed, isolated young man who was orphaned at an early age because of his parents untimely death. *The Zoo Story* was the beginning of Albee's career as a professional playwright. The plays that followed are some of the most important and influential in American dramatic literature. Three of his greatest are *Who's Afraid of Virginia Wolff?*, *Three Tall Women*, and *The Goat, or Who is Sylvia?* Albee has received numerous major awards including the New York Press Association's Best Play, the Lola D'Annunzio Award, the New York Drama Critics Award, a Tony Award, and three Pulitzer Prizes.

Albee's plays bring to life contemporary human conflicts in a style that is rhythmically poetic. Some believe that human beings are as leaves in the

wind, blown around against their will, but Albee believes that if an individual is unsatisfied, he or she has the power to make a change.

Feature Section
An Interview with Playwright Edward Albee

What inspired you to become a playwright?

I was inspired to become a playwright by failing in all other branches of writing. This came by the time I was 22.

How do you approach writing a new play?

I tell myself that I'm thinking about a play, I think about it, then I write it.

What, if any, advice would you have for novice playwrights?

Most importantly: be sure that playwriting is essential to you, for it's a tough racket.

Wendy Wasserstein (1950–2006)

Wendy Wasserstein's mother, Lola Schleifer, was an amateur dancer and her father, Morris Wasserstein, was a textile manufacturer who moved from Poland to Brooklyn because he was accused of being a spy. Wendy, the youngest of four children, was born in Brooklyn. She was educated at Mount Holyoke (B.A., 1971) and City College of New York (M.A. in Creative Writing, 1976).

Not long after graduating from City College, her play, *Any Woman Can't*, was produced by an off-Broadway theatre. Wasserstein then decided to study playwriting at the Yale School of Drama, where her classmates were all male and included the well-known and successful Christopher Durang (*Marriage of Bette and Boo*). Wasserstein received an M.F.A. in Playwriting from Yale in 1976.

Wasserstein went on to write a number of successful and critically acclaimed plays, including *Third*, *Old Money*, *The Sisters Rosensweig*, and *Isn't It Romantic*. Her work covers a wide variety of subjects—feminism, ethnicity, and pop culture. In 1989, she received a Tony Award and the Pulitzer Prize for *The Heidi Chronicles*. Wendy Wasserstein died of lymphoma in 2006.

Playwright Nicky Silver

Nicky Silver was born in Philadelphia. When he was very young his parents took him to a play. This exposure peaked his interest in the theatre. "I wanted to be a part of it (the theatre.)" He wrote his first play while in high school simply because he and his friends were frustrated by the types of plays that the school was producing. At 16, knowing he wanted to be a part of the theatre, he was accepted into New York University where he focused his study in NYU's Experimental Theatre Wing. The faculty at the ETW was drawn from Charles Ludlum's Ridiculous Theatre Company, The Mary Overlie Dance Company, the Iowa Theatre Lab, and Ann Bogart's theatre program.

Silver has written a number of successful plays: *Pterodactyls, The Food Chain, Raised in Captivity, Fat Men in Skirts, The Maiden's Prayer, The Eros Trilogy, The Altruists,* and *Beautiful Child*. *Pterodactyls* and *Raised in Captivity* were both nominated for the Drama Desk Award for Outstanding Play.

Nicky Silver

Photograph courtesy of Nicky Silver.

FEATURE SECTION
An Interview with Playwright Nicky Silver

What inspired you to become a playwright?

While at school in New York, in the mid to late 70s, I had the opportunity to see Broadway productions written by then-contemporary playwrights, Wendy Wasserstein, Christopher Durang, and Joseph Papp. I enjoyed some of their work but longed for novelty. Still yearning to "be a part of the theatre" and without formal training in playwriting, I began writing plays.

I learned how to write by reading plays written by a variety of different playwrights. Reading plays can help a novice playwright determine what types of plays (realism, farce, experimental, etc.) that he or she enjoys and connects with, thereby defining his or her own taste and writing style.

How do you begin writing a new play?

I begin writing a play by formulating a question that I want to find the answer to. The question is based on a subject that I know well enough to write about but not so much about that I will become bored. Next, I determine the situation—where and with whom will this search for an answer take place? Then I wait, patiently; I wait a good deal of time. I ruminate on my initial thoughts about the play before I begin writing. If I start writing before my ideas formulate, it is a frustrating experience. Writing should feel like floating.

After I complete my first draft which can take, in some cases, less than a month, I read my play aloud numerous times, listening to the musicality of the words, the rhythm of the sentences. Paying attention, special attention, to every sound made (the words) and unmade (the punctuation).

What is most challenging about playwriting?

I believe that there is too much focus on perfection and the drive for perfection squelches one's interest in attempting playwriting.

If a student were interested in becoming a playwright, what would you recommend?

Playwriting is an autocratic art—making it a "user-friendly" art. Anyone can do it; all you need is an image in your mind. Focus on putting the image that is in your mind into words and onto paper. Do not focus on whether or not the play will be any good or if anyone will like it. If you like it, someone else will too; and because art is subjective, no matter how grand your play is, someone else will undoubtedly hate it.

The Lifestyle of a Playwright

Because playwriting is an independent art form, you can have a career and write in your spare time.

Once the playwright has finished writing his or her play, a staged reading might be in order. There are a variety of places where a staged reading might be performed, including university, college, or high school theatre programs and community theatres. After the staged reading, the playwright may want to have it fully realized in a production. Again, educational theatre programs and community theatres may be interested.

There are many playwriting competitions, here and abroad, that can be entered. Frequently, these competitions will offer prizes—cash, a guaranteed staged reading, or a workshop production. The Internet provides a good deal of information on the many annual playwriting competitions.

A novice playwright usually needs to rely on other jobs for support. Perhaps the aspiring playwright has a career and is interested in writing as a hobby. Because playwriting is an independent art form, it is possible to have a career and simply write in one's spare time.

Summary

Plays contain several key elements—central characters, objectives, obstacles, a climax, and a resolution. Plays are written with the intention that the audience will become emotionally involved in the story and its characters. Thus, background information in the form of exposition is presented early in the play. Foreshadowing is another technique that playwrights use in order to highlight a person, place, or thing which will assume significance at a later point.

There are several methods used to approach the writing of a play. One of them is brainstorming. If an individual is interested in writing a play, it is best to write about people, places, and situations with which he or she is reasonably familiar. It can take years to compose a well-written play but the experience can be personally satisfying and in some cases, very lucrative. There are a number of successful playwrights around the world. This chapter has examined only a few of the best.

The Theatre in Your Career

I. Brainstorming

Brainstorming is a technique frequently used to generate new ideas and to solve existing problems. In brainstorming, do not judge but simply write down the ideas. Many playwrights brainstorm when devising the structure of their plays, but brainstorming can also be used to solve problems in the workplace and in school.

II. Story Development

Developing a story that has a clear, descriptive beginning, middle, and end is an essential skill for playwriting, but it is a skill that is vital in other vocations. For example, sales presentations need to have a well-defined beginning, middle, and end. Job interviews are most effective when the interviewer poses questions in a clear and concise fashion, and the interviewee provides responses that have a definitive beginning, middle, and end.

Active Learning Assignment
"Bringing Theatre to Life"

I. **The Final Group Project—Playwriting Section**

   Each group will write a short play (5–10 minutes) in the style of a selected period or genre such as Roman, Medieval, Symbolist, Music Theatre, etc. Each group is responsible for first selecting the style of theatre to be produced. The group may choose a period or style that has been discussed in class or any other period, style, or genre that captures its interest.

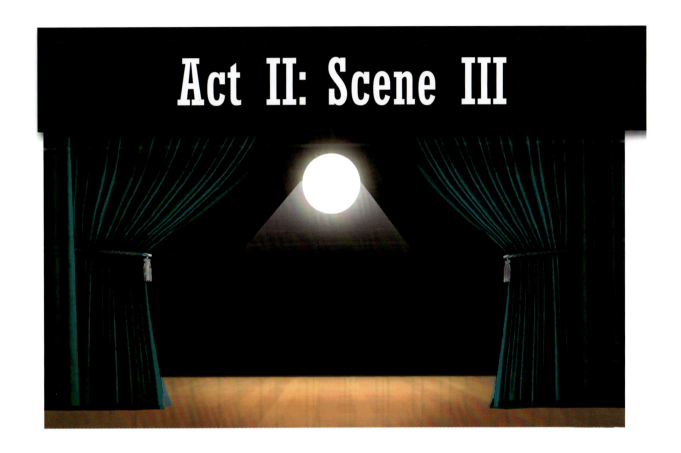

Producing and Directing the Play

Financial Classifications of Theatres

From a financial perspective, there are four types of theatre organizations—commercial, regional, community, and educational. New York City is the center of the commercial theatre in the United States, although there are commercial theatres in other parts of the country. New York City commercial theatre is divided into Broadway, Off-Broadway, and Off-Off Broadway. Regional Theatre companies are not-for-profit, meaning that the operators can take no profits themselves but must reinvest all profits in the theatre itself. Community theatres are not-for-profit organizations; however, they differ from regional theatre companies in that they are amateur organizations. Educational theatres are also not-for-profit organizations. Usually they are located in high schools, community colleges or universities, and their primary purpose is education.

The Producer's Role in Theatre Production

Producers are responsible for every facet associated with play production.

Producers, sometimes known as Executive Directors, are responsible for every facet associated with play production. This includes securing a playscript, hiring artistic and managerial staffs, raising money, contract negotiations, securing the rehearsal halls and the theatre, and overseeing publicity. It can cost millions of dollars to produce a play on Broadway and not all plays are successful. In order to insure that a Broadway production will be successful, most playscripts, especially original playscripts, will be produced first by a regional or an Off-Broadway theatre company. Producing a play in a small venue costs less money and gives the playwright an opportunity to view a live production of his or her playscript, read critical reviews, and re-write weak portions of the playscript. Once the play has been revised and has received positive reviews, a producer may select to option the play for a run on Broadway. An option is a contract that specifies performance dates (the length of the run) and the sum of money that will be advanced to the playwright. All of this is negotiated between the playwright's agent and the producer.

Once the playscript has been optioned, the producer will secure locations for rehearsals and performances, hire the artistic and managerial staff, and continue to address issues related to fundraising and promotion of the production. Producers must be effective leaders who can organize, multi-task, and manage both finances and people.

Broadway plays are almost wholly dependent on positive reviews. The morning after a production opens, the producer will read the theatre critics' reviews. If the production receives negative reviews, the producer immediately has to decide how to proceed. He or she can run the production as planned and take a chance, make adjustments to the production, or close the show. The old saying, "it is lonely at the top" has some validity. Often, producers hire persons who are not only consummate theatre professionals but also close personal friends; however, if a person is not benefiting the production, the producer has to remove him or her.

If the production receives rave reviews, it will most likely enjoy a long run—and there is a great deal of money to be made in a successful Broadway production. If becoming a theatre producer is intriguing, a number of universities offer degrees in theatre management, and many regional theatre companies offer internship programs in theatre management which provide an appropriate foundation for future producers.

Commercial Producer A. Max Weitzenhoffer

A. Max Weitzenhoffer has enjoyed a distinguished career which began at the La Jolla Playhouse, San Diego, as general manager (1963–64). In 1965, he became president of Weitzenhoffer Productions, Ltd., with headquarters in both New York City and in London, England. In the same year, he was appointed the vice president of three important organizations: New Dramatists, Theatreworks, and The Theatre Investment Fund.

Also in 1965, Weitzenhoffer became a member of the board of directors of Circle Repertory Theatre, a member of the board of trustees of The American Academy of Dramatic Arts, and the treasurer of The Stage Directors and Choreographers Foundation, Inc. In addition to his professional activities, he has dedicated himself to education as an adjunct professor of drama and producing director of musical theatre at the University of Oklahoma.

Weitzenhoffer serves as a member of the board of governors of the League of American Producers and Theatre Owners and also holds memberships in Actors' Equity Association, Players Club, Century Association, Delta Kappa Epsilon, Screen Actors Guild, and the Friars Club.

A. Max Weitzenhoffer has been received numerous prestigious awards including Tony Awards for *Dracula*—best revival (1978) and for *The Will Rogers Follies*—best musical (1991). He received a Distinguished Service Citation from the University of Oklahoma in 1988, and in 1994, Weitzenhoffer was inducted into the Oklahoma Hall of Fame.

FEATURE SECTION
An Interview with Commercial Producer A. Max Weitzenhoffer

What inspired you to become a producer?

I think that is was a logical outgrowth, a natural process, although I didn't realize it at the time. I tried acting and I wasn't any good. I was interested in designing and I wasn't as good as I needed to be. I needed to be great. Everything is based on how well you can do it. If your goal is to be on Broadway, you have to find some way that will get you there. Good producers know all of the theatrical disciplines well. If you don't you won't be able to hire the right people. You have to do it well. I did learn ("hands on") about all of the disciplines and my knowledge led to producing.

What is the most challenging part of your job?

Finding a property that I want to do—it is difficult because there aren't any. I want to find something to produce that interests me—something that appeals to me.

What is the most pleasant part of your job?

When I find a property that someone else likes—my peers, the audience. It is not about being financially successful, although that's important. Also, finding properties that will bring in younger audiences—rejuvenating the audience.

Do you have a favorite project? If so, what?

Will Rodger's Follies. It is all about where we come from (Mr. Weitzenhoffer is an Oklahoman). It is the most significant production about this area, other than *Oklahoma*. It showed this region in a positive light. It looked good. It felt good, and made us feel good about ourselves. People liked the production. It was beneficial.

What recommendations do you have for a student who would like to become a producer?

First, learn firsthand what everyone in the theatre does (designers, directing, acting, and etc.). You will not be able to recognize talent and hire the right artistic team if you do not thoroughly understand what they do. Learn it at a college level. Then find work in an entry-level position—mail room—at a theatre, say a regional theatre. I began in an internship position at the La Jolla Playhouse. The key becoming a producer is networking. People have to learn your name, in a positive way. How else can they hire you if they don't know who you are? The key is networking.

Executive Director Louis G. Spisto

Louis Spisto was hired in 2002 as the Executive Director of the Old Globe Theatre in San Diego. Since that time, he has produced several world-premieres, including Dr. Seuss' *How the Grinch Stole Christmas!*, *Dirty Rotten Scoundrels*, and *Chita Rivera: A Dancer's Life*. The last went on to win several Tony Awards after it opened on Broadway.

Spisto has engineered several fundraising campaigns for the Old Globe, including "Securing a San Diego Landmark," a campaign to raise $75 million by the Theatre's 75th anniversary in 2010. The campaign, which began in March 2006, reached 61 percent of its goal by May 2007. Spisto is also directly responsible for a dramatic increase in ticket sales.

Louis Spisto's previous leadership positions include Executive Director of the American Ballet in New York City, President of the Detroit Symphony Orchestra, Executive Director of the Pacific Symphony Orchestra, Director of Marketing for the Pittsburgh Symphony Orchestra and Director of Operations and Development for the Performing Arts Center, University of California, Berkeley. He received his Masters' degree in Arts Administration from the University of Wisconsin and his Bachelors' of Business Administration from Notre Dame University.

FEATURE SECTION

An Interview with Executive Director of The Old Globe Theatre, San Diego, California— Louis G. Spisto

Have you always wanted to be a producer?

I started performing in bands and musicals in high school from age 14 until I was about 22. While I was in college, I directed musicals and, between college and graduate school, I was both an actor and theatre manager. I attended the University of Wisconsin and studied Arts Administration, because, yes, I always wanted to be a producer.

What are your responsibilities at the Old Globe?

Jack O'Brien (Artistic Director), Jerry Patch (Resident Artistic Director), and I choose the season. I am responsible for organizing and managing the entire theatre, including a $19 million budget and fundraising and marketing campaigns. I hire and oversee the administrative staff and artistic staff—well over 100 people. I work with commercial producers to secure projects that *The Globe* is interested in producing. I have to work out all of the details including what the commercial producer is willing to pay to have *The Globe* realize their production. I am very involved in the community, Balboa Park (we are located in the park), and the arts.

What is the most difficult part of your job?

It is important that I am always aware of the needs of the community—specifically, the leaders of the community. It is important to know and address the needs, objectives, and desires of the community without compromising the theatre's goal. I must work in concert with the community. We are in a very competitive market here and we are working toward long-term financial security.

What is the most pleasant part of your job?

I enjoy working with our staff, bringing great new work to San Diego. It is exciting to bring new works to the stage . . . new musicals.

What recommendations do you have for a student who would like to become a producer?

One has to be a great multi-tasker and very good at detail. You need to be able to see the whole picture. One must be diplomatic while also remaining true to a vision. One should be comfortable leading. When working with artistic talent, they like to lead, they have egos—they need to be partnered.

History of Directing

Between the sixteenth century and the early nineteenth centuries, actors would typically rehearse their roles on their own.

Between the sixteenth century and the early nineteenth centuries, actors would typically rehearse their roles on their own. The entire cast would rehearse together only a few times; a stage hand or a stage manager would coordinate complex blocking sequences, sound effects, and the location of hand properties. This individualistic approach to mounting a production was probably effective for the time since language and poetry were valued above all. Also, the lack of modern electric lighting meant that the audience could not clearly see the actor's faces, thus language had to incorporate and communicate emotions. In an effort to keep the audience's attention and move the story along, the actors had to perform at a reasonably rapid pace.

Science and technology have played important roles in the development of all art forms.

Science and technology have played important roles in the development of all art forms. For example, the computer and digital graphics have made a major impact on the movie industry. The same impact was felt in the theatre when the incandescent light bulb was invented. The first theatre to use electricity to illuminate both the stage and the auditorium was the Savoy Theatre in London (1881). The introduction of electric lighting and the change in style to realism (which required more nuance) gave birth to the modern director.

Richard Wagner (1813–1883)

Wagner's unified approach to theatre production is the basis for all realistic modern-day productions.

Raised in a family that worked in the theatre, Wagner always preferred myth and magic to realism. He wrote music-dramas (*not* operas) and in his attention to all aspects of the production sought to create what he called *Gesamtkunstwerk* or "master art work." Wagner's unified approach to theatre production is the basis for all realistic modern-day theatre productions. Among his many production innovations, he is also responsible for inventing a new type of seating arrangement. Completed in 1876, Wagner's Festival Theatre in Bayreuth replaced the common box seating with a new fan shaped seating plan. It is a seating plan that is still used in many modern theatres and movie houses.

Georg II, Duke of Saxe-Meiningen (1826–1914)

The Duke of Saxe-Meiningen made several contributions to theatre production.

The Duke of Saxe-Meiningen began to oversee the Meiningen Players when he succeeded to the throne in 1866. He made several notable changes in the company. The first was to appoint company member and comedic actor Ludwig Chronegk (1837–1891) as stage director. Chronegk worked tirelessly for the company, arranging a number of performance engagements outside Saxe-Meiningen, which contributed to the company's reputation. One of the company's actresses, Ellen Franz (1839–1923) married Saxe-Meiningen in 1873 and assumed the responsibility for selecting and adapting the company's plays. The company was dissolved in 1890 when Chronegk became quite ill. By that time, it had earned a worldwide reputation for excellence.

One of the most valuable contributions Saxe-Meiningen made to the theatre was creating productions noted for their historical accuracy. Prior to Saxe-Meiningen, performers provided their own costumes or made alterations to the ones given them by the theatre. The Duke insisted on using used, authentic fabrics and materials such as real chain-mail to create the costumes. His scenery was painted in vivid colors using three-dimensional techniques and the floor was included in the overall design. The stage picture was completed by using actual antique furniture.

One of Saxe-Meiningen's most significant contributions to staging was intricate direction of large groups of supernumeraries (extras). He created detailed staging and assigned lines of dialogue to each actor. Then he painstakingly coordinated the entire scene. The effect was awe inspiring to audiences. It is because of Saxe-Meiningen's concern for unified production that he is often called "the first modern director."

Director's Role in Theatre Production

The director is responsible for bringing the play to life, but this is not a solo role. Similar to the creative development and execution of an innovative corporate product, many people are needed to bring a play to life. In the corporate world, a team leader or CEO of a corporation may want to "one up" a competitor by introducing a new product line. The leader or CEO will begin by researching the market to find out what makes the competitor's product so popular and to determine how a current product from his or her company product can be altered to generate consumer interest and excitement. Once the research has been completed, the project is turned over to specialized teams. These teams collaborate with one another to create the final product. Theatre directors work using the same approach as corporate leaders—research and collaboration.

The director is responsible for bringing the play to life.

Research

Research for a director begins with reading the play, not once but many times. He or she wants to get a complete sense of the play and asks these questions: What does the play mean? What emotional response should the audience have to the play? What world do the characters live in? What is the style of the play—realistic, fantasy, presentational, etc.? What are the playwright's intentions?

After reading the play and answering these questions, the director will probably read other plays by the same playwright to get a feel for his or her work—many playwrights develop a noticeable style that is recognizable from play to play. The director may seek out reviews and pictures of other productions. If a period play is being produced, he or she may spend time studying the customs and culture of the period through examining paintings, reading histories, and listening to music. Additionally, if the playwright is available and willing, he or she may advise the director.

The designers will base their designs on the director's concept/theme.

Conveying the Overall Concept/Theme for the Production

During the first production meeting, the concept/theme needs to be concisely expressed to the other members of the artistic team. Many directors devise an emotionally charged sentence or two which conveys the entire concept/theme, illuminating both the meaning of the play and the intended emotional response from the audience. All of the designers base their work on the director's concept/theme.

Production Meetings

Several production meetings take place before the rehearsal period begins, and subsequent meetings take place once a week during every week of rehearsal. In a production meeting, the designers share their progress, trouble shoot, and ask questions of one another and the director. These meetings are important, not only for artistic collaboration, but also for the continuity of the production. It is crucial that all of the design elements compliment one another in bringing to life the director's vision. Similar to a board meeting in the business world, each member of the team must communicate clearly, concisely, and respectfully, while always being willing to compromise.

A few production meetings will take place before the rehearsal period and subsequent meetings take place once a week for every week of rehearsal.

Casting the Play

After analyzing the play, the director writes a brief description of each character. These descriptions will be used in all casting call announcements. Casting calls also include the date, time, and location of the audition, and what the actor should prepare—perhaps two contrasting monologues not to exceed two minutes. Professional theatre companies employ a casting director to make the audition arrangements because, in most cases, time constraints make it impossible for every auditioner to be seen by the director. A short list of potential performers is selected.

On the day of the auditions, the director arrives with a pad of paper and a pencil to make notes. Water and snacks may be on hand since it will be a long day. In most cases, the performers will audition individually for the director. While the actor is auditioning, the director takes brief notes. In an effort to get to know the performers personality and more accurately judge their abilities, the director may ask to see an additional monologue or suggest that the actor explore a new approach to the original monologue.

At the end of auditions the director creates another short list of actors. This is referred to as a call-back list. The actors on this list will return on another day to read specific scenes from the play. After the call-back audition, the director casts the play, arranges to notify the actors, and schedules rehearsals.

At the end of auditions the director will create another short list of actors called a call-back list.

Rehearsals

Before rehearsals begin, the director will score the play. He or she identifies elements such as the crisis, the climax, the resolution, and also notes each character's objectives and obstacles in an attempt to access the overall arc and intention of the story. The director will then devise a rehearsal schedule, perhaps allowing extra time for difficult scenes. Rehearsals in the professional theatre are typically two weeks, and four to six weeks in the non-professional theatre. During rehearsals, the director is solely responsible for creating a unified production, filling the play with emotional and intellectual stimuli, and illuminating the playwright's intent. This is hardly an easy task and is one which is best approached in a collaborative, yet firm, manner.

After the call back audition, the director will cast the play, notify the actors, and schedule rehearsals.

Play rehearsals are typically four to six weeks long.

Typical Schedule of a Four-Week Rehearsal Period

First Week

The first rehearsal includes introductions, brief discussions of the director's concept and the set design, and a read-through of the play. What is done for the remainder of the first week varies from director to director. Some prefer to keep the actors seated at a table reading the script. This approach is particularly useful for classical texts since it encourages the actors to focus on the language of the play. Other directors introduce improvisational exercises designed to help the actors better connect with their characters. Some directors *block* (*blocking*—where and when the actors move on stage) the scenes during the first week of rehearsal; others allow actors to discover their own blocking. The collaborative approach is probably best, combining the director's blocking with the actors' discoveries.

Second and Third Weeks

Effective directors have a clear vision of the overall production and how each of the characters should be portrayed. During the second and third week of a four-week rehearsal period, most directors focus on the acting. Some use a dictatorial approach—yelling and demanding instant results. Others spend the majority of rehearsal time "coaching the actors"—asking questions related to the characters, such as given circumstances, objectives, obstacles, and relationships. Still others create improvisations designed to allow the actors to explore—many of theses discoveries end up in the final production. Still other directors combine these approaches—less the yelling. No one responds well to verbal abuse. Of course, the director is at the helm and must have complete control, but he or she is best served by practicing patience and courtesy.

Somewhere between the first and third week, most of the actors' blocking is set. Blocking is a practical necessity in any production. Practically all plays call for simple physical movement. If one of the characters is having a pizza for dinner, he or she must bring the pizza in from the kitchen, sit at the table, eat the pizza, and take the pizza box back to the kitchen. Some plays include scenes that require complex physical movement—sword fights or dancing. A scene with many characters, such as a wedding, makes blocking a particularly challenging task for the director.

The director has to make sure all of the characters are seen, while also drawing the audience's attention to the central characters. If the audience's focus is not drawn to them, much of the story will be lost. There are many techniques that directors use to give the focus to a central character. Some include: placing an actor near or on top of the largest piece of furniture, placing an actor in a doorway, placing an actor downstage center, having the other characters look at or away from one actor or costuming one actor in a bright color and having the rest of the cast in muted colors.

When blocking a play, the director must consider the overall stage picture. The stage picture includes the actors, the setting, and the furniture and the properties in a scene. The stage picture changes from moment to moment as the actors move about the stage. As with any well-framed photograph, the stage picture must have an interesting and well-balanced composition.

Blocking also defines relationships and the changes in relationship dynamics. For example, at the beginning of the play, before the dialogue begins, a man and a woman are sitting close together on a love seat. This establishes an intimate relationship for the audience. In the following scene, the same couple is sitting at opposite ends of the room, not looking at each other, creating tension and a feeling of distance.

Blocking is not confined to the theatre but is an important part of most vocations. While in the work-place, the individual employees must consider spatial relationships when interacting with others. For example, it is inappropriate to move into another's personal space (your co-worker or customer will feel invaded), carry on important one-on-one conversations from a distance of more than four feet (much of the conversation will be lost), or address a large group from a distance of less than five feet (the entire group will not be able to see you).

End of the Third Week and Fourth Week

During the end of the third week the director will call for a *run-through*, which means the entire play is performed without stopping for any reason. *Run-throughs* give the actor and director an opportunity to insure that the rhythm (some moments will have a quick tempo, some will linger) and the arc—objectives, conflicts, obstacles, crisis's, climax, and resolutions—are being fully realized. Notes are given to the actors after every run-through in an attempt to *polish* (improve) any weak points in their performances. If any major elements are being missed, the director may call the troubled scenes in for more work. Otherwise, rehearsals will consist of *run-throughs* until the technical rehearsals which begin during the final week.

Opening Night

The director's job is finished on opening night. At this point, all the director does is praise and congratulate the actors for their hard work. Some directors give small gifts or thank-you notes to the actors. Many times, a party is organized after the opening performance to celebrate the success of the production.

Director John Doyle

John Doyle received his theatre training at the University of Georgia. As a professional director, he has over 200 productions to his credit, including *Female Parts* (Arts Theatre, London), *You're Gonna Love Tomorrow* (Palace Theatre, London), and *Driving Miss Daisy* in both Zurich and Vienna. He has guest directed at many prominent theatres including the Dundee Repertory Theatre, Edinburgh Lyceum Theatre, and the Glasgow Kings Theatre.

Doyle has developed a reputation as a teacher as well as a theatre artist, and has lectured at several prestigious European schools and theatres such as the Moscow Arts Theatre, the Royal Scottish Academy of Music and Drama, and the Royal Academy of Dramatic Art. He also wrote *Shakespeare for Dummies* which includes an enthusiastic foreword by Dame Judi Dench.

John Doyle has received numerous awards, including the Irish Times Award for Best Musical—*Gypsy*. His production of *Sweeny Todd* earned both Tony and Drama Desk awards (2006).

> **FEATURE SECTION**
> ## An Interview with Director John Doyle

What inspired you to become a director?

Gosh—It is almost too long ago to remember. I studied theatre here in the UK, then went to the University of Georgia, and there studied with two directors, both European, who had a big influence. Like so many influences though, you only recognize them in retrospect.

What do you feel is the most challenging aspect of directing?

Keeping your sense of humor, finding your vision. Keeping hold of your vision. The people are nearly always great, but keeping everybody feeling "safe" is probably the greatest challenge.

What is the most rewarding aspect of directing?

Seeing people develop. Seeing growth in other artists.

How do you approach a new project?

Every project is different. You just have to search for the "truth" in everything. You have to look for what the piece "says" to you, and you have to stop your ego from allowing itself to stand in the way of the story you are telling.

If a student were interested in becoming a director, how might he or she begin?

Gosh—all you can do is try. You must set up your own projects and don't expect anybody else to provide you with the situation to allow you to express yourself. That is your own responsibility. There will be so many disappointments, all of which make you a richer artist and, indeed, a richer human being.

Director Scott Aaron Palmer

Scott Palmer, a native Oregonian, is a professional Theatre Director and Development Consultant with experience working in the Cultural Industries across the world. Scott received his education in theatre and performance from the University of Oregon, a Masters' Degree from Oregon State University, and he studied for a Ph.D. in Theatre, Film and Television at the University of Glasgow in Scotland.

As a theatre director, he has directed critically acclaimed theatrical productions in the United Kingdom including William Shakespeare's *Richard III*, *As You Like It*, *Henry V*, *Antony and Cleopatra*, *King Lear*, *The Tempest*, *Measure for Measure*, *Titus Andronicus*, *Twelfth Night*, *Romeo and Juliet*, Richard Greenberg's *Eastern Standard*, Susan Somte's *Seen and Not Heard*, and his own original adaptations of Shakespeare's work (including *Lear*, *Henry*, *Kabuki Titus* and *Infinite Variety*) in New Zealand (including the New Zealand premiere of the original script *Infinite Variety* and various performance art works such as *Magpie*, *Pigeon*, and *Touch* for the Wellington

International Festival) and the United States (including Noel Coward's *Blithe Spirit* and *Private Lives*, Ben Jonson's *The Silent Woman*, the Reduced Shakespeare Company's *The Complete Works of William Shakespeare (abridged)*, the North American premiere of Adrian Osmand's *Just One More Dance* for OSU's Holocaust Memorial Week, *Shakespeare's Macbeth*, *The Taming of the Shrew*, and *Much Ado About Nothing*, and the world premiere of a new, original adaptation of *Romeo and Juliet*).

As a fundraiser and development consultant, Scott has worked for some of the largest and most prestigious arts and non-profit organizations in the United Kingdom, New Zealand, and the United States. He worked as the Development Director for the Arches Theatre Company, one of the United Kingdom's largest multiform arts venues located in Glasgow, Scotland, and was directly responsible for a $15 million capital refurbishment campaign for the venue. Scott also worked as a fund-raising and development executive for the Royal Scottish National Orchestra, the Glasgow Art Fair, Scotland's National Performance Festival Big in Falkirk, the Performing Arts Foundation of New Zealand and Toi Whakaari, the New Zealand National Drama School. Scott was also the founding Artistic Director of Glasgow Repertory Company, Scotland's only Shakespeare-dedicated theater company where he raised initial start-up funds for the company and directed a number of critically acclaimed outdoor Shakespeare performances.

Scott is continuing his love of directing outdoors, site-specific Shakespearean performances as the Director of Oregon State University's annual Bard in the Quad summer performance festival, and as the Artistic Director of the Rose Theatre Project (a public-private partnership examining the feasibility of building a replica Elizabethan stage in the greater Portland, Oregon, metropolitan area).

Director Scott Aaron Palmer
Courtesy of Scott Aaron Palmer.

FEATURE SECTION
An Interview with Director Scott Aaron Palmer

What interested you in becoming a director?

I have always been an avid consumer of theater. My first experience with the theater was in third grade when my class was asked to perform a traditional Melodrama for our school (a maiden tied to the train-tracks, demands for the rent from an evil landlord, lots of twirling mustaches, dashing third grade hero, etc.). Throughout the rehearsal process,

I found myself becoming more and more frustrated that, as an actor in the show, I wouldn't get to see the performance as an audience member. In fact, I said to my teacher, Mrs. Peterson, "How can I know if I'm doing right if I can't watch myself perform?"

I think that is where my first directorial urges began to manifest themselves.

As I grew older, and became involved in theater in junior high school and high school, I became aware of the wide range of elements that are necessary for a theatrical production to be a success. I always felt like a theatre show was, essentially, a very complicated puzzle that needed to be put together. If you have ever worked alongside your siblings or friends on a jigsaw puzzle, you will know that it always helps to have some people start on the corners and edges while others work on specific items or images in the puzzle. But the most important part of the co-operative puzzle process is to make sure someone is in charge of looking at the whole picture. I always wanted to be that person; the one who (although not necessarily skilled in lighting design, sound design, or set design) was meant to see how the lights, working in conjunction with the set, and with the addition of a sound-cue, could create a particularly expressive moment for the audience. For me, theatre has always been a puzzle in need of a solution and I was drawn to theatre, and to theatre directing, because I believed I had some creative ideas about how to solve those challenges.

And I always wanted to make sure I was in the audience to see it all come together.

How do you approach directing?

Most of my professional life in the theatre has been devoted to working with classic texts, and more specifically, Shakespeare and other Elizabethan playwrights. As a result, I believe that my approach to directing has two important components: begin with the script itself and then create a vision with the audience in mind.

It is crucial, in my opinion, that a director of classical drama be very familiar with both the text (its history, influences, production history, meaning, original sources, and various critical responses) and with the mechanics of the language. Understanding verse and verse speaking is hugely important for a director and a commitment to the poetry and its structure is at the heart of all my directing work. Once I have explored the text in detail, I generally begin working on adapting the script with my vision of the play and the audience in mind.

My approach to directing, and my love of theatre, has always been based on the performance and its relationship with the audience. Actors and designers I have worked with tell me that I direct shows that I would want to see as an audience member, and I think that is an accurate description of my overall approach to directing. An audience-centered approach, one that has at its core a conception of what the audience wants and needs to have in order to enjoy and understand the performance, has always been at the heart of my work.

My work with actors is a combination of encouraging experimentation and fostering the inherent skills of each actor. I prefer to work with actors in discovering the characters and the play rather than placing a structure on the work before-hand. Providing the actors and other artists with a "direction" and an understanding of my vision is crucial, but so is the recognition that there are many different ways to achieve that vision. Relying on the inherent skills, training, and talent of the artists I work with allows me to achieve my directorial vision of the play collaboratively. As a result, I have generally found my work to be filled with a communal sense of commitment and satisfaction that, as a team, we have been able to create something greater than the sum of our parts.

What do you particularly enjoy about directing?

My two great joys as a director are the adaptation process and working with actors. As someone who is fascinated by language, poetry, and verse, I am consistently drawn to scripts and writers who have a heightened appreciation for the mechanics of the English language. Some of my favorite memories of being a director involve a bottomless cup of coffee, a worn out pencil and a copy of *The Complete Works of William Shakespeare.* The intimate relationship that can be created between director and text is a truly powerful one and I have always found the weeks and months before the rehearsal process to be one of personal fulfillment and excitement as I read through the text, evaluate different options, understand the original source materials, and begin to allow the script and the play to take shape in my mind.

Once that process is underway, I am always incredibly impatient to begin working with the acting team to find new and inspiring ways to reach my goals. Working alongside other artists with a similar commitment and love of the language is enormously fulfilling while, at the same time, challenging for me as a director and audience member. I never tire of watching actors discover, for themselves, the power of the language and the inherent beauty in the script.

I love opening nights.

What do you dislike about directing?

I am an impatient person and one of the things I have struggled with throughout my directing career has been learning that all artists work at a different pace and speed. I have spent a great deal of time training myself to "wait." I have had to learn to work with actors and designers in a way that is as respectful of their own individual processes as I expect them to be of mine. As someone with inherent control issues, this can be difficult at times.

I hate closing nights.

If a student were interested in becoming a director, what steps would you recommend?

First, see as much theatre as you can. The theatre community is a never ending source of inspiration and excitement for me. I always make a point of going to theatre wherever I am . . . while traveling to direct or while on holiday, seeing local theatre is always a part of my plans. Students who are interested in directing can find enormous motivation and creativity in the work of other artists.

Second, learn the mechanics of theatre. When given the opportunity, volunteer to be a stage manager, an assistant in the scene shop, run the light board, make props, sew buttons, do the laundry, iron the pumpkin breeches, hand out flyers, usher. Understand that theatre is a process that isn't always glamorous but that requires the dedication and hard work of many individuals, all of whom must be respected and admired for their craft. The more you understand about the business of theatre, the better you will be at making theatre.

Third, *make* theatre. Don't wait for a directing assignment or your student directed one-act festival. Find a script, grab some actors, do a show. The most important lessons of being a director are those that you uncover yourself while trying to make your vision manifest on stage. Rely on your colleagues, trust in their own talent and passion for theatre, and just make it happen. The lessons you learn will shape and instruct your life both in and out of the theatre.

Infinite Variety: Shakespeare Women Real and Imagined

Glasgow Repertory Company, 2005. Director Scott Aaron Palmer.

Summary

Producers and directors hold leadership positions in the theatre. The producer is responsible for securing a playscript, hiring artistic and managerial staffs, raising money, contract negotiations, securing the rehearsal halls and the theatre for the performances, and overseeing publicity. The director is responsible for developing the artistic concept, casting, rehearsing the actors, and collaborating with the artistic staff. The critical success of the production dictates the length of the run in the commercial theatre. If the production receives negative reviews, it may be forced to close early, or some of the artists, even the director, may be replaced. Commercial theatre is an expensive venture and it is crucial for all involved to work as a team.

The Theatre in Your Career

There are several directorial techniques that you can apply to your own career, particularly if you are required to give oral presentations—lectures, training sessions, sales pitches, budget reports, etc. As you are already aware, the most effective presentations are visually stimulating, esthetically pleasing, and move along at an efficient pace. The following section examines some of the techniques that theatre directors use, all of which can be adapted for any oral presentation, specifically *Picking Up Cues* (pace), *Composition* (esthetics), and *Cheating* (eye-contact with the audience).

Active Learning Assignment
"Bringing Theatre to Life"

I. **Staging Techniques to be used in the Final Group Project**

Relationships and conflicts may be enhanced and clarified by using simple blocking techniques. The groups will explore staging techniques—**creating a balanced stage picture, defining relationships through blocking, controlling focus on the stage, and giving stage directions to actors.**

Creating a Balanced Stage Picture

Composition is as important onstage as it is in other visual art. Two examples: triangles are more interesting than straight lines; different heights help to create an interesting stage picture (if the actors are placed at different levels on stage, it is much more interesting than if all the actors are standing on floor level).

Defining Relationship Through Blocking

On stage and in real life, the physical distance between people defines their relationships. Suppose the opening scene of a play shows a couple snuggling together on a loveseat while watching television. Even before the dialogue begins, we can assume, because of their physical relationship that they are either dating or married. However, if the opening scene of a play includes several characters sitting around a table and one character who is standing in the corner of the room, we will focus on the lone character and question his or her isolation.

Controlling Focus on the Stage

Here are a number of standard techniques to gain focus on stage:

I. All of the actors can look at another actor on stage.

II. An actor can stand alongside a large piece of furniture, in a doorway, or in front of a window.

III. All of the actors can face front except for one actor who has his or her back to the audience.

IV. Color can draw focus—all of the actors can wear blue, except one actor wearing red.

V. Levels can draw focus—all of the actors can stand except for one who is sitting.

VI. The actor downstage center will usually have the focus.

Giving Stage Directions to Actors

Theatre, as with any other business, has its jargon. Here are standard terms that directors use to communicate with actors:

Cross—another word for walk

Cue—the last portion of the line of dialogue just before your line of dialogue

Pick Up the Cue—begin to speak your line of dialogue *immediately* after you hear your cue

Lights Up—you may begin acting the scene

Cheat Out—when performing, and keep your face and body open to the audience.

Producing and Directing the Play   165

The illustration below provides you with specific areas of the stage. Directors use these areas to communicate movement to actors.

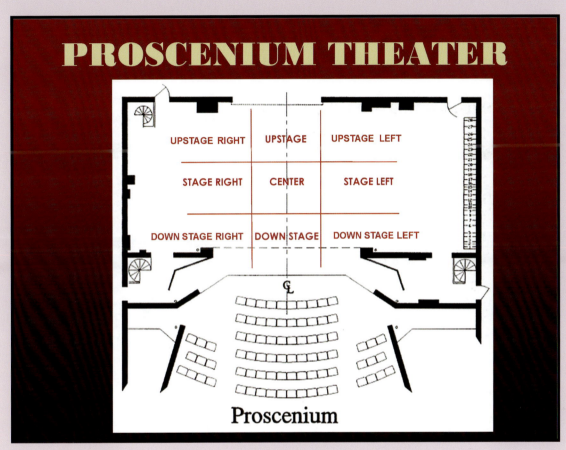

Illustration by Christopher Domanski.

Whether or Not You Want to Be an Actor, Achieve Your Personal Best

To be an actor or not to be an actor, that is the question; but what is the answer? Professional actors have experienced varying levels of respect and criticism throughout history. Storytellers were valuable members of ancient tribal communities, maintaining history and providing entertainment; but Elizabethan actors were regarded as immoral and could be denied burial in church cemeteries. Today, very popular modern actors are considered "stars" and treated with respect and admiration; while unknowns may be ridiculed because of their profession. In this chapter, we will examine how modern day actors care for themselves and gain employment. We will also examine a few of the modern theatre's most influential actors. The techniques in the following section can help an individual succeed in any profession.

Personal Preparation: Improving Your Self-Esteem, Appearance, and Interpersonal Communication Skills

The Look: Diet and Exercise

One of the characteristics that actors strive to acquire and maintain, regardless of age and physical type, is optimal physical condition.

At one time or another, many of us fantasize about becoming a world renowned actor, a "star." Even if that is just a passing fancy, anyone can use an actor's techniques to further his or her chosen career. One of the characteristics that actors strive to acquire and maintain, regardless of age and physical type, is optimal physical condition. Star actors adhere to rigorous exercise programs and diets developed by personal trainers and nutritional experts. These diets and exercise programs may even be adjusted to physically prepare an actor for a particular role. Serious amateur performers may also participate in daily exercise and diet regimens. They may be able to afford a personal trainer and a nutritionist, or they may create their own regimen. Certainly, before one begins an exercise diet regimen, it is important to discuss the plan with a physician.

Effective exercise programs combine cardiovascular and strength training. A diet should consist of lean protein, fruits and vegetables, whole grains, healthy oils, and plenty of water. There should be minimal consumption of unrefined sugar products, alcoholic beverages, and sodas. There are numerous "crash" weight loss programs on the market such as liquid diets and diet pills; but "crash" diets usually do not have a lasting effect on weight loss or weight control.

Because the acting profession is so competitive and stressful it is imperative that the actor have a positive self image and be able to handle rejection.

Because the acting profession is so competitive and stressful, it is imperative that the actor have a positive self image and be able to handle rejection. Proper diet and exercise have been proven to have a significant impact on emotional well-being and mental health. Cardiovascular exercise causes endorphins (chemicals in the body that act as natural pain killers) to be released. A regular release of endorphins helps one to relax and cope with anxiety. In addition, physical exercise strengthens the body and helps one look "long and lean," thus improving self-esteem.

The Smile

Because actors audition in intimate spaces, take many close-up photographs, and rehearse and perform in close proximity to others, healthy teeth and gums are crucial. Unless the actor is one of those rare individuals born with perfect teeth, he or she must work to achieve that award-winning smile. Braces, bonding, and whitening are some of these, although each can cost hundreds or even thousands of dollars. Even after the desired look is achieved, one must maintain the dental work through daily dental care. Most actors discover early in their careers that the "perfect smile" is essential to getting work.

The Hands

Producers, directors, and agents notice the actor's hands during an interview. Nails that have been chewed and bloody or torn cuticles make the actor appear nervous and insecure. Acting is a competitive business; it is imperative to be well groomed. Nail salons provide both men and women with a variety of services such as manicures, pedicures, and acrylic nails. Actors and actresses are always best served by clean, natural nails—medium length for women, short length for men.

Acting is a competitive business; it is imperative to be well-groomed.

The Scent

Men and women in acting professions should use a minimal amount of cologne or perfume. A director, agent, or producer may find a strong fragrance displeasing. It could bring back unpleasant memories; or it is possible that he or she is allergic to the fragrance. Of course, the actor always needs to be bathed and fresh when working with others; but it is best to be a minimalist when it comes to fragrance.

The Skin

Healthy and attractive-looking skin is important to everyone, but it is especially important to the actor. It is essential to apply sunscreen with a SPF (Sun Protection Factor) of at least 30 to all exposed body parts everyday. Of course wearing sunscreen decreases the risk of skin cancer, age spots and wrinkles; but actors shooting a film or a television show are expected to maintain the same skin color for the sake of continuity. Sunburns and deep tans are difficult for the make-up artist to conceal, and they add unwanted (and expensive) time to the shooting schedule.

© Jupiter Images Corp

Body Language and Eye Contact

Actors must use effective non-verbal communication—body language and eye contact—when auditioning for a role. Auditions are stressful but the talent (actor/actress) must appear calm, confident, and charismatic. Nervous behavior includes such gestures as crossing the arms. Although it provides the individual with a sense of security, crossed arms may be perceived by others as defensive. It is much more effective to allow the arms to hang naturally by the side while standing and to rest gently on the lap when sitting. Appropriate eye contact is another important skill to learn and practice. During interviews, make eye contact with the interviewer, especially when answering questions. Avoiding eye contact gives the impression of dishonesty or anxiety.

Actors must use effective non-verbal communication—body language and eye contact—when auditioning for a role.

Time Management

> *It is extremely important for actors to be excellent time managers and organizers.*

It is extremely important for actors to be excellent time managers and organizers. Once an actor has "booked" (acquired) a job, he or she must always be on time and ready to begin work when "called" (scheduled). Unless the actor has been involved in a serious emergency, he or she may be fired. This can result in a ruined reputation because the theatre is actually a small, close-knit business. Directors, agents, and producers are constantly in communication with one another. In order to avoid being late or missing an appointment, accurate records of auditions, rehearsals, and performances must be kept. It is imperative that these records include the location of the appointment and accurate directions. Ideally, a couple of different routes should be listed to avoid unexpected delays such as traffic accidents or public transportation delays. It is also a good idea to allow extra time for travel—rushing creates anxiety.

Personality

Since a plays is typically rehearsed for six to eight weeks in a confined space, directors and producers consider the individual's personality. Hiring someone who is respectful and outgoing is important because acting requires emotional intimacy. Cast members must feel as though they are safe from judgment and ridicule when rehearsing. Other valuable personality traits include being upbeat, friendly, and approachable. Everyone enjoys working in a pleasant, non-confrontational atmosphere. There are many actors vying for the same roles. It makes sense that those who display positive personality traits will secure most of the work.

> *It makes sense that those who display positive personality traits will secure most of the work.*

Listening

> *Listening is an important skill for actors to master both onstage and in everyday life.*

Listening is an important skill for actors to master both onstage and in everyday life. The speaker wants a listener to not only hear what they say but fully understand and genuinely respond to what is being said. Good listeners are active listeners. While listening, they respond with non-verbal and verbal communication cues including nodding the head, using facial expressions, and interjecting brief verbal comments such as, "Yes" or "I see." Unfortunately, real listening is difficult. It is very easy to get distracted by the environment or by ones own thoughts. Becoming a good listener makes one appear more charismatic. How? People tend to talk about subjects that have personal significance and really listening validates a speaker's thoughts, feelings, opinions, and desires. Active listening empowers the speaker and gives him or her a feeling of self worth; in turn, the speaker views the active listener as charismatic.

As mentioned in the first chapter of this book, one of the most important theatrical conventions is the spectator's willing suspension of disbelief. It is the unspoken understanding between the audience members and the performers in which everyone pretends that what happens on stage is real. This agreement allows the audience to get involved in the production and become emotionally invested in the characters. Actors use a variety of techniques to create this "willing suspension of disbelief." The most critical is listening. If an actor does not use active listen skills, it appears as if lines are being recited. There are three major steps in active listening: 1) really hearing what a person is saying, 2) allowing what was said to affect you, and 3) responding. Active listening is also a crucial skill to use when *networking*.

Networking

There are literally thousands of professional actors looking for work at any given time, and one way to secure an acting job is through *networking*. In the theatre, as well as in business, this old adage applies: "It's not what you know, but who you know that counts." Networking does not usually cost any money and can even be fun to do. The basic premise is that you attend social gatherings, dinners, lunches, parties, etc., and become acquainted with as many people as possible. At these events it is beneficial to utilize the interpersonal communication skills already discussed, paying special attention to active listening. You want to, as Dale Carnegie says, "Win Friends and Influence People." When an actor is at a party, he will learn the names, interests, and professions of as many people as possible and get their contact information. It does not really matter if the people you meet are casting directors or not. Networking means that you exchange information. Many times a person who is not "in the business" can introduce the actor to someone who does work in the theatre. Upon leaving the event, actors should write down and catalogue all of the information about their new acquaintances and follow up by contacting each shortly after the event, perhaps even arranging another meeting. Networking may help an actor land an audition or secure an agent.

There are literally thousands of professional actors looking for work at any given time, and one way to secure an acting job is through networking.

Agents

Agents seek employment for actors. Screen Actors Agents franchised by The Guild receive a daily fax or e-mail called a "breakdown." The "breakdown" informs agents which productions are currently casting and provides detailed information about each of the roles available. After reviewing the breakdown, agents will examine their list of clients and determine if anyone fits the description of the upcoming roles. If the agent represents performers appropriate for the roles, he or she will "submit" the client to the casting director. This is done by putting the client's headshot and resume in an envelope with a note identifying the role/roles the talent would suit and sending it to the casting director. Some submissions are sent via e-mail. To the right is an example of a client's headshot and her resume appears on the following page.

Agents seek employment for actors.

Kelly Kiernan

Photograph courtesy of Kelly Kiernan.

Kelly Kiernan
(*AEA*)

BiCoastal Talent Phone: (407) 839-4313

Height: 5'3" **Weight**: 140lbs

Professional Experience

Film	The Real NCIS	Lead	Investigation Discovery
TV/Industrial	Montana Rides Again	Featured	Parabolic Pictures
	CSX Transportation	Lead	Spectrum Films
	St. Vincent's Medical Ctr	Lead	Barton Productions
	Gas Co of New Mexico	Principal	Sterling Grant-Director ("The Big Easy")
	Vystar	Featured	Kohl-Lindsey Entertainment
	Creamland Dairies	Principal	Sunrise Productions
	Southwest Toyota	Principal	Sunrise Productions
Regional Theatre	Murder in the Cathedral	Woman of Canterbury	Stratford Festival Theatre; Dir-Louis Burke
	Much Ado About Nothing	Margaret	Bridgeport Free Shakespeare; Ellen Lieberman
	The Comedy of Errors	The Courtezan	Shakespeare in Santa Fe; Dir-Mark Cuddy
	Romeo & Juliet	Lady Montague	Shakespeare in Santa Fe; Dir-Steven Schwartz
	Laundry & Bourbon	Hattie	Cowgirl Hall of Fame; Dir-Nicholas Ballas
	Reckless	Pooty	Santa Fe Actor's Theatre; Dir-Nicholas Ballas
	Billy the Kid	Abrana	NM Outdoor Drama Assoc; Dir-Richard Waite
	Ruffian on the Stair	Joyce	Corral Playhouse, Portales NM
Tour	A Midsummer Night's Dream	Titania	Shakespeare in Santa Fe, Outreach Program
	Macbeth	1st Witch	Shakespeare in Santa Fe, Outreach Program
	Shakespeare's Fools	Ensemble	Shakespeare in Santa Fe, Outreach Program
Staged Reading	Ophelia's Mother	Queen Gertrude	Orlando Shakespeare Festival, Playfest 2005
	Shatter the Sky	Helen of Troy	Invictus T.C., OSF Playfest 2005
	The Ebony Ape	Eugenia Presbury	SFT Celebrity Play Reading; w/ Douglas Sills
	Toes	"New Singer"	SFT Celebrity Play Reading; w/Celeste Holm
	Twelfth Night	Maria	Stratford Festival Theatre Fundraiser
University Theatre	Witness for the Prosecution	Romaine	ENMU Mainstage
	The Dining Room	Actress #3	ENMU Mainstage
	Broadway Bound	Kate Jerome	ENMU Mainstage
	All My Sons	Kate Keller	ENMU Mainstage
	Chicago	Annie	ENMU Mainstage
Community Theatre	Good Woman of Setzuan	Shen Te/Shuia Ta	Santa Fe Playhouse, Santa Fe NM
	A Macbeth	Lady Macbeth	Studio Experimental Theatre Group
	Brighton Beach Memoirs	Blanche	Studio Experimental Theatre Group

Professional Training

BFA **Theatre Arts** **Eastern NM State University**

Film: Mark Mullen & Rus Blackwell, Mullen Casting, Orlando FL
Lynn Britt, Eugene O'Neill Theatre Center
Sande Shurin, Sandee Shurin Studios NYC, "Beyond Sense Memory"
Shakespeare: John Barton, Royal Shakespeare Co, participant in "Playing Shakespeare USA"
Louis Burke, Stratford Festival Theatre, Broadway Director/Producer
Chekhov: Professor Murray Biggs, Dept of Theatre Studies, Yale University
Dance: 7 yrs Jazz; 2 yrs Ballet; 2 yrs Modern; 2 yrs Theatrical

Special Skills

Horseback riding, Swimming, BikramYoga, Teach Shakespeare Workshops

Resume Courtesy of Kelly Kiernan

Ideally, agents have developed positive relationships with casting directors and will be able to "go to bat" (call the casting director and talk positively) for their clients.

If a casting director selects an actor or actress to read for a role, he or she needs to be reasonably certain that the actor will read well and not be an embarrassment. The casting director's job is as fragile as an actors. If a director decides to cast an actor or actress in a role, then the agent will negotiate the client's contract. The types of contractual arrangements include the client's title (star, co-star, etc.) name placement, the size of the font in publicity materials, and accommodations for the client during rehearsals and performances. Contractually, agents get 10 percent of what the actor is paid.

How to Get an Agent

Agents need to be familiar with their clients' acting abilities and have a sense of their "types"—the kinds of roles that they are best suited to play. If the agent believes that the new actor is talented enough to secure employment, the agent will review their current client "types" to insure that he is not already representing other actors in the same category. It is impractical to have several actors of the same "type" at the same agency because the clients would be forced compete with one another for the same jobs. If there are no apparent conflicts, the agent will call the actor in for an interview. The agent may also ask the actor to perform a monologue or two so that he may confirm the acting ability of the potential client.

Unsigned actors who want to become visible to agents perform in venues such as non-union plays, independent films, and stand-up comedy houses. Actors network with the hope that a friend or acquaintance will make a recommendation to an agent. Unrepresented talents also submit their headshots and resumes to agents by mail, and some agents even accept and review these unsolicited submissions.

Once a performer has signed, the agent strives to secure work for their new client. If the talent "books" a job performing at a theatre or on camera, the agent will notify Actors Equity Association or The Screen Actors Guild.

Actors Labor Union: Actors Equity Association

Actors Equity Association was created on May 26, 1913, to protect professional actors and actresses from unfair and unsafe working conditions. In 1919, Actors Equity Association was given a charter by The American Federation of Labor (now known as the AFL-CIO) and in that same year Equity held its first strike. Since it's inclusion in AFL-CIO, Actors Equity Association has acquired numerous benefits for members—health and pension plans, minimum salaries, payment for rehearsals, regulation of theatrical agents, restrictions on the employment of foreign actors, and insuring that principles and chorus members who do not have agents have an opportunity to audition for productions.

In 1947, Actors Equity Association played an important role in the civil rights struggle. The National Theatre in Washington, DC, did not allow African Americans to attend its performances. Actors Equity Association responded by removing its actors from the stage. The dispute was eventually resolved, and a non-discrimination policy was put in place at the theatre.

Training

There are literally thousands of professional, card-holding actors seeking employment at any given time. If an actor intends to book a job, it is imperative that he continue training. Actors are like athletes—always "working-out," refining techniques, and investigating new approaches. Actors typically enroll in formal study at a university, college, or private studio, each of which offers students different opportunities. Some private studios offer their students' opportunities to audition for casting directors, agents and producers; some colleges and universities offer not only a degree but also professional acting opportunities. For example, the University of San Diego collaborates with the Old Globe Theatre, in San Diego, to create professional acting opportunities for students while they are working toward a Master of Fine Arts degree.

The three main areas of study for an actor are voice, movement, and acting.

Regardless of the school, actor training programs have definite similarities. The three main areas of study for an actor are voice, movement, and acting. Over the years, many teachers have developed their own methods in order to train actors in each of the three areas. The next part of this chapter focuses on five renowned acting teachers and presents brief overviews of their approaches to training actors.

The Father of Modern Acting Training—Konstantin Stanislavsky (1863–1938)

Konstantin Sergeevich Alekseev was born into a wealthy Russian manufacturing family who instilled in him a love of theatre. Unfortunately, many actors had been serfs during the nineteenth century, and even after serfdom was abolished, actors were considered second-class citizens. As a youth, Konstantin acted and directed in many productions and found he could not live without the theatre. In 1844, not wanting to tarnish the family name, he assumed the stage name of his favorite ballerina, Stanislavsky.

In 1897, Vladimir Nemirovich-Danchenko, a playwright and educator who was unhappy with actor training practices, invited Stanislavsky to join him in founding The Moscow Art Theatre. Together, they set out to develop a new approach to actor training. Traditionally, actors were trained in a presentational style, using conventional vocal techniques and physical gestures. For example, putting a hand to their forehead to indicate sorrow and laying a hand on the heart to signify love. Stanislavsky's System differed—its goal was to train actors to access and express genuine emotions. Stanislavsky's philosophy approached acting holistically—the mind and body are one and emotions are not separate from physicality.

Konstantin Stanislavsky

Stanislavsky taught actors to connect their emotions to physical behavior. He wanted them to appear as though they were truly living in the moment. He accomplished this, in part, by submitting his performers to long rigorous rehearsal periods during which the actors would seek to find a balance between personal "sense of self" and textual character analysis. Stanislavsky was also interested in Yoga and derived much of his approach from this discipline. He created exercises to help the actor get in tune with his body, imagination, emotions, and concentration. All of this was an effort to become more skillful at communicating—not just the text but also the *subtext* of the play.

The *subtext* is the unspoken underlying desire of the character. Stanislavsky's System also took an analytical approach to the text. Actors were taught to research the character in order to better understand who the character was, where he or she came from, and what he or she wanted. He required his students to dissect the play into bits (now called *beats*) which are moments of completed actions. He also created a unique acting technique called the *magic if*. In order to use the *magic if*, the actor had to ask, "What if this was really happening to me? What would I do? How would I behave? How would I solve the problem?"

Stanislavsky's attention to emotional expression on-stage reflected the early twentieth century interest in Freudian psychology. He went on to write his autobiography, *My Life in Art* (1942), *An Actor Prepares* (1926), *Creating a Role* (1948), and *Building a Character* (1950). Published in numerous languages, his books still serve as the basis for many professional actor training programs.

Stanislavsky's innovative approach inspired his former students and other theatre practitioners and teachers to develop their own methods of training. Often, these methods incorporate much of Stanislavsky's original philosophy. Some of these acting teachers have included Lee Strasberg, Stella Adler, Sandford Meisner, and Michael Chekhov.

The Method

In 1923, two of Stanislavsky's students, Richard Boleslavsky and Maria Ouspenskaya, introduced an approach for training actors that was new to Americans. They based their method of training on Stanislavsky's System, and it quickly gained popularity. One of their students, Lee Strasberg, helped form The Group Theatre. The members of The Group Theatre were interested in producing new plays written by Americans, and Strasberg's interpretation of the Stanislavsky System was used to train actors for these productions. Strasberg's approach became known as the *Method*. The System and the Method both sought to train actors to play their roles realistically, with human complexity and genuine emotional depth.

Strasberg's Method focused on the actor's inner life, a natural stage presence, and an ensemble approach to productions. Method practitioners believe that genuine emotional moments should occur during the performance, but in a controlled manner. For example, if the scene calls for a character to cry, the actor must produce real tears, but, the actor must control the emotional release in order to complete the performance. Method actors use *personalization* as a mean of expressing their emotions on-stage. *Personalization* in Method acting means that actors access their own emotions and feelings

about their own life experiences and re-create them onstage. For instance, an actor might be playing a character whose father has just died, but the actor has never lost a father or a close family member. The actor has, perhaps, experienced the death of a close friend, so the actor substitutes his real-life emotional response to that death when portraying the character's loss.

The members of The Group Theatre also believed that *physical activities* should actually be performed by the actors during the performance. If the character is supposed to be reading a book, then the actor should actually be reading a book. If a scene calls for the actor to eat dinner, real food should be consumed.

Method actors must always *motivate* their dialogue, their relationships with the other characters in the play, and their onstage physical activities. Motivation is fueled by the character's *intentions* (personal goals), and as in real life, motivation creates urgency.

The Method also examines the *subtext* which is a part of real life conversation. Pretend that a single woman named Jane Doe is at work in her office when a handsome man comes in to deliver her mail. She is on the job and feels that she must address him professionally. She says, "Thank you for bringing my mail," but since she finds him attractive, her body language and vocal intonation imply a subtle flirtation. The way actors find and convey this subtext is by analyzing a character's *given circumstances*. In the example above, Jane Doe's given circumstances are that she is single and works in an office. The subtext (subtle flirtation) would change if Jane Doe's given circumstances were different. For example, if she were a married woman working in her husband's office.

Finally, Method actors strive to portray their roles with *spontaneity* and to give their audiences the impression that the action onstage is happening for the first time. As mentioned earlier, listening is the key to creating natural behavior onstage. In real-life conversation, we do not appreciate someone who is not really listening but is instead thinking of what to say after we are finished. If an actor is not listening and delivers his lines before the other character finishes, the audience is reminded that they are watching a play and this destroys the *suspension of disbelief* (Act I Scene I).

For The Group Theatre, complete preparation was vital; and improvisational exercises always constituted a significant portion of the rehearsal period. These improvisational exercises helped the actors personalize the text. It ignited their imaginations, freed up their emotions, and taught them to listen and respond to one another.

Over the years, some members left The Group theatre and went on to develop their own variations of the Method. Lee Strasberg, Stella Adler, and Sandford Mesiner were three individuals who made significant contributions to American acting training. Each created his or her own improvisational approach. For example, Strasberg instructed his students in the use of nonsensical words to act out scenes in the play; Adler's actors were taught to paraphrase the text; and Meisner had his actors utilize a series of repetition exercises.

The Method has received its share of criticism by some acting teachers as being psychologically dangerous because it encourages performers to tap into their personal memories. Other teachers have viewed the Method as self-indulgent, resulting in mumbled speech patterns that are difficult to understand. However, there is no doubt that there have been numerous successful Method actors—Marlon Brando and Marilyn Monroe to name just two.

Michael Chekhov

The great playwright Anton Chekhov wrote several plays that were produced by The Moscow Art Theatre during Stanislavsky's tenure. Anton's nephew, Michael Chekhov, was only seven years old when The Moscow Art Theatre began. Michael spent a good deal of time at the theatre while he was growing up and eventually became a student of acting at the *First Studio,* directed by the acting teacher Sulerzhitsky. Sulerzhitsky taught Stanislavsky's *System* and Michael Chekhov was receptive to the approach. He eventually became an admired actor and acting teacher who used much of Stanislavsky's approach in his own classroom; but Michael Chekhov modified the *System* to reflect his personal taste.

Michael Chekhov went on to create his own actor training methodology. Among other techniques, his students were encouraged to create an *atmosphere* where their characters resided—an atmosphere in which the actors performed physical activities in a way that best reflected the environment. A meal eaten alone in the privacy of one's own home is different than a meal eaten in an expensive restaurant in front of friends or colleagues. Because the *atmosphere* has changed, the manner of dining must change. When an actor allows the imagined *atmosphere* to affect his or her behavior, the performance becomes more truthful and that was what Michael Chekhov was aiming toward.

The *Psychological Gestures* was another of Michael Chekhov's contributions to actor training. Human beings are multifaceted and to portray them accurately, actors must reveal an individual character's idiosyncrasies. *Psychological Gestures* help actors to reveal the complexity of the characters. Michael Chekhov developed a variety of exercises intended to teach actors how to use *Psychological Gestures* in their performances. One such exercise was to ask the actor to make a physical gesture while speaking their lines such as waving enthusiastically to the other character in the scene. The actor would then be asked to do the scene again, but this time to remain physically still and imagine that he or she is enthusiastically waving to the other character in the scene. It is the imagining of the gesture which is referred to as the *Psychological Gesture*.

Michael Chekhov also developed *qualities of movement* which he called *molding, radiating,* and *flying.* Imagination is the key to utilizing these *qualities of movement.* For example, an actor would use his or her psychological inner strength or will to "mold" the air molecules when walking over to pick up a book. The actor would then pick up the book while focusing on *flying* and then on *radiating.* Each of these psychological images elicits a different bodily feeling. *Molding* the air molecules gives an individual a sensation of strength/power; *flying* and *radiating* tend to make a person feel light and easy. These qualities are useful to an actor because they help him or her to better define the character's physicality and intentions.

Michael Chekhov made significant contributions to the theatre as an actor, teacher, and writer. He authored several influential books. One of them, *To the Actor,* was completed in 1942 and finally published in 1953 after a great deal of editing. In 1990, a more inclusive addition *On the Technique of Acting,* was published.

Arthur Lessac, the Creator of the Lessac Kinesensic Voice and Body Training

Arthur Lessac

Photograph courtesy of Arthur Lessac.

Arthur Lessac, Professor Emeritus of Theatre, State University of New York at Binghamton, has taught voice training for more than 80 years to a wide variety of students. His approach draws from his personal experience as a teacher, theatrical performer, professional singer, director, and speech and voice therapist. Lessac has been involved with the training of the Lincoln Center Repertory Company in New York (including Faye Dunaway, Frank Langella, Christopher Lloyd, and Martin Sheen), with Broadway productions and with many other productions across the United States and around the world. Currently based in Santa Monica, California, where he oversees the Lessac Training and Research Institute, Lessac continues his research, occasionally teaches at the Lessac Summer Intensives, gives workshops, and is collaborating on his next book.

FEATURE SECTION

An Interview with Arthur Lessac, the Creator of the Lessac Kinesensic Voice and Body Training

How did you get involved in voice, speech, and body training?

I had to go way, way back to find out when it first became of interest to me. At that time I was a lad of 10, which was 88 years ago.

Two things I remember happening: I found out that I had a singing voice. Not a big voice, but a good voice. I sang in choirs and at synagogues and other places. I remember thinking, when I was singing, that singing felt good. I remember at the time feeling tingling sensations. Which I now know were resonance and wave reflections. My singing voice obviously was carrying over to my speaking voice.

When I work with the voice today, I say, "When you speak, do you feel like you are singing?" I have had voice clients that stutter when they speak. But when they sing they do not stutter. When they experience and feel the musicality in their speech—the music that was not there before—they do not stutter.

I also knew that I loved to run, climb, and to play one wall hand ball. I loved feeling myself throwing a ball. I had a sense of floating, balance, and rhythm and even gracefulness. I loved it. I was also experiencing ambidexterity—the right hand teaching the left hand to do something, and the left hand teaching the right hand to do something.

Body work is the very foundation of my *kinesensic* work.

(Kinesensic: *kine* for movement and motion; *esens* for basic meaning, nature, cognition; *sens* for spirit, inner energy, involvement; *sic* for familiar occurrences—definition from *The Use and Training of the Human Voice: A Bio-Dynamic Approach to Vocal Life* by Arthur Lessac.)

What is most challenging and most enjoyable about your work?

The challenge is that there is no stagnation (end) to movement, motion, or to creativity. (There is no end of possibilities or discovery within my work.) This is also the real excitement. At my age, I get excited every time I think of something new.

My work is great for actors but there is a greater potential for my work in such fields as geriatrics, therapy, and interpersonal relationships. There is work to be done (overall in the world). The work will not be done with money, not by leaders and not with religion. It is going to be done with a desire to use this work (my work) to achieve optimal health and wellness and to recognize poisons that can enter the human organism from the outer environment.

We can use my work to achieve a genuine connection and communing with others. When I say communing it is different than communication. Communication implies the intellect. While communing starts and ends with the feeling process. The feeling process is the road to cross-cultural relationships. The idea of feeling through the senses is the foundation of my work. (In conversation,) if we become truly aware of the other person's tone of voice and the look in their eye then no matter where we are in the world we will realize that we are all the same, we are all human beings. We are all family. Thereby, hopefully ending the most serious poison of war and easing suffering.

Acting Coach Jolene Adams

Jolene Adams is the Artistic Director of Actors Art Theatre (a member of The Los Angeles Stage Alliance) which she founded in New York City. Jolene produced her first Equity production, *The Runner Stumbles,* at the Collective Actors Theatre in New York City and has since produced and directed over 50 productions. She produced, developed, and starred in the Drama-Logue Award winning *Adam & Eva Marie* at Actors Art Theatre. She also developed and directed the critically-acclaimed, Ovation Award nominated hit, *Boiler Room* by Dan Fante at both AAT in LA & The Pantheon in New York City, (selected as one of the most notable plays of the year by Don Shirley of *The LA Times*) and Cathy Ladman's solo show, *Scardeypants,* for HBO Independent Productions/The U.S. Comedy Arts Festival in Aspen. She directed and co-wrote AAT's last four productions, *F Buddy* (BackStage

Jolene Adams

Photograph courtesy of Actors Art Theatre. Photograph by Gloria Grant.

West Critic's Pick), *Resignation* (featured in DailyCandy and recommended by *The LA Weekly*), *One Crazy Lady*, Jenica Bergere's (*Drew Carey Show*, *Men Behaving Badly*), solo show, and developed Mike Dugan's (Emmy Award-winning comedian) *Men Fake Foreplay*. Jolene starred as "Dolores" in the critically-acclaimed, world premiere of Edward Allen Baker's *Crying Rocks* at The Laurelgrove Theatre and "Gretty" in *Gretty Good Time* at Garry Marshall's The Falcon Theatre, directed by Joe Regalbuto. She's featured in Larry Silverberg's book, *Guide to Qualified Acting Coaches*, and taught for the NYU Theatre Program at the Harold Clurman Theatre. Among the several screenplays she has written, co-written, or has in pre-production are *Vampingo* (co-written with Ariana Johns), *F Buddy* (co-written with Danielle Weeks), *Sight Unseen*, *Resignation* (co-written with Terry Brown), and *Catching Hell*.

FEATURE SECTION
An Interview with Acting Coach Jolene Adams

What inspired you to become an acting coach/teacher?

After a demanding BFA program, I continued to study acting in NYC with Martha Jacobs who taught a Sanford Meisner-inspired technique. She told me that I had a unique ability to both act and communicate how I did what I did which she believed gave me the ability to be an effective teacher.

I co-produced and co-created a two-woman show at Playwright's Horizons in NYC after I finished her program. I played several characters from a teenage rap artist to a middle-aged Midwestern housewife. My performance was well received by the industry and I had never felt so free and alive on stage. Several of my college classmates saw the performance and wanted to know what I had learned in the two years after graduation regarding character work and dealing spontaneously with the audience. I agreed to teach them what I'd learned from my wonderful teacher plus some tools that I invented for myself to access deeper states of relaxation and inspiration. So I would say that my friends' enthusiasm for my work and my teacher's belief in me were what inspired me to teach.

What do you enjoy most about teaching?

I love the work, the script analysis, the improvisations, and the discoveries of new tools. It is so gratifying to help develop the craft of a passionate artist. When one of my clients embodies a character and is able to consistently live truthfully in the moment, I can't help but feel proud. I love watching a client become authentic and compassionate towards themselves and others. When I see them flourish personally from the gifts of acting, I can't help but feel fulfilled and useful!

What is most challenging?

It's always challenging to take a person with a superficial interest in acting and inspire them to connect to a deeper understanding of the art.

If a student were interested in becoming a coach/teacher of acting what advice would you give them?

The advice I give to students who want to become teachers is . . . don't do it for money! I think that if you are a good teacher/coach type of person, your career will start naturally. People will seek out your council because they respect your work and feel a connection with you. If you do good work as an actor and know how you do it and can't help but share it, chances are you will be a good, successful coach.

For more information about Jolene Adams contact her at **www.actorsart.com**

Actor/Acting Coach Larry Silverberg

Larry Silverberg

Larry Silverberg is one of the most widely published actors/acting teachers in the world today and he is considered the foremost authority on the Sanford Meisner technique of acting through his internationally acclaimed four volume series, "The Sanford Meisner Approach: An Actors Workbook," and his book, "Loving To Audition." Larry's newest book has just been released, "The 7 Simple Truths of Acting for the Teen Actor."

Larry is a graduate of the Neighborhood Playhouse School of Theatre where he studied with legendary acting teacher, Sanford Meisner. Since then, Larry has worked professionally as an actor and director across the United States and in Canada. Recently, he received high praise from the New York Times for his performance as "Don" in Athol Fugard's "People Are Living There" at The Signature Theater in New York City, and he won the Seattle Critic's Association "Stellar Acting Award" for his portrayal of "Teach" in the Belltown Theatre Center production of "American Buffalo."

Larry teaches acting in his world renowned professional actors training program, "The Meisner Intensive Training Program" which he runs at Universities, Colleges, and Acting Studios around the globe. In the summers, Larry trains professors to teach the Meisner Approach in his "Meisner Teacher Certificate Program" which he holds at Eckerd College in St. Petersburg, Florida. Most recently, Larry was invited to introduce the Meisner work to the country of Brazil at FAAP University in Sao Paulo. Larry can be contacted through his website address, **http://www.actorscraft.com**.

Feature Section
An Interview with Actor/Acting Coach Larry Silverberg

What inspired you to become an actor?

I was a very fat child and very self conscious. If I had to stand in front of the class, I would become so nervous I would turn red—this was in elementary school. I was attracted to film making and after giving up on becoming a race car driver, I really thought I was going to be a film director. Then I went to college, I was a film studies student and I began making movies. This girl I knew from high school was attending the same college and she talked me into taking a Beginning Acting class. We had to work on scenes. I was working on a scene with a girl in class and at the end of the semester, we had to perform it. Something happened that was so revolutionary . . . so profound. For the first time in my life, I got my attention off of myself and I began to free-up and experience parts of myself that were previously restricted. The best way to describe it was a "falling in love." After that, I auditioned for a two person show and I got the part. Acting unleashed the part of me that wanted to express itself. And then I got very involved in the Theatre Department, taking every acting class that was offered and acting in all the plays.

The turning point in my life, (from film making into acting) was:

I made a film at college for which I won the largest grant the school had ever given for a student project like this and I entered it into a national film competition—*The Warner Brothers: Young Film Makers Award*. I was one of eight people in the country chosen as the winners and the eight of us received an offer to come to the Warner Brothers lot, all expenses paid, to work with professional directors. But I had also applied to sweep the theatre at a summer stock in return for taking acting classes and being a member of an intern company where I would get to act in the intern shows. Well, much to the shock of my parents and friends, I turned down Warner Brothers and went to the summer stock theatre.

Right after I graduated from college, I took a short workshop with an acting teacher in New York. After the workshop, I went to the teacher and asked him what I should do to become a professional actor. He said, "Get to Sanford Meisner." I knew that I had learned certain skills in college but I felt that I really was not yet prepared to be a professional actor. So, I listened to the teacher and I applied to Sanford Meisner's school, the Neighborhood Playhouse. I had never heard of Sanford Meisner before but when I arrived at the playhouse and began looking at the pictures of his students on the wall—actors like Gregory Peck, Jeff Goldblum, Mary Sternbergen, Steve Mc Queen, Robert Duvall, Joanne Woodward, Eli Wallach and others—I began to understand the magnitude of who Sanford Meisner was.

After I graduated from the Playhouse, I began acting in numerous Off-Broadway shows. Then, I was down in Florida acting in a play and certainly, the last thing I thought I would do was teach acting. But some people told me that they were starting a new theatre company and they wanted me to coach them. The thought of sharing what Sandy (Sanford Meisner) taught me was exciting. I decided to teach the company members and, in my mind, I went over my classes with Sandy, and I began to teach. Simply, I fell in love with teaching, it was like coming home. Then a conservatory in Florida invited me to teach a Meisner class and I did.

While as I was working on a play, I met my wife and she got pregnant. We didn't want to stay in Florida or bring up the baby in New York City, so we headed up to Seattle, Washington where we had heard there was a lot of theatre activity. Before we moved, I found an acting studio, and made an arrangement with the owners to rent the studio to teach an acting class there. I took out an advertisement in the local newspaper offering a Meisner class and then we drove from Miami to Seattle. By the time we got to Seattle the class was totally full! I had to turn people away! I realized there was a great need for Meisner classes and that the Seattle actors were hungry for this kind of work. After teaching this class, My wife and I opened a professional theatre and acting studio in downtown Seattle.

The other thing that happened when I was in Seattle teaching that first class, was that an older actor (who was also a very famous writer) who had spent time studying with Sandy many years before, said to me, "You must write a book on how you teach this work."

My reaction was, "I can't. I don't know how to write a book."

"Yes, you can," he said.

"No, I can't," I replied.

"Yes, you can," he demanded.

So I listened to him and wrote the first of my books. The only way I could write the book was to write as if I were talking to a student in class. When I had half of the book done, I sent it to my dear friend Horton Foote. He loved it. He sent it to Smith and Krauss and they wanted to publish it.

So I sent the book to Sandy for his approval. I was nervous because Sandy wasn't crazy about acting books. When I sent it to him, I never expected to get his permission but he gave it to me.

After the first book, I called my publisher and said, "Thanks, it's been nice to know you."

"You're not finished, you have other books to write," my publisher responded.

"No, I don't," I said.

"Yes, you do!" my publisher emphatically replied.

Now I have written six acting books and have signed a contract to write another.

The incredible thing about these books is that I get e-mails from people all around the world, from every country and from actors in the big cities as well as the most unusual places, telling me that they are using my books to learn and to teach acting. High schools and colleges have been using my books. It is an incredible gift to share the work and I am so grateful that the books have become useful—useful to so many people. Of course, the books, in and of themselves, are not the way to learn acting; you have to be in an acting class too.

What do you enjoy most about acting and teaching?

As far as acting, the great joy is that when I act I "disappear." It's a sense of such freedom and mindlessness, where all of the neuroses of the mind fade away. It's also the joy of going through the absolute pain of giving birth to this thing called the character. I love rehearsals; I love collaborating with other great artists. I love the journey, finding my way inside these imaginary circumstances and deepening the experience with the other actors and the director. I love working as a team, all of us aimed at creating something wonderful together, and that only happens when the script, actors, and director truly come together.

Whenever I act, there is always this point in rehearsal that it is so painful that I don't know if I'm going to make it. The only thing that keeps me going is that, from experience, I know that I will find a way through; that on the other side of the pain there is utter joy. I approach performances as a continued rehearsal process which makes the continued exploration fun and free. By the end of the run, I feel like I am just "getting to know this guy (this character) and I want to keep going!

I love the unknown of the performance and entering the unknown every night with people I can trust. Acting is the art of human expression, and expressing oneself fully is just plain. . . fun. It is necessary for human beings to express themselves while being witnessed by others, this is a basic human need and so it is that theatre only happens with an audience. We (actors) live out the circumstances of the play, we truly experience these events in each moment, and we are witnessed by the audience having these experiences.

My joy of teaching? I do find incredible joy in teaching. You know, for me, teaching is a lot like acting; it is a deeply collaborative process. I have to be as involved with my students as I am with the other actors when I am acting. Teaching demands that I am fully present every moment while I am in the classroom. For a student actor to move through all of his/her struggles and come out on the other side is an inspiration to me. To see a student come in at one level and to then see that person be able to stand on his/her own two feet is extremely rewarding. It is not my intention for them to become more like me, but to fully become who they are as human beings. It is rewarding beyond words and I feel very fortunate to spend my life working with actors in this way.

Challenges. . .

One of the biggest challenges for an actor is the work itself. Students need to understand that the work of being an actor, a true actor, is more grueling and difficult then they could ever imagine. If a person wants to study acting, he/she will soon discover the cost is high and the cost is personal. There is one crucial component to being successful in your studies and that's working VERY hard. That is difficult when things get rough. Most people tend to run the other way when things get difficult. Acting is very much three steps forward and two steps back, five steps forward and three steps back. The important thing to remember is that it is the three steps back that makes the next leap forward possible. Of course, it's very important that they have a teacher who is a human being, a teacher who is simple, direct, and compassionate. Students must be very aware that if they land in a class where the teacher is in any way mean, disrespectful, manipulative, cruel to students, or likes to talk about himself more than he likes to teach, they need to run in the other direction as fast as possible!

A note to actors on working hard:

All of us have certain gifts we were born with. There is nothing we can do about the gifts we were born with, it is out of our hands. The ONLY thing we can do is to WORK HARD so that we can FULFILL the gifts we have been given.

For the student who wants to know how to become an actor:

The young actor must wake-up and stay awake. Stay aware of the world around you in order to strengthen your ability to be available to others, not just in the classroom but in all of your life. Actors must be curious and interested in what is happening around them and in the lives of everyone they encounter. Actors must also refuse to allow other people, or their own critical thoughts, to make them feel less than adequate. Last, actors must remember that they are here to make a difference and that if they strive to be simple, human, and authentic; if they take the time and work very hard to develop their skills so that they know what it is to fight for something with every ounce of their being both in life and on the stage; if they can move the ego aside and want to work in communion with other human beings in order to create something of lasting value, then they will certainly make a difference in the lives of the people who come to see them work. And in this very troubled world, a true voice is needed more than ever.

Actors/Actresses

Untold thousands of actors have "trod the boards" over the centuries. Many of these actors have made valuable contributions to the theatre. The following looks at the lives and careers of three important figures from the modern theatre. Those examined include Laurence Olivier, Meryl Streep, and Sidney Poitier.

Laurence Olivier (1907–1989)
From Hungry Actor to Baron Olivier of Brighton

One of the most successful actors of the twentieth century and one of the most celebrated actors of all time was Laurence Olivier, the son of Gerard and Agnes Olivier. Gerard Olivier, ordained in the Church of England in 1902, possessed an elegant appearance and gave his sermons a dramatic flare. Agnes Olivier was a beautiful, intelligent woman with a wonderful sense of humor. Laurence was born at the height of the Edwardian era and, although many of the Victorian customs were still practiced, change was underway, particularly in the attitude toward the theatre. Queen Victoria had knighted Henry Irving the first actor to be so honored. Her successor, King Edward, loved the theatre and contributed to making it a popular and respected art.

After a vocal audition, Laurence Olivier was enrolled in All Saints, a school with an excellent choir. Father Heald gave Laurence his first role in a play. He was cast as one of the citizens in *Julius Caesar;* but when the young man playing Brutus was unable to perform the role to Father Heald's satisfaction, the role was given to Laurence, who was the youngest and smallest in his class. Air raids occurred frequently during rehearsals for the production; nevertheless, Laurence determined to succeed in his role and hid under a table in the crypt to memorize his lines. The world-renowned actress Ellen Terry was in the audience when Laurence performed Brutus. When the production ended and everyone was doting over the young men who played Caesar and Anthony. But as Donald Spoto recounts, in his book *Laurence Olivier A Biography,* Ellen Terry, said "No. . . . The boy who played Brutus. . . . The dark little boy—He is a born actor."

When Laurence was 17 years old, he was admitted to The Central School for Speech and Drama. The school's main objective was to train students to have a natural and healthy speaking voice. Laurence received a full scholarship, but it gave him only one pound a week to live on. As a result, the now five-foot-ten Laurence was very thin and hungry most of the time. But the emptiness in his stomach did not dissuade this young talent from striving for excellence in his work. He diligently approached his studies with energy and enthusiasm. So much so, his class performance of Caliban from Shakespeare's *The Tempest* made one female classmate faint, another leave the room, and the rest of his classmates gasp. Olivier biographer, Donald Spoto, provides an example of young Olivier's attention to detail. When Olivier read Shakespeare's description of Caliban, "a freckled whelp, hag horn, not honoured with a human shape," Laurence covered his body in green slime and attached colored plasters to his face simulate oozing boils. Throughout Olivier's career, makeup, which he generally applied himself, was one of the ways he defined his characters.

In 1925, Olivier finished his training at the Central School for Speech and Drama, taking with him the Dawson Milward Cup award for most popular actor. His first professional role was Armand St. Cry in *The Unfailing Instinct*. For this, he received two pounds a week. Laurence continued in this fashion, playing non-leading roles in mostly failing productions, until he was 22 years old when he was offered a role in a Hollywood film. Actors generally viewed film to be a lesser art form, but Olivier, needing money and hoping for fame, left for Hollywood.

Laurence Olivier found fame and fortune in Hollywood and eventually became an internationally renowned actor. He acted in well over 100 major plays and film productions around the world. Some of his stage roles include Caesar in *Caesar and Cleopatra*, Antony in *Antony and Cleopatra*, the title role in *Othello* and his portrayal of Hamlet is legendary. But he did not perform only in Shakespeare. His talents brought to life other playwrights' work such as Ioensco's *Rhinoceros*, Noel Coward's *Private Lives*, and Ibsen's *The Master Builder*. Of course, he starred in countless films, including *The Marathon Man*, *Spartacus*, and *A Little Romance*. He was also a consummate director and was responsible for numerous stage and film productions.

Olivier received more accolades than any other actor or actress in history. He became Sir Laurence Olivier in 1947. He was the first director of the National Theatre of Great Britain, and his valuable contributions there earned him a Tony award (The Antoinette Perry Award) in the United States. The most prestigious acting award in the London theatre is named the Olivier. In 1970, he was named a *Life Peer*, a lifetime member of the British House of the Lords. His title was Baron Olivier of Brighton.

Meryl Streep (1949–)

On June 22, 1949, pharmaceutical employee Harry Streep and commercial artist Mary Louis became parents to Mary Louise Streep (Meryl became their daughter's nickname at birth) in Summit, New Jersey. At age 12, Streep, a talented singer, began taking lessons from Estelle Liebling in New York City.

Streep was an awkward looking teenager—thick spectacles, braces, and a distinctive crooked nose. Upon entering high-school, Streep was determined to shed her "ugly duckling" image, so she covered her hair in lemon juice and peroxide and intentionally broke her glasses. Streep's striking new look and natural talent resulted in leading roles in school plays. She earned her first standing ovation playing Marian in a high school production of *The Music Man*, one of her favorite plays.

Streep attended college at Vassar where she played several leading roles, including the title role in Strindberg's *Miss Julie*. Her senior year she transferred to Dartmouth College to study directing and set design. Dartmouth had recently become co-ed, 6,000 men and 60 women. Feeling a bit out of place at Dartmouth, she joined a theatre group in Woodstock, Vermont. She transferred back to Vassar to complete her undergraduate studies and graduated with honors in drama.

Streep earned a three-year scholarship at The Yale School of Drama. She played several major roles at Yale, including Alma in Tennessee William's *Summer and Smoke,* Helena in *A Midsummer Night's Dream,* and the daughter in Strindberg's *The Father*. During her third year at Yale, she was cast in six out of the seven productions at the Yale Repertory Theatre. During all this, she worked part time to support herself.

After graduating with a Master of Fine Arts, Streep began working at the O'Neil Playwrights' Conference in Waterford, Connecticut. She subsequently played Imogen Parrott in *Trelawney of the Wells* at Joseph Papp's Public Theatre. While in rehearsal for *Trelawney*, she auditioned at the Phoenix Theatre and won two roles, a 180-pound woman in Tennessee Williams *27 Wagons Full of Cotton,* and a sexy secretary in Arthur Miller's *Memory of Two Mondays*. Meryl's performances in these diverse roles were so impressive that she won awards from both The Outer Circle Critics and Theatre World, plus she received a Tony nomination.

Streep was on the rise to stardom when Joseph Papp cast her in *Henry V* and *Measure for Measure* in New York's Shakespeare in the Park, but it was her portrayal of Kate in *Taming of the Shrew* opposite Raul Julia's Petruchio at the New York Public Theatre that was charged with sexual chemistry. Filmmaker Karel Reisz, who was preparing his upcoming film, *The French Lieutenant's Woman,* saw the production and felt Streep had the quality of ". . . a swash-buckling musketeer, with a special kind of daring."

Streep's first film was *Julia* starring Jane Fonda. Meryl was considered for the title role but, being an unknown, was given a small part in the film, the role of a wealthy socialite. Unfortunately, most of Streep's one scene ended up on the cutting room floor. But she did not need much time on screen to make a lasting impression. She had a 15-minute scene in the movie *Kramer vs. Kramer* and won the Oscar for Best Supporting Actress. It was Steep's performance in *Kramer vs. Kramer* that launched her career as leading lady.

Streep's first lead in a film was that of Sarah Woodruff in Karel Reisz's *The French Lieutenant's Woman*. Reisz remembered her from *Taming of the Shrew*. Shortly afterwards, she starred in the title role in *Sophie's Choice,* which won her the Academy award for Best Actress, along with a Golden Globe and New York Film Critics best actress awards. She was again nominated for a Best Actress Oscar, for her portrayal of Karen Silkwood in the film *Silkwood*.

Streep is generally considered to be one of the best American actresses of our time. She has been rewarded with 13 Oscar nominations for Best Actress. Her repertoire is diverse and includes both stage and film performances such as Eleanor Shaw in *The Manchurian Candidate* (film/2004), Gail Hartman in *The River Wild* (film/1994) and the voice of Blue Mecha/A.I. Artificial Intelligence in the film *A.I. Artificial Intelligence* (film/2001).

Sidney Poitier (1927–)

Sidney Poitier was born prematurely in Miami, Florida, where his father, a tomato farmer from Cat Island in the Bahamas, was selling fruit to the Miami Produce Exchange. His father, Reginald, and mother, Evelyn, had already lost several infants at birth. Thus, Reginald resigned himself and bought a tiny casket, the size of a small shoebox, for his sickly son. But Evelyn was desperate to affirm her baby's well-being and paid a soothsayer 50 cents to read the small infant's future. The grey-haired seer told Evelyn, "He will survive and he will not be a sickly child. He will grow up to . . . travel to most of the corners of the earth. He will walk with kings. He will be rich and famous. Your name will be carried all over the world. You must not worry about that child."

Poitier was raised on Cat Island with his six siblings. The family lived in a three-room stone hut with a thatched roof and no plumbing. Poitier spent his childhood working in the fields, feeding chickens, fetching water, grinding grits and doing other household chores. When work was finished for the day, he wandered around the island, caught fish, mixed them with peppers and lime and cooked them over a fire on the shore. He grew to love the sea and spent his spare time gazing out into the ocean and daydreaming.

Even as a young boy, Poitier loved to act. He would take the clothes off his mother's clothesline and dress himself up so that he could portray a variety of characters. Despite the obvious hardships of his childhood, island life was an excellent environment in which to develop his imagination, self-reliance, and physical prowess—all of which benefited him later as a professional actor.

Poitier grew up in a time of racial prejudice. The early movies, many of them "Westerns," typically featured a black man as a side-kick whose ignorance provided the white audience members with laughs. The early Hollywood film that epitomized racism was D. W. Griffith's *Birth of a Nation* (1915) which featured black characters who were not only ignorant, but also rapists and murderers. Despite all of the racial stereotypes, Poitier said later that he learned a great deal from movies. After the young Sidney saw a movie, he would return home and act out the entire story for his family, thus providing himself with home-made acting lessons.

There was so much poverty on the island that in January 1943, Poitier, with only the clothes on his back and a passport, traveled by boat to Miami, Florida, to make a new life. His first job was at a pharmacy. He was hired to make deliveries, by bicycle, to homes in the all white upper-class neighborhoods. Unknowingly, he attempted to deliver his first package at the front door of one of the homes. The woman who answered the door told him to make his delivery at the back door. He did not know that blacks were not permitted at the front door. Later that evening, the Ku Klux Klan, intending to punish him for his insolence, marched through the area where Poitier lived.

After moving to Atlanta, Georgia, and spending six weeks of 12-hour days washing dishes and doing other manual labor jobs at a resort, Poitier had earned $39. He used the money to buy a bus ticket to Harlem in New York. It was said that Harlem had opportunities for African Americans that the rest of the country did not.

The 16-year-old Poitier found a job in New York City, as a dishwasher in one of the popular restaurants. He soon tired of washing dishes and auditioned for the American Negro Theatre (ANT). He was rejected because of his illiteracy and strong island accent. Determined to be an actor, Poitier returned to his one room apartment and every night after work, he listened to the radio announcers and imitated their speech. He poured over newspapers in an effort to teach himself to read. Finally, he had another opportunity to audition for the ANT and was selected as an apprentice. Poitier replaced his night job with daytime employment, and took ANT acting classes in the evening. Unfortunately, following his three-month trial period, he was asked to leave the program. The faculty did not feel he had improved. Poitier wanted to continue to study at the school and offered to assume janitorial duties in exchange for another chance. His offer was accepted. Poitier worked days at one job, took class in the evening, and cleaned the school after class. His hard work and dedication finally paid off. He was given the understudy role in *Days of Our Youth,* and when the young man who had the role, missed a private rehearsal for Broadway director James Light, Poitier stepped in and gave a flawless performance. James Light offered Poitier a role in his upcoming Broadway revival of an all black production of Aristophanes' *Lysistrata*. All-black casts of traditionally white plays were trendy during this time period.

Poitier's first film role was as an extra (no lines) in the all-black film *Sepia Cinderella* (1947). In the spring of 1949, he was hired to perform in an Army training film intended to teach young recruits about how inappropriate behavior can lead to contracting venereal disease. Poitier received $100 for three days of shooting the training film.

In 1949, Poitier won his first lead on Broadway in a musical about South Africa called *Lost in the Stars*. Not long after he had been cast in *Lost in the Stars,* Twentieth Century-Fox began screen testing for a movie, starring Black actors, called *No Way Out*. Poitier auditioned for the leading role in *No Way Out* and was offered the part, but both of the projects were scheduled at the same time. Poitier's agent wanted him to do the film since it paid ten times the salary that the play offered. The agent gave the Broadway producers an opportunity to match the film's salary. They declined and Poitier began filming *No Way Out*. He received excellent reviews for his performance.

Poitier was next cast in a leading role in the controversial film *Blackboard Jungle* (1954). Although the film earned over $8 million by 1957, Poitier was paid just $3,000. The film also won the St. George Statuette at the Venice Film festival because of its humane message. Poitier's career was blossoming, and in the process, he was changing the perception of the Black American and creating acting employment opportunities for Black actors.

There were still many films produced that represented African Americans as ignorant and uneducated such as George Gershwin's folk opera *Porgy and Bess,* in which the leading character was a gin drinking gambler. Samuel Goldwyn offered Poitier the leading role, but Sidney was against portraying African Americans in this manner. He had worked hard to garner roles that would improve the way his race was viewed. During the contract negotiations for *Porgy and Bess,* Poitier was offered the lead in a film that challenged racial prejudice, Stanley Kramer's *The Defiant Ones*. Poitier, a contract player at Samuel Goldwyn's studio, had to request release time to do *The Defiant Ones*. Goldwyn made a deal with Poitier—if he accepted the lead in *Porgy and Bess,* Goldwyn would give him release time to shoot *The Defiant Ones*.

This bitter-sweet deal won Poitier the Silver Bear Award at the Berlin Film Festival for his performance in *The Defiant Ones*. The film went on to win numerous awards from organizations such as the New York Film Critics, the Film Critics' Circle, and the British Film Academy. It won nine Academy Award nominations, including a Best Actor nomination for Poitier. Although he did not win the Oscar, the nomination was a milestone for racial equality in film.

In 1960, Poitier was nominated for a Tony Award as Best Actor for *A Raisin in the Sun,* a role that he re-created in the film version. In 1963, Poitier was again nominated for an Academy Award for his performance in *Lilies of the Field*. Other nominees that year included Paul Newman, Rex Harrison, Richard Harris, and Albert Finney. When Mr. Poitier was announced as the winner of the Academy Award, "The audience's tremendous roar acknowledged not only Poitier's performance, but also the toppling of a racial barrier." The following

year, as the civil rights movement was gathering momentum, stars Marlon Brando and Laurence Olivier barred their films from being shown in segregated theatres. Poitier received an honorary Academy Award for lifetime achievement at the 74th Academy Awards ceremony.

Actress Kaitlin Hopkins

Kaitlin Hopkins

Photo Courtesy of Kaitlin Hopkins.

As an actress Kaitlin has worked extensively in theater, film, television, and radio for 25 years. Some credits include: Broadway: *How the Grinch Stole Christmas*, *Noises Off*, and *Anything Goes*. Off Broadway, she originated the role of Meredith in *Bat Boy—The Musical* receiving Drama Desk and Ovation Award nominations. She also appeared in *BARE*, *The Great American Trailer Park Musical*, Nicky Silver's *Beautiful Child*. Others include: Disney's *On the Record* (National tour), John Adams opera, *I Was Looking at the Ceiling and Then I Saw the Sky* (International tour/Edinburgh Festival/Lincoln Center) directed by Peter Sellars, *The Opposite of Sex* and *Party Come Here* (Williamstown Theatre Festival), *The Philanderer* (South Coast Repertory/Ovation nomination), and *She Loves Me* (Reprise Series/Ovation nomination). Radio: *The Heidi Chronicles*, *Working* and *Proof*. Television and film includes: *The Nanny Diaries*, *How To Kill Your Neighbor's Dog*, *Crocodile Dundee in Los Angeles*, *Rescue Me*, *Six Degrees*, *Law and Order: SVU*, *Law and Order: CI*, *The Practice*, *Spin City*, *JAG*, *Star Trek—Voyager* and three years as Dr. Kelsey Harrison on *Another World*. Training: Carnegie Mellon University (musical theater), The Royal Academy of Dramatic Arts, London. Kaitlin is a proud member of Actors Equity since 1984. For more info visit www.kaitlinhopkins.com.

FEATURE SECTION
An Interview with Actress Kaitlin Hopkins

What do you find most challenging and rewarding about acting?

Probably just making a living, coping with the stress of auditioning, and dealing with "no, you didn't get it" all the time when you have bills to pay. Often the biggest challenge we face as artists is finding ways to feel like an artist no matter what you're doing—or not doing. How to find a way to feel like an artist when you are playing a reindeer in a Christmas show in a dinner theater to pay your bills and make your (equity-required) health insurance weeks, or worse, waiting on the people attending the show—that's a challenge.

Let me make one thing clear: making a good living as an actor is hard. The people you see on television or in the movies that you assume must be rich—I've got news for you, they struggle, too. I have been a working actor for 25 years and it is still a struggle, and I work all the time! Sometimes, it is challenging because I choose to do new plays and musicals in Off Broadway theaters and the pay is very low. Sometimes it is because New York is such an expensive place to live and if you don't work for a few months, it can be difficult to get by until the next acting gig. Regardless of the reason, call me crazy, I still choose a profession that has no guarantees. There is always the stress of knowing that the audition process never ends, there is very little stability and there is constant change. I think it takes a certain kind of person to be able to live like that and still be happy. Sometimes you make a lot of money, and sometimes you make no money. That is the nature of this business and it is just that, a business. Mainly, it takes a willingness to do other types of work to support your acting habit. One thing is certain: life is never dull.

Concerning the stress of auditioning: well, there are many things that you will discover that help. For me, I find that if I think of the audition process as an opportunity for two things, I always succeed, even if I don't get the job. The first thing I do is look at it as an opportunity to do what I love for 10 minutes that day—or 30 seconds, or half an hour. It's maybe the only time that whole week I get to do that and what a great opportunity! It helps me bring so much joy to that experience which is important on so many levels. The second thing I do is use it as an opportunity to get better at what I do. If I take "I need to get this job" out of the equation, I find I do much better work. If I know I have done good work, I let that be enough. I rarely ask my agents for feedback because I know how I did. We must try not to give our power away. What I mean by that is, you must know who you are and what you bring to the table. You can't look to the casting director or the director in the room for validation that you did well. They are just casting their show and praying you are "the one"—after all, if you are, they can stop looking. Some of the best work I have ever done has been in an audition room for three people for a job I didn't get. I had to find a way for that to be enough for me. If you only see your success as "getting the job" or in relationship to how you see other actors doing, well, quite frankly, you will go crazy.

The truth is, we audition a lot—sometimes more than we work—so we have to look at that as part of our career, our process, and as an essential part of our growth as artists. The best advice I can give any actor is to find a way to LOVE the process not the RESULT. I promise you, that's where your gold is—that is where true artists live. Most painters will tell you that the final result of what ends up on the canvas means little to them, their process of the hundreds of drawings that got them there was when they were alive. If you look at Picasso's sketches, he did dozens for each painting; one realizes the incredible process he went through to find his way to ultimately what ended up on the canvas. As an actor, I much prefer rehearsals to performing. I love the discovery process—that is where I feel alive and creative. I admit learning to embrace the process as "enough" is hard to do, but getting the job needs to come as icing on the cake, second to the goal of doing your work and getting better at your craft. Bottom line is that auditioning and rehearsing are as much a part of the job as any performance I'll ever do.

So. My agent calls me. "No, you didn't get it." Hmmmmm. The challenge is understanding that "no" doesn't mean you are not good, you are just not right for the role. That one role. Over the years you develop a thicker skin, and now it rarely bothers me any more. It's part of the job. The only time it's painful for me is when you get "so close" and you know it was between you and the actor who booked the job. Often, in those cases, the audition process was long and required enormous amounts of work. It is hard not to get emotionally invested in the role. Those times it hurts a little more. You can't help but care about not getting it. Those moments are inevitable and it is okay to spend the day in bed with a pizza and watch bad TV movies to lick your wounds. Auditioning takes so much out of us, especially when the stakes are high and especially if it is a lead in a Broadway show, for example. The only advice I have (and I have a hard time practicing what I preach) is that I figure for

me to get that close, I have to be pretty damn good—there are thousands of actors who wish they even had a shot at that job. At least I had the chance to get in the room and get that close. Most didn't, including some of my established and respected peers. It is important to remember when you do not get a job that all the work you did was not wasted. Every minute you spent preparing was an investment in your craft and your career.

In regard to feeling like an artist, especially when I am not working, I have found the challenge is owning and accepting how I choose to live in the world, and using that to my advantage. What that means to me is enjoying my life outside of my work, which requires a balance. I find life often happens and is most exciting when we are not working, and that's an opportunity. I must look at unemployment as an opportunity to live, to refuel, to grow, to love and be present—look at it as a gift. It is challenging because we get frightened about not working again, not having enough money, but you won't get the next job or, if you do, be any good at it if you always function from a place of fear. The best work comes from being brave and fearless, which may seem obvious, but few in our business actually live in that dynamic, fearless place. I have learned that I have to find ways to nurture and support that attitude in my life. I need a life outside of being an artist to actually be a successful one. We make the business so important and then we lose sight of the most important things in our lives. I like to think of it this way: At my funeral, I want people to talk about the kind of person I was and how I lived, not about the work I did or my resume. It sounds simple and a little morbid, but you get my point. At the end of the day our careers are only important to us. We should never deprive ourselves of recognizing our growth as artists because we're focused on the jobs we didn't get. Don't let life pass you by because you are so focused on being famous. Being famous has nothing to do with being a great actor, and it has even less to do with being happy. I know. I've lived with and around famous people my whole life. It doesn't guarantee anything. One of the greatest performances I ever saw in the theater was by a regional actor I had never heard of in Washington, years ago—a performance and an actor I will never forget. On the other hand, I have seen many famous actors give embarrassingly bad performances on the stage over the years which I've tried diligently to forget. Enough said.

All that being said, I must also say something about how rewarding a career as an actor can be. I always tell my students, if you can live without acting and be happy doing something else, I highly recommend that. If not, hang on, 'cause it's a wild ride. Truly, there are so many ways to have creative outlets in this world, in our community theaters and churches, one doesn't need to pursue being a professional actor to have the exact same creative experience I have on a Broadway stage. Theater is theater, no matter where it is done and, honestly, the location is unimportant if it is really about doing the work. There is great work done all over this country, every day on stages in churches, schools, community theaters, regional houses, as well as Broadway. The things I ultimately find rewarding have little or nothing to do with the success I have achieved as an actor and have everything to do with the life I have lived because I am an actor. I have had the opportunity to travel all over the world. I have met and worked with amazing artists from whom I have learned so much. And the best part is, I have an opportunity to teach others and pass along to the next generation of actors and singers what I have learned—that is an amazing gift.

If you are interested in becoming an actor, I suggest reading as many plays as you can get your hands on. Read all the great books written about acting, as well as all the great books in literature. Study every acting technique you can find. There is no one way or right way to do it. The more tools you have, the more choices you have to serve each character, and, in the long run, if there is a long run, the better you will be. Personally, I think the most important thing to develop as an actor and the most overlooked is the voice. Study voice and speech. You cannot be a good actor, or a successful one, without a good, strong instrument. It is impossible to do eight shows a week if you are not trained in voice and speech, period. You need to be physically strong, flexible, and relaxed—study Alexander technique, or Pilates, or Yoga. Go to the theater, go to museums, see art, listen to music, go for walks. Look for inspiration in nature, in architecture, in everything. Study people—their behavior, their emotions, their mannerisms, their inflections. Go to the zoo, study the behavior of the animals, study psychology, learn to read music, go the ballet, treat yourself to the opera. The life of an artist, though difficult, is a great life, full of adventure, discovery, and constant change. I wouldn't change my choice, even on my worst day, for all the stability and predictability in the world. But that's just me. And you're just you. And that's why every actor is one of a kind. Peace.

Actor/Acting Teacher Steve Eastin

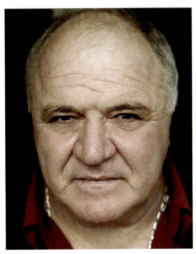

Steve Eastin grew up on the plains of eastern Colorado. He appeared in his first play at the age of six. From then on, he felt the pull of performing. He always felt his destiny lay in the coastal mountains of Southern California. He developed an affinity for such icons as Burt Lancaster and Robert Mitchum. He received his Actors Equity card at 16, when he appeared in two musicals choreographed by Michael (A Chorus Line) Bennett. In 1970, Steve graduated cum laude with a degree in English Literature Ed. from the University of Northern Colorado. While at UNC, he appeared in several productions at The Little Theater of the Rockies; a company which also boasts Nick Nolte as one of its alumni.

After completing his undergraduate work, Steve received a Fellowship to teach at the University of Arizona. While at the U of A, he was cast in his first SAG role opposite Clint Eastwood in the Universal film Joe Kidd. Subsequently, while in Tucson, he appeared in seven episodes of the NBC/ Paramount series Petrocelli with Barry Newman. In 1975, Steve fulfilled a dream by moving to Hollywood.

Upon his arrival, Steve enrolled in the Charles Conrad Studio, where he studied for four years. While there he was in Conrad's teacher training program. Soon, he began to book. He guest starred in such classic shows as *Little House, Hill St. Blues, NYPD Blue, The Gilmore Girls, The A-Team, Without A Trace* and over two hundred others. He also found himself in the ranks of the top commerical actors, having appeared in numerous spots such as Morgan Stanley, General Electric, and New York life. His feature film career has also been blessed with such films as *Field of Dreams, Bound By Honor, Austin Powers, The Scout, Con Air, Catch Me If You Can* (with Leo DiCaprio), *A Man Apart* (with Vin Diesal) and *Matchstick Men* (with Nick Cage). In 2005, Steve is re-curring on *The Gilmore Girls* and appearing in *The Black Dahlia* with Hilary Swank and Scarlett Johannsen.

Steve continues his acting career while keeping the acting school as his top priority. He teaches with a deep affinity for his students. He remembers where he came from and knows what they are up against.

http://www.imdb.com/name/nm0247611

Steve's Reel: www.SteveEastin.com

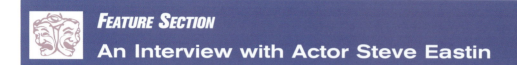

FEATURE SECTION
An Interview with Actor Steve Eastin

What inspired you to become an actor?

When I saw the movie *The Adventures of Robin Hood* with Errol Flynn at the age of six, I had as much of an epiphany as a small boy can have. I asked my parents if we could wait outside the small town theater (Wray, Colorado pop. 1800) for the actors to "come out from behind that sheet" so I could ask them how they got to do that. Then I played the lead in my first grade play *The Tenderfoot*. Me getting the part probably had something to do with my Mom being the only parent that could accompany the play on piano. At the end of the play I sang "I'm an Ol' Cowhand," heard the applause, and from that point forward, the die was cast.

What is most challenging about being an actor?

Getting to work consistently and using your time when you are not working constructively are the two greatest challenges I have faced as an actor. It is an extremely competitive environment. And it is often unfair. I have seen many actors allow this to effect their spiritual core over the years. Then this bitterness infects their work and a vicious cycle is created.

What is most enjoyable about being an actor?

What is the joy in dreams of flying? What is the joy in training yourself to experience detailed, nuanced, mixed emotion on demand? What is the joy in base jumping, extreme skiing, fighting a bull? As I've gotten older, I've come to realize that joy is not about anything specific. It is a moment to moment experience that comes to you when you are following your bliss. When your work is your worship. I have had many more powerful "religious experiences" in a darkened theater, on stage, on a movie set, and in a good class than I ever had in church. It is my feeling that you are never as close to the creator than when you are creating. I also love and respect the actor's archetypal, historical link to the ancient shamans and storytellers, to the English romantic poets, to the impressionistic painters, and all other artists. What some people consider to be a narcissistic, shallow vocation (acting) is actually a noble, high calling. Our work, when it is good, literally lifts the spirits of people and can bring about massive social change. It also is an avocation that can continue to fascinate a human being for their entire life. The act itself never gets repetitive or tiresome no matter how old you get. In fact it is just the opposite; Deepak Chopra and other neuroscientists have confirmed that exercising one's creative intelligence only enhances and extends a human life. Being a part of the tapestry of actors is also filled with wonder. We are gypsy knife fighters, at a campfire under a full moon. We are the dreamers and the sharers of dreams. In Jungian psychology we are the wild woman archetype. We are the women who run with the wolves, with only our instinct and intuition to guide us. It is truly a labor of love that brings the experience of love as you do it. It is a return to childlike wonder where there is poetry and beauty all around you. What we feel, not what we think, is the most present centered thing in our moment to moment existence. How a heart feels is one of the great mysteries of the universe. And the actor gets to spend his life immersed in that glorious mystery.

If a student was interested in becoming an actor what would you recommend that they do?

First of all they should search for ANYTHING ELSE that can fulfill them. It is not an easy, economic life. If it absolutely has to be acting like salmon have to spawn, you should read, read, read. Find everything fascinating. History, great novels, biographies. Make sure you have a way of making money while you pursue your career. Desperation and poverty are not good for your creative process. Being a "starving artist" is over romanticized and no fun. Come to know yourself. There has been a lot of scientific breakthroughs in the last five years that is drastically changing many of the holy edicts of Stanislavsky, Strasberg, and the other dinosaurs of acting instruction. An example would be a lecture on **www.Tedtalks.com** by Harvard neuroscientist Jill Bolte Taylor entitled "A Stroke of Insight." Take advantage of all the school and parks opportunities to act. You'll learn something from all your experiences whether they be good or bad. Avoid classes where they have you doing exercises. Acting is handling dialogue with velocity and assurance. So train somewhere where you handle dialogue from the very first day. If they are asking you to be a cold glass of milk, or think about the time your grandma died so you can be sad, I would get away from that as quickly as possible. And if the time comes and you make the daring leap to LA, you are welcome to come to my school (**www.eastinstudio.com**) for a free audit and see how it feels. I teach almost every class (though this week—4/21/09—I am flying to St. Louis to shoot one great scene with George Clooney in the new Jason Reitman film "Up in the Air.") I guess that's not bad for a farm kid from eastern Colorado who wanted to grow up to be Robin Hood.

Luis Salgado—Actor, Dancer, Choreographer

Luis Salgado grew up and studied acting in Vega Alta, Puerto Rico. As a teenager he started a dance academy in the local gym, and in 2001 his students were invited to perform at New York's Puerto Rican Day Parade. Following this production he moved to New York.

Since that time, Salgado has had ensemble roles in an off-Broadway production of *Fame*, *Aida* at Westchester Broadway Theatre, and *Evita* (starring Felicia Finley) at the Helen Hayes Theatre in Rockland County. He has danced in Madison Square Garden concerts by pop stars Thalía and Paulina Rubio, and in the free outdoor "Dancing for Life" performances presented in the summer by Dancers Responding to AIDS. Luis Salgado has also worked for Sociedad Educativa de las Artes, a bilingual youth theater company and arts education program. He

Luis Salgado

Photo Courtesy of Luis Salgado.

performed in SEA's revue of Latino music, ¡Tropical!, and choreographed its original musical *Los Desertores/The Dropouts*.

In 2007, he was cast as an ensemble member and as the assistant to the choreographer in the Broadway production of a new Broadway musical, *In the Heights*.

His film credits include: dance double for star Diego Luna in 2004's *Dirty Dancing: Havana Nights* and roles in *American Gangster* and *Enchanted*.

Feature Section
An Interview with Actor/Dancer/Choreographer Luis Salgado

What inspired you to become an actor/dancer/singer/performer?

For me, performing was a way of freedom. I started in elementary school in an after-school program called "enlace." After coming back from my first experience in the States, my grades were low because I didn't speak the language. When I returned to Puerto Rico, I met someone special who became my mentor over the years, and thanks to him I developed a passion for the arts.

Everything having to do with acting, singing, and dancing was a huge dream for me; it was something I wanted to accomplish, and until this day it still is. It is my profession and I have been making my living from performing for a long time, but I look at it with the same desire or more than before. Art IS FULL OF LIFE AND DOING THINGS so you can never know too much. There is always more to learn!

It was not until I closed my dancing school and moved to NY that I fell so strongly in love with musical theatre. Ever since then it has been like a constant quest for learning that I know will always be part of me, and that makes each job very fun. "Training is everything; we have to be ready for when the opportunity comes." I think that that opportunity is life and it's in front of me every single day.

What do you feel is most challenging about performing?

There are two ways for me to see this question. Sometimes the challenge is to have either too much or too little of the work.

In Puerto Rico it was very difficult to let go when involved in a project. The shows take a long time to build and sometimes they run for only three performances. I just visited the island (Puerto Rico) last year to do *A Chorus Line*. I was there for only a month, but the cast worked on it for almost six months (rehearsing) and did a total of only seven performances . . . so, that is hard and it's also passion.

In NY it is the opposite. I think the challenge is being really aware of your body when doing a show for so long. Your voice and body are the tools that make the show happen and doing eight shows a week can become a hard task on them both. Sometimes you are doing other jobs at the same time and it's important to know how much extra work to put on your self without risking your show. For me teaching is also a passion, but it affects my chords for the singing, so when I am active in a show I cut down my teaching the most I can.

What is most rewarding regarding performing?

Wow! I think the opportunity to grow, to learn. There is so much that every single show I do adds to my own self. Every show has some kind of human understanding, a point of view, and when you jump on board, your own self is jumping into a growing process. You can take the journey or not; it is up to you, but there is something that always ends up striking you big time. In my case that one moment affects me for life in most cases pushing me to be better.

There is also the blessing of the audience. It is not only the fact that we give out talent and it's valued as shown through the applause, the e-mails, the comments; but it is really giving something away to the world and you see it, you are a part of it.

I remember how theatre changed my life. The first time I saw Pinocchio I could not sleep for a few days. Now to have the honor of doing that, of giving that emotion, that excitement, that thing to someone, that is BEYOND BELIEF!

Shows like *In the Heights*—where I work at the moment—make my people feel proud of who they are. It celebrates a culture and makes everyone to want to be better. That is priceless.

Do you have a favorite role? Is so, what? Why did you like it?

I enjoyed going home to Puerto Rico a lot and having the challenge of playing Bobby in *A Chorus Line*. That is a "miscast" in the states, but it was gold for me on the island and I had a lot of fun doing it.

I remember the time I did Joe Vegas in *Fame* on 42nd Street with fond memories because my mom saw me for the first time in NYC doing a role and she can never forget it. . . . Everything she has seen after that for her has been good, but it has not been that experience and joy of the first time seeing her son in NY.

If a student was interested in becoming an actor/performer how might he or she begin?

I would say the best way to start is starting! A lot of times people wait too long to do something. And if it really is a passion, you just have to get on it. I think I am an extremist, because for me it is all or nothing. I think life is serious, but I take it as a great game and I play living! It works for me!

When I teach workshops, I always tell people about how much tension there is when trying to get a job. If you just go to the audition thinking it is like taking a class, you come across much more relaxed and people see YOU. That in a lot of cases will get you the job. So enjoy the process, live to the fullest, and PLAY!

A note from Luis Salgado

Theatre is for me a lot more than entertainment. It serves that purpose and it does not always have to be too heavy, but I think an artist always has to have a mission. There are a lot of people who come into the business because they want fame and money. I would say look into your heart, search if there is really that passion, and if that passion and desire in you are honest, then immerse yourself in it. If not, then look for your true passion; don't hurt the arts . . .

Summary

Actors practice healthy eating habits and incorporate exercise, and dental and skin care into their daily regimen. Actors also strive to master interpersonal skills such as active listening, networking, organization, and time management. Becoming a professional actor may not interest you, but anyone can benefit from a healthy lifestyle and interpersonal skills. If you are

interested in acting as a profession then you will need to enroll in an actor training program, solicit an agent to represent you, and join one or both of the actors' unions. Perhaps with a little luck and a great deal of hard work, persistence, and self-discipline, you will become an Academy award winning actor. Or you can apply the skills that actors use to become successful in another profession. But keep in mind that acting can also be a rewarding hobby and you can always audition for plays at your community theatre.

The Theatre in Your Career

I. Getting the Job—No Matter What Your Vocation

Before going to an interview, research the company, the current employees, and the specific job. Assess your skills and the needs of the company. Be prepared to explain how your specific skills will benefit the company and its employees.

During the interview, wait to sit down until you are offered a seat, call each person by his or her name (research ahead of time to learn the names), use active listening skills, and use eye contact and open body language. When leaving the interview, wait to be offered a hand-shake, do not offer one yourself, since some people do not like to shake hands.

After the interview, write and send a brief thank-you note to the interviewers. Tell them that you appreciated their time and interest and that you look forward to hearing from them.

Active Learning Assignment
"Bringing Theatre to Life"

I. **Character Analysis**

As a group, create a brief description of each of the characters in your play. A character description includes information such as age, race, religion, marital status, amount and type of education, occupation, living arrangements, relationship to the other characters, and any other traits that define the character.

II. **Voice and Body—Warm-up**

Actors warm up their voices and bodies before rehearsing on-stage. If you are not an actor, warming up before an important presentation or job interview will help to relax you. Let us experience the benefits of stretching while we sit in our chairs.

A. **Hand and Wrist Stretch**

1. Massage your own hands.
2. Next, make small circles with your hands by turning them at the wrists. Make the circles in different directions.
3. Make fists.
4. Flex out your hands as if your fingers were reaching for something.
5. Make fists.

6. Flex out your hands.

7. Release.

B. **Head and Neck Stretch**

1. Place your feet on the floor in front of you.

2. Allow your hands to rest on your lap or hang by your side.

3. Imagine that there is a large balloon attached to your right wrist.

4. Allow the balloon to float right up, until it is fully extended above your head.

5. Remember to keep breathing, your jaw relaxed, lips slightly parted.

6. Now, allow your right hand to rest on your left ear. The weight of your right hand will draw your head and neck down, so that your right ear is close to your right shoulder.

7. Breathe so that you feel in the left side of your neck.

8. Allow the right hand to float off of your left ear and allow your head and neck to float back to its original position.

9. Repeat. This time the left hand will rest on the right ear. Don't forget to breathe deeply.

C. **Shoulder Stretch**

1. While breathing deeply, roll both of your shoulders forward. Do this for several rotations.

2. While breathing deeply, roll both of your shoulders backward. Do this for several rotations.

3. While breathing deeply, roll your right shoulder forward. While the right shoulder is rolling forward, roll your left shoulder backward. Do this for several rotations.

4. While breathing deeply, roll your left shoulder forward. While the left shoulder is rolling forward, roll your right shoulder backward. Do this for several rotations.

D. **Facial Stretch**

1. Open your eyes and mouth as much as you can.

2. Close your eyes and mouth as much as you can.

3. Repeat steps one and two a couple of times.

E. **Voice Massage**

1. Hum the letter "M." Experiment with high and low pitches, and loud and soft volumes.

2. Hum a song you like.

Note: How Hollywood Got Its Name

H. H. Wilcox, a Kansas prohibitionist, laid out a portion of Los Angeles as a real-estate subdivision known as Cahuenga Valley where he had settled on a huge ranch in 1887. A year later his wife renamed it Hollywoodland after a friend's home in Chicago.

Act II: Scene V

Designing

The Performance Space

Before a production can be mounted, a performance space has to be secured.

Before a production can be mounted, a performance space has to be secured. Commercial companies frequently rent theatres for their productions; most regional theatre companies own complexes that include two or three different types of stages; college and university theatres also have several performing spaces. The following section discusses traditional and non-traditional stage configurations.

Traditional Theatrical Spaces

Traditional indoor theatres most commonly use one of three stage configurations: the proscenium arch, *the* arena *stage, or the* thrust *stage.*

Traditional indoor theatres most commonly use one of three stage configurations: the *proscenium arch* or picture frame stage (similar to a movie theatre); the *arena* stage in which the audience sits on all sides; or the *thrust* stage, which allows for seating around three sides.

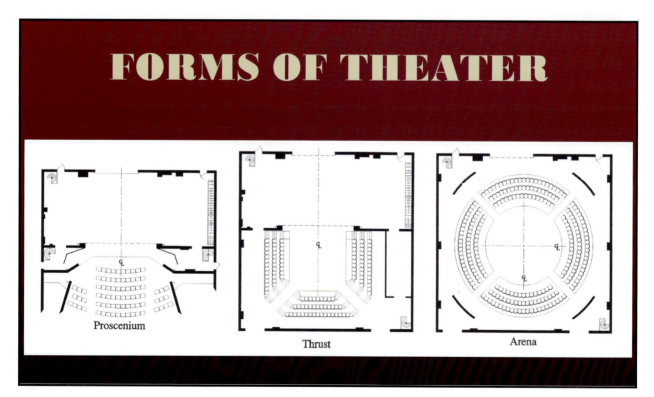

Illustration by Christopher Domanski

Designing   203

Black Box Theatre

Another theatrical space is a flexible theatre or, as it is commonly known, a black box. This is typically a small square or rectangular space which is often painted black. The seating arrangement in a black box can be configured into a proscenium space, an arena space, or a thrust space to suit the particular play—being mounted. Black box theatres are often used to produce intimate (small cast) plays or experimental works.

Another theatrical space is a flexible theatre or, as it is commonly known, a black box.

Other Theatrical Spaces

Amphitheatres feature outdoor stages; some even have canopies over the audience to protect from inclement weather. Occasionally, a production is performed without a traditional stage. These spaces are referred to as *environmental* and the performance may take place virtually anywhere.

Amphitheatres feature outdoor stages.

A production performed without a traditional stage is referred to as environmental.

Courtyard of a University Campus

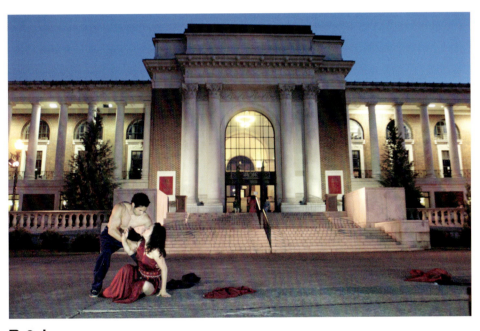

R & J

Directed by Scott Palmer. *Photo courtesy of Oregon State University.*

Theatre may be performed in any space accommodating at least one actor and one audience member.

The Classroom as a Theatre

Theatre may be performed in any space accommodating at least one actor and one audience member. Even the average classroom can accommodate a performance, and many are equipped with computers and a screen intended for PowerPoint presentations. Productions staged in a classroom may be enhanced by using PowerPoint images as scenic backdrops.

Active Learning Assignment
"Bringing Theatre to Life"

I. The Theatrical Space

One of the members in each group tells a short story to the rest of the group who have arranged themselves in a configuration similar to that of an arena stage. Afterward, the members will reconfigure themselves to simulate a thrust stage, then a proscenium stage, and last an environmental space. Each time, a different speaker tells a new story. All of the group members take turns as the speakers.

Critical Thinking in Class Discussion

I. What was it like for you to watch a performance in arena and thrust settings?

II. How do they differ from performances you have seen in a proscenium setting?

III. What was it like to perform in the arena and thrust settings?

IV. Were the arena and thrust stages more or less difficult to perform in? Why?

V. Which arrangement did you prefer? Why?

VI. Which space would be the most effective to stage your final group project? Why?

Designing the Production

Once the location for the production has been determined, the scenic, lighting, costume, properties, and sound designers can begin to flesh out the director's concept.

Once the location for the production has been determined, the scenic, lighting, costume, properties, and sound designers can begin to flesh out the director's concept. This section of the chapter provides an overview of the techniques used by designers who specialize in each of the disciplines. Although each discipline has its idiosyncrasies, there are also commonalities directly relating to the continuity and truthfulness of the production.

The Playboy of the Western World

Directed by Dr. Charlotte Headrick. Production from Oregon State University. *Photograph courtesy of Jim Folts.*

Commonalities—Designers and the Realization of the Director's Concept

Design artists strive to create designs that are stimulating and imaginative while also following the director's production concept. During the initial production meeting, the director communicates his or her concept by providing the designer with a brief description, a visual image, or both. For example, a director working on *Into the Woods* might describe his or her concept for the production as "*Cirque Du Soleil* in a fairytale land." If a director prefers to present his or her concept for Samuel Beckett's *Waiting for Godot* by using visual images, he or she might provide the designers with a picture or painting—say a Salvador Dali. There are directors who prefer to dictate the entire look of the design—"everyone should wear light blue leotards and pink ballet shoes"—but such an approach can hinder the production since it leaves the designers little room for creativity.

After the initial meeting, the designers research the director's concept as it relates to the overall production. In addition to compiling formal research, they will also take numerous production elements into consideration, including the time period, location (country, city, state, house/hotel, park, etc.), and the cultural and social status of the characters. The designers will also need to consider special technical requirements such as quick changes and the functionality of each design element.

Several production meetings take place during the course of the production's development, but the agenda of the meetings is similar—designs are presented, discussed, and adjustments are made. Ideally, all designs should be finalized early in the production process in order to provide a sufficient amount of time to construct the scenery, costumes, etc.

Designers must communicate effectively with one other in order to insure that the designs enhance one another. Particular attention is given to the overall colors and textures used in a production. Finally, all of the designers must insure that their designs can be fully realized within the budgetary constraints of the production.

Design artists strive to create designs that are stimulating and imaginative while also following the director's production concept.

After the initial meeting, the designers research the director's concept as it relates to the overall production.

The designers will also need to consider special technical requirements such as quick changes and the functionality of each design element.

An Overview of the Techniques Used by Designers

Scenic Artists

The first steps in designing scenery for a production include drafting a ground plan and making a sketch and/or a three-dimensional model of the design.

These are shown to the director and the rest of the artistic team at a production meeting. Oftentimes, the director or a member of the team will have questions or comments for the scenic designer. This is where the research gathered early in the design process aids the designer in explaining to the artistic team why, for example, the design features or emphasizes certain scenic elements. The director may ask the designer to make adjustments if the concept has been altered or if new scenic requirements have appeared since the initial meeting.

Ideally, all designs should be finalized early in the production process in order to provide a sufficient amount of time to construct the scenery, costumes, etc.

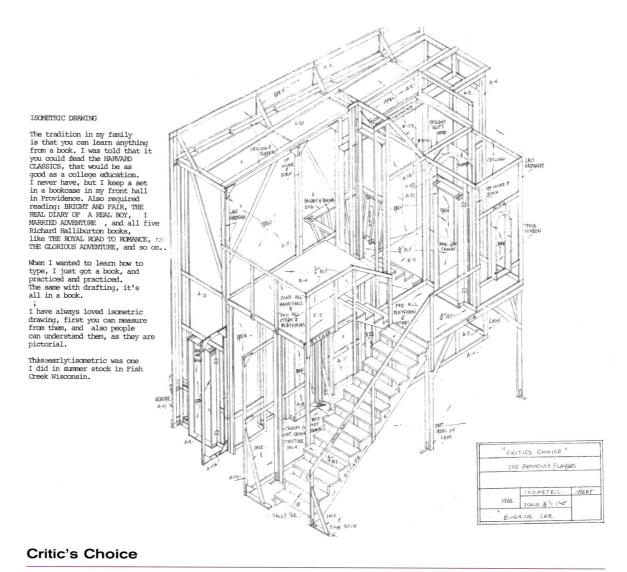

ISOMETRIC DRAWING

The tradition in my family is that you can learn anything from a book. I was told that it you could read the HARVARD CLASSICS, that would be as good as a college education. I never have, but I keep a set in a bookcase in my front hall in Providence. Also required reading: BRIGHT AND FAIR, THE REAL DIARY OF A REAL BOY, I MARRIED ADVENTURE , and all five Richard Halliburton books, like THE ROYAL ROAD TO ROMANCE, THE GLORIOUS ADVENTURE, and so on..

When I wanted to learn how to type, I just got a book, and practiced and practiced. The same with drafting, it's all in a book.

I have always loved isometric drawing, first you can measure from them, and also people can understand them, as they are pictorial.

This early isometric was one I did in summer stock in Fish Creek Wisconsin.

Critic's Choice

Isometric Drawing/Design and Explanation by Eugene Lee. *Courtesy of Eugene Lee.*

Building the Set

Once the scenic design is finalized, the design is turned over to the technical director who is responsible for its construction. Of course, other individuals work with the technical director to realize the design. These include the shop foreman, carpenters, and scenic painters.

Particular attention is given to the overall colors and textures used in a production.

Eugene Lee

Photograph courtesy of Constance Brown.

Scenic Designer Eugene Lee

Mr. Lee has been the resident designer at Trinity Repertory Company since 1967 when he was hired to design *The Threepenny Opera* by Adrian Hall. He has B.F.A.'s from The Art Institute of Chicago and Carnegie Mellon University and a M.F.A. from The Yale School of Drama, and honorary Ph.D.'s from DePaul University, Rhode Island College, and The Rhode Island School of Design. He has won many awards including: The Tony, The Drama Desk Award, The Outer Critics Circle Award, The Pell Award, The American Theatre Wing's Design Award, The Lucille Lortel Award, The Theatre La Ovation Award, The Boston Critics Circle Award, the Rhode Island Governor's Arts Award, and was recently inducted into the New York Theater Hall of Fame. Mr. Lee designs *Saturday Night Live*, and is represented on Broadway with *Wicked* and *The Pirate Queen*. He is visiting professor at Brown University at the Oenslager Studios, and lives on Providence's East Side with his wife, Brooke, and their dog, George.

Feature Section
Eugene Lee Comments on His Art and Career

The Graduate Design Program Created by Eugene Lee

The three-year graduate program at Oenslager Studios offers a practicum in design for stage and media.

Eugene Lee, founder of the Oenslager Studios, sets out his vision for a pedagogy of practice:

> "It is most important to create an environment where impossible things happen, where young designers, in a COLLABORATIVE, PROFESSIONAL studio, work together with the candor, openness and sense of play that produces the very best theatre. . . ."

The Oenslager Studio is:
Devoted to the Practice of Believing Impossible Things

Believing the Impossible: Eugene Lee Solving Scenic Problems

Brother to Dragons, was kind of classic Adrian Hall. The set was kind of an abstract barn, and the story was from the epic poem by Robert Penn Warren, about a nephew of Thomas Jefferson who killed and butchered one of his slaves, for breaking a pitcher in his master's house. It was story telling at its best. It brought to question of how to kill a person on stage. We finally decided that we might hang the black actor (Ed Hall) by his feet if he agreed, and then bring on a large butcher block and a side of meat, and that chopping the meat would be "real business," and the company would make all the sounds, (Adrian almost never used recorded sound effects) of the flesh being tossed into the fire. There were many wonderful moments: a dead woman who opened and sat in her own grave (every night before the performance the actor would go and dust her grave), a storm created by a large caged swinging light, and apple bobbing, which always sent water into the fifth row of the audience. The only thing missing was a large cannon. Adrian never had an office in the theatre, much less a board room; we would meet at his house or some restaurant. There were no production managers, and no production meetings. The set was developed out of work with the actors. A very different time than now and very creative.

Eugene Lee Remembers His First Tony Award

I first met Harold Prince when I was asked to design *Candide,* at The Chelsea Theatre in Brooklyn. Harold was on the board and he was to direct a revival of *Candide* which had played on Broadway, but was not a success.

Having already flattened their floor for *Slaveship,* I did it again. I drew a little courtyard-like space, with a small proscenium stage at one end, and a thrust stage at the other. In the center I put a little platform, and I connected these with little road-like ramps, and bridges. The audience sat on benches on the sides and stools in the middle. The orchestra was in three locations. I did the lighting in my usual way, and got myself into trouble with the director. I usually have a very specific idea for particular moment and hung the lights accordingly, i.e., little hanging bulbs when Candide wanders through the audience. So I showed him that, he said, "that's nice, but I can see something else" and of course I was in big trouble. But of course it became a hit and we moved it to Broadway the best we could. For the design I won my very first Tony award, and the Chelsea staff screamed from the top balcony, (the only seats that they could afford) at the Shubert Theatre, a sweet moment.

As it turns out Harold Prince has been my neighbor at Rockefeller Center these many years. His is one of the last, (maybe last) old time offices, it is great to see George Abbot on the door. I count him as one of my good friends, he once gave me a tour of Rome, our paths have crossed and crisscrossed over the years, I love him dearly.

Thoughts on Scenic Design by Eugene Lee

Set design! Best job in the world!
Every project is different.
I get up early, have some coffee, and read *The New York Times*.
I am in my studio by 8.
I tend to work on a number of projects at once.
I usually have a few kids working with me, I try to suggest them for jobs I can't do.
I have dinner at 7.

Designs by Eugene Lee

Courtesy of Eugene Lee

The Homecoming by Pinter

Typical photo of a set model. I take the picture with my faithful Pentex K1000. One of the best and very simple camera. I have a little collection. I buy them when I can find them. They are often used in first year photography classes at The Rhode Island School of Design.

I use just standard color print film. After they are developed I often work on the photo a bit with felt tip markers. Then I print them in black and white on my PH printer. Different speeds, give various results. (Written by Eugene Lee)

Act II: Scene V

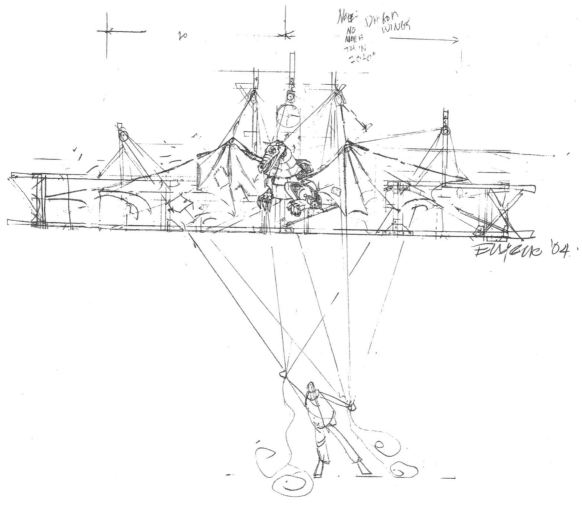

An Early Draft for *Wicked*

Mauritis

One fine day my phone rang, on the other end was the playwright Theresa Rebeck. I like her very much, and I had designed her play THE BELLS, at the McCarter in Princeton. She asked if I could design a play she had written that was being produced by the Huntington Theater Company, in Boston. It turned out to be a sweet little play called MAURITUS. It was mostly set in a dusty stamp collectors office, but it also had a short scene in a diner and another in a shabby livingroom. Since she had written NO transitions, I decided to have the diner and the livingroom, just pull out of the walls of the office. It was a fine idea and worked quite well. (Written by Eugene Lee)

Active Learning Assignment
"Bringing Theatre to Life"

I. **Designing Your Set**

Begin by measuring the area of the classroom that will be used as the stage. On a piece of plain or graph paper, draw (with a pencil) an overhead sketch (*a ground plan*) indicating where each set piece will be located—attempt to make the ground plan as close to scale as possible (1/8″ or 1/4″ for every 1′ of actual floor space.) You need to be certain that there will be room for your set pieces and for the actors to move freely in the space. Some productions may have more than one location. Draw one ground plan for each location. When you are finished with your plans, examine them for composition, the same way you would if you were taking a photograph. You want to create a set that is not only practical but is also visually interesting. If you are not satisfied with the composition, erase the objects and begin again. Once you are satisfied, share your plans with the rest of your group, making sure that all are in agreement.

II. **Building Your Set**

More than likely, these in-class productions will not have a budget but sets can be created with old boxes, borrowed furniture, and a little imagination.

First, survey your classroom and surrounding areas to determine what furniture is there that might be used to create your set. If there is a particular set piece that cannot be found nearby, a suitable substitute may be found in a friend's dorm room. Of course, you need to ask before borrowing furniture and return it promptly in its original condition. Keep in mind that set pieces can also be inexpensively built using cardboard boxes, paints, glue, and other craft items.

III. **Using Computer Images as Backdrops**

Many classrooms have computers and screens for PowerPoint presentations. If your classroom is so equipped, you can burn a compact disc with images that can serve as a backdrop for your production. Of course, when an actor walks in front of the projection the image will be distorted, but your audience should be employing the "willing suspension of disbelief." (Note: If projected images are used someone will need to be assigned to run them.)

IV. **Scene Changes**

If your production has multiple settings, be sure to assign running crew members to move the set pieces. The changes need to be rehearsed so that they run smoothly and safely.

Costume Designers

After the research has been compiled and analyzed, a sketch is made of each of the costumes on body forms resembling the actors' sizes and shapes. The sketches are colorized with water colors, gouache, pastels, and/or other artist's media. The designer also attaches a *swatch* (a small piece of the actual fabric) to each sketch to give the director and the team an idea of what the costumes will look like and how, due to the weight and cut of the garments, they will move with the actors. (The way that the costume is constructed, particularly the way that the fabric is cut, whether on the bias or not, affects the way the garment will hang and move with the actor.) Some costume designers, such as William Ivey Long assemble a *collage* incorporating the designs that all of the characters will be wearing on stage at any one time. This collage may also contain some of the early research materials. Collages help designers create an overall stage picture that is both attractive and cohesive.

These sketches or collages are shown to the artistic team during a production meeting. Often, the director or a member of the production team will have questions for the costume designer. Again, the research that was gathered early in the design process will aid the designer in explaining to the artistic team why the design was created to feature certain elements. The director may ask the designer to make adjustments if new costume requirements have presented themselves since the initial meeting. Once the design has been finalized, the costume designer will turn it over to a costume technologist for the actual construction. (In the professional theatre, the costume designer designs the costumes and oversees construction, but in most community and educational theatres, the designer is also responsible for building the costumes.) Much like the technical director, the costume technologist has several assistants including *drapers* and *stitchers*.

Building the Costumes

Usually the first item of business after the designs have been approved is to measure all of the actors. These measurements are often taken during the first rehearsal, and after an initial fitting, the actors will come in to the costume shop periodically to try on their costumes during various stages of construction.

After measurements are taken, the next step for costume designers is the creation of a pattern with which to cut and sew the fabric into the final project. In some cases, two or more prefabricated patterns may be combined to

Ben Jonson's "The Silent Women"

Adapted and directed for Oregon State University theatre by Scott Palmer. *Photo Courtesy of Oregon State University.*

create the desired look, but many designers create their own original patterns for the costumes.

Draping is another method used in costume design. This technique involves laying a piece (or pieces) of fabric on a life size body form and manipulating (cutting and pinning) the fabric into the desired shape. Many times, if a costume is to be made of an expensive material, a mock-up is first constructed of muslin or scrap material. If the costume designer is on a tight budget or time constraint, he or she may select to alter existing costumes, use donated items, or rent or borrow costume pieces.

Costume Running Crew

Although the costume designer's job is complete when the production opens, numerous running crew members are needed during the production to insure that the actors get into their costumes easily and on-time. Costume running crew members pre-set costumes on the stage if characters actually use them in a scene and function as *dressers* to help actors with quick changes—an actor might have less than a minute to change into a new costume. Running crew members repair costumes in emergencies (perhaps an actor tears his or her slacks during a scene). Running crew members also make sure that costumes are hung up in appropriate places at the end of the performance and see to it that underwear and other garments are washed or cleaned before they are used again.

Costume Designer William Ivey Long

William Ivey Long

Photograph courtesy of William Ivey Long.

Born in 1947, William Ivey Long pursed a degree in Art History at the University of North Carolina at Chapel Hill. During his studies visiting professor Betty Smith suggested that he apply to the design program at Yale University. While at Yale he met Sigourney Weaver (his roommate), Christopher Durang and Meryl Streep. He also studied with renowned designer Ming Cho Lee—a mentor to Long. Since graduation he has designed numerous productions. Long has won Tony Awards for his costume designs of the following *Nine*, *Crazy for You*, *The Producers*, *Hairspray* and *Grey Gardens*. He is the recipient of a Drama Desk Award for *Hairspray, The Producers, Guys and Dolls, Lend Me a Tenor* and *Nine*. He was inducted into the Theatre Hall of Fame in January 2006.

A Quote by William Ivey Long Regarding Costumes

"Costumes are like New York City taxis. Taxis look like cars, drive like cars, run like cars, but to be in New York City they must withstand more than any other car in any other city must withstand with all the traffic, scrapes, bumps, and bangs, and at the end of the day it must still be a car ready for the next day. Costumes are quite similar. While they have to look like a suit or dress, wear like a suit or dress and fit like a suit or dress, they must endure constant pulling, zipping, stretching—much more than 'normal' clothing, and still be ready for the next performance."

Costume Designer Theoni Aldredge

Theoni Aldredge

Photograph courtesy of Theoni Aldredge.

Theoni V. Aldredge was born in Athens, Greece, in 1932. She is a renowned costume designer in the theatre, opera, ballet, film and television. Aldredge received her formal training at the American School in Athens and at the Goodman Theatre in Chicago. Her first Broadway design credit was for Geraldine Page's in Tennessee Williams' *Sweet Bird of Youth* in 1959. Since then she has been the recipient of an Oscar and a British Academy Award for her work on *The Great Gatsby* (1974). Aldredge has designed over 150 productions including the original Broadway production of *Hair* (1967) and *A Chorus Line* (1975). Aldredge has been the recipient of three academy awards—*Annie (1977)*, Barnum (1980) and *La Cage aux Folles* (1984).

FEATURE SECTION

Thoughts on Costume Design by Theoni Aldredge

Theatre is a common effort by a lot of people, all of them working towards a common goal, the play and the director's vision. Born in Greece I was exposed to theatre at a young age—I was eight years old when my father took me to see *Oedipus* and *King Lear*. The actors playing the two leading roles were friends of my fathers. I knew them but they looked so different in clothes I had never seen before. It was magic! This feeling stayed with me

all these years. It's still magic! Go to the theatre as often as you can. You learn a lot every time the curtain goes up anywhere! Don't let anybody tell you "it can't be done" yes "it can."

And when I get depressed, we all do one time or another, I sing to myself, the last few lines of my favorite show *A Chorus Line* ". . . won't forget, can't regret, what I did for love . . ." And then I know why I do what I do.

Active Learning Assignment
"Bringing Theatre to Life"

Note: This activity is intended to give all students an opportunity to explore *basic* costume design techniques—not the actual rendering techniques that a professional designer would use. The exercise is based on cutting and pasting in order to afford those students without drawing skills the opportunity to successfully participate.

I. Designing the costumes for the final project

   A. The play that you have written for your final presentation will be the subject for your costume designs.

   B. You will need magazines that contain lots of pictures of people, scissors, glue, colored pencils or pens, and several sheets of plain white paper.

   C. Cut out figures from the magazines to represent each of the characters in your play. Try to select figures that are standing (include the head and feet) and who are wearing clothing that is form fitting. Outline each of the figures on separate sheets of paper and mark the character's names under the figures. If you are an artist, feel free to draw your own figures.

   D. Decide what you think the theme of the play is. For example, perhaps you feel that *A Doll's House* is about liberation and self reliance. Then, as a group, agree on a theme and a concept for your play.

   E. Imagine the type of clothing each character might wear. What colors would the character wear? Remember to consider the time period in which the play is set, the time of year, and the time of day.

   F. Look through magazines to find clothes that resemble your ideas for the first scene of the play. If you cannot find exactly what you are looking for, trace figures on a separate sheet of paper, sketch the costumes, cut them out, and paste the items of clothing that you have selected on the appropriate characters. Do this for each scene in the play.

II. Collecting, Building, and Altering the Costume Pieces for the Final In-Class Project

Once each group has decided what costumes will work best for their respective productions, it is time to collect, build, or alter existing costumes. Since there is not a budget for these final group projects, the costume design process will become a sort of treasure hunt. Don't allow a lack of funds to discourage the group. Remember that many theatre companies, particularly community and educational organizations, commonly use borrowed and/or found costumes.

   A. First, examine the group's designs.

B. Begin the costume "treasure hunt." Ask around. Very often friends may have old Halloween costumes or other accessories that may be used. If someone does lend the group some clothing, then, of course, they will need to be returned in their original condition (be particularly careful of makeup stains). The group might even consider listing the donor in the program.

C. Some costume pieces may need to be purchased; if so, patronize thrift or discount stores.

D. If the group finds a costume that is reasonably close to the desired design, minor alterations can be made very simply. If a costume is too big, use safety pins; if it is the wrong color, perhaps it can be dyed or painted; hobby stores carry different types of paints or other materials that can be effective.

E. Finally, remember that this is a class project; it does not have to be perfect. The costumes will work well for the project if they have been assembled with thought and creativity.

III. **Costume Running Crew**

If a group's production requires quick costume changes, a running crew should be formed. An individual does not have to be just on the costume running crew. He or she can double as an actor and/or a scenic running crew member, etc. The idea is that all members of the group work together as a team in order to ensure the smoothest possible production.

The Theatre in Your Career

Costuming is a part of our everyday lives. Everyday, we each dress in a particular manner and our choices are based on research—the weather, the time of day, the time of year, and the occasion. Other factors include the person's ethnic background, age, sex, occupation, and city, state, and country of residence.

I. **Color and Clothing**

Color has been proven to have an emotional impact on individuals; thus, it is important to consciously consider color when stocking a wardrobe.

Blue denotes trust and respect, which is the reason attorneys and police officers wear blue. Blue is an excellent color to wear to job interviews.

Red is an attention getting color, but if over used, it can appear "cheap."

Pink is a calming color and is used to reduce anger and stress in some prisons and jails.

Brown suggests openness and friendliness.

Black clothing suggests power, wisdom, and authority—priests and judges wear black.

White apparel with black accents is viewed as a very sophisticated combination.

Yellow is the epitome of happiness.

Green denotes warmth and friendliness.

II. **Styles for Job Interviews**

When selecting what to wear to a job interview, research the potential employer. Most businesses these days have sites on the Internet and, frequently, these include pictures of employees. When you interview, "costume" yourself in a similar fashion.

The following is a list of suggested clothing pieces that can be worn to most job interviews. (To save money, patronize thrift and second hand shops.)

Men: a pair of dark colored slacks, a dark brown or black leather belt with matching hard soled shoes (clean, polished, and with new laces), a button-down dress shirt—free of stains and wrinkles (look for permapress), a tie, a sports jacket that coordinates with the slacks or perhaps a dark colored suit.

Women: a pair of dark-colored, loose fitting slacks or a dark-colored skirt (that will hang at least three inches past the knee), a button-up blouse, a jacket that matches the slacks or skirt, a dark leather belt, and a pair of matching dark-colored heels (not spiked—no more than a 2-1/2-inch heel), and nude or dark-colored hose.

Lighting Designers

Lighting provides illumination, but it also enhances mood, delineates seasonal and time changes, adds dimension and texture to the overall composition, draws the audiences attention to a desired area on the stage, and provides theatrical spectacle. The lighting designer will typically approach a new production in the same manner as other designers, through research and production meetings. He or she will then create a *lighting plot* which will indicate where the lighting instruments will need to be positioned in order to create the desired lighting effects.

The lighting plot will also include information about the color of the *gels* (specialized "cellophane-like" plastic that, when inserted in front of the lamp, changes the color of the light) and/or *gobos* (pieces of metal that have been cut into a shape, perhaps a window frame, which when illuminated will cast the shadow of the shape) that will be inserted into the instruments. New lighting technology includes moving lights, although not all theatres have them, which can be programmed to create special effects such as "moving" water and "dancing" fire. The use of a fog machine in certain lighting designs can add an eerie quality to the overall look.

Before the lighting designer begins to design a production, he or she must first determine what lighting instruments the theatre owns or intends to rent. He or she must also determine where the instruments can be

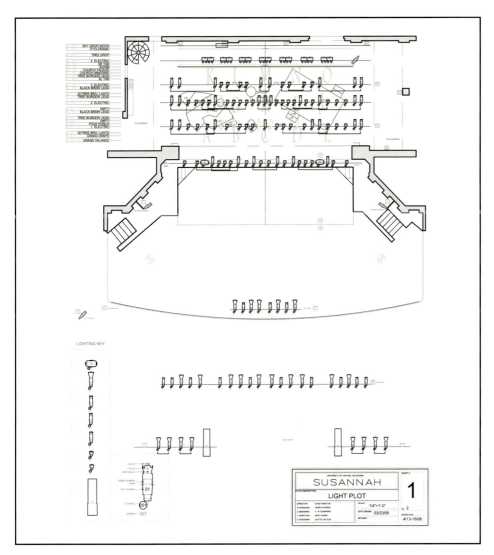

Lighting Plot for *Susannah* (opera)

Designed by Christopher Domanski. *Photograph courtesy of Christopher Domanski.*

mounted—lighting trees, overhead electrics, or lighting grids. The lighting designer and the scenic designer must work very closely to insure that a lighting instrument will not be blocked by a piece of scenery.

Other lighting design considerations include the colors and textures of the set and the costumes. For example, if the set and costumes are neutral in color, bold color gels will stand out, while pale color gels will blend in. Soft-sided or textured scenery tends to absorb more light than hard-sided scenery.

After the design plot has been created and approved, the master electrician will hang the lighting instruments and mount all *practical lights* (table lamps, for example, operated by the actors on-stage). The lighting instruments are then *focused* (positioned for optimal illumination and effect). Once the lights have been focused, the light *cues* (the point in the production that lighting instruments will be turned off or on) will be programmed into a lighting control board. During the production, the light cues will be called by the stage manager.

Lighting Designer Jennifer Tipton

Jennifer Tipton is one of the most distinguished lighting designers of the modern theatre with hundreds of professional credits to her name. Born in Columbus, Ohio, she received a B.A. in English from Cornell University. After graduation, she moved to New York to pursue a life in dance, a field that introduced her to her true love—lighting. In 1963, she began working with the Paul Taylor Dance Company, but it was her stunning design for Jerome Robbins' *Celebration: The Art of the Pas de Deux* (1973) at Spoleto, Italy, that solidified her reputation as one of the modern theatre's most exceptional lighting designers.

Jennifer Tipton has designed celebrated productions around the globe. Some of her representative work include: *For Colored Girls Who Have Considered Suicide When the Rainbow Is Enuf* by Ntosake Shange, directed by Oz Scott, The New York Shakespeare Festival, and the Newman Theatre, New York City (1976), *The Nutcracker* choreographed by Mikhail Baryshnikov, American Ballet Theater (1976) *The Cherry Orchard* directed by Andrei Serban, New York Shakespeare Festival (1977) *Happy End* by Bertolt Brecht and Kurt Weill, directed by Robert Kalfin, BAM & The Martin Beck Theater, New York City (1977) *Bosoms and Neglect* by John Guare, directed by Mel Shapiro, The Goodman Theatre, Chicago (1979) *The Catherine Wheel* choreographed by Twyla Tharp, Wintergarden Theater, New York City (1981) Verdi's *Falstaff*, the Dorothy Chandler Pavillion, Los Angeles, Royal Opera House, London (1982) *A Winter's Tale* directed by Frank Galati, The Goodman Theater, Chicago (1990) *Medea* directed by Garland Wright, Guthrie Theater, Minneapolis (1991) *Necessary Weather* by Dana Reitz with Sara Rudner at the Kitchen, New York City (1992) the da Ponte Mozarts, Glyndebourne, UK (2000) Eugene Ionesco's *The Chairs*, directed by David Gordon, Barbican, London, BAM, New York City (2004) *The Fever* by Wallace Shawn, Acorn Theater, New York City (2007), among many others.

Jennifer Tipton has been honored with numerous prestigious awards including Drama Desk Awards for *The Cherry Orchard* and *For Colored Girls Who Have Considered Suicide When the Rainbow Is Enuf* (1977), a Tony Award for *The Cherry Orchard* (1977), an Obie Award for sustained excellence in lighting at the Public Theater (1979), a Bessie Award for sustained excellence in lighting dance (1984), a Bessie Award shared with Dana Reitz for *Circumstantial Evidence* (1987), a Tony Award for Jerome Robbins' *Broadway* (1989), a Drama Desk Award for Jerome Robbins' *Broadway* and *Waiting for Godot* (1989), the Common Wealth Award in Dramatic Arts (1989), an Olivier Award shared with Twyla Tharp for *In the Upper Room* (1991), a Distinguished Artist Award from the Theatre Program, the National Endowment for the Arts (1991), and an Obie Lifetime Achievement Award (1998).

In addition to her professional career, Jennifer Tipton teaches at the Yale School of Drama and several of her students, owing no doubt to her tutelage, have already begun to make significant contributions to lighting design. Tipton has also given workshops around the world including such sites as Beijing, Shanghai, and Manila.

FEATURE SECTION
An Interview with Lighting Designer Jennifer Tipton

What inspired you to become a lighting designer?

I don't know if you could say I was inspired. I was the rehearsal mistress for a company that danced for children. I had to watch the performances so I could critique the dancers. I looked at the bigger picture and that was made by light. I fell in love with it (lighting) and I have been in love with it ever since. I think that what makes me able to be the lighting designer that I am today without formal training is my ability to "look at the bigger picture."

What is the most pleasant part of your job?

I enjoy going from situation to situation. I work in all genres: dance, opera, and theatre. I love going from one to the next. Each production has its own needs and nuances. It's great to work with a variety of people. I call theatre "the dirty art" because it takes so many people to create it and if the chemistry between those people is "just right," it is a fantastic experience.

What is the most challenging aspect of lighting design?

I don't know if challenging is the proper word. The most necessary thing to get right is the focus of the lights. I hate to focus but it is the only time that I get a chance to see what happens with each and every light. So I do it myself; I do not use an assistant.

Do you have a favorite project?

It was Jerome Robbins' *Celebration: The Art of the Pas de Deux,* Spoleto Festival, Italy, 1973. It was a miracle time. Thinking back there is really nothing I would have changed.

What recommendations do you have for a student who would like to become a lighting designer?

They must be "stage struck"—nothing is more important. There are many other things to do that make more money and offer more rewards. Lighting is not an easy life. I just spent eight days in a row working from 8:00 A.M. until midnight—long, exhausting hours. If that is what you want, great; but if not, then stay away.

I feel strongly about the fact that it is the art of lighting for the stage. So many people think that it is only technical. I call it "music for the eye." It has the same form and structure as music. Once you establish a theme, the possible variations are endless.

(Theatre) is important. It allows us to go into a room together and mirror ourselves.

Just the fact that we are doing this play, this way, and the whole debate that occurs during the production process is important. How does it (the way we chose to do the play) affect who we are and how we see ourselves? If we limit ourselves to one or two possibilities, then our final choice is poverty stricken. If we choose from many possibilities then the final choice is rich with content and meaning.

> **Active Learning Assignment**
> **"Bringing Theatre to Life"**
>
> I. Designing the Lights for Your In-Class Production
>
> Only limited lighting design can be done for most in-class productions because the majority of classrooms are equipped with large florescent lights that can be turned only on or off. The group may want to consider flashlights and/or small lamps to use in the production. Portable strobe lights and black lights can also be used. Caution: if a strobe light is used, it is IMPORTANT to warn all actors and audience members since strobe lights can trigger seizures in some people. Do not use candles—they are not safe.
>
> If the group elects to turn off the lights and perform in darkness for a portion of the performance, rehearse this effect with the actors before in order to avoid injury. Mark your light cues in the script and assign an individual to control the light switch.

Sound Design

The pre-production for sound design follows the same process as other designers—research and production meetings. Depending on the production, the sound designer may be responsible for some or all of the following: pre-show, after-show, intermission, underscoring (music played while a scene is being performed), and sound effects such as doors creaking, gunshots, wind, thunder, etc.

Most theatres have a collection of compact discs containing a variety of sound effects. For example, one compact disc may include several gunshots from different guns—shotgun, pistol, cannon, etc. Remember that it is important for the sound to match the type of gun seen in the production in order for the effect to seem real.

The music used for the production may also be found in the theatre's CD collection or a sound designer may select to compose his or her own. If a sound designer cannot find or compose the desired sound effects or music, he or she may search the Internet, library, or music stores.

Once the sound effects and the music have been selected and the volume and length of each cue have been determined, the sound designer will program the cues into a sound control board. In some productions, *practical sound cues* (for example, a stereo switched on by an actor on stage) are also needed. The sound designer will work with the scenic designer and the properties designer to create these effects.

Sound Designer Bruce Ellman

Over the past 30 years, Bruce Ellman has been the sound designer for countless shows (well, you could count them if you like) on Broadway, Off-Broadway, and regional theatres. Credits include—Broadway: *Absurd Person Singular, The Tale of the Allergist's Wife*; Off-Broadway and Regional: *Iron, Rose's Dilemma, Bad Dates, Last Dance, Polish Joke, Kimberly Akimbo, House & Garden, Comic Potential* (Drama Desk nomination), *Fuddy Meers, Full Gallop, Four Dogs and a Bone, Beggars in the House of Plenty, The Waverly Gallery, Mambo Mouth, Fully Committed* (Los Angeles Drama Critics Circle Award nomination), and *To Gillian on Her 37th Birthday*. Bruce is an adjunct faculty member of the New York City College of Technology in the Entertainment Technology department.

Bruce Ellman

Photograph Courtesy of Bruce Ellman.

FEATURE SECTION
An Interview with Sound Designer Bruce Ellman

What inspired you to become a sound designer?

The initial inspiration was that it was a good way to meet "chicks," which is what we called young women back in my non-PC day. I was a biology major at the City College of New York and most of the good-looking girls were in the theatre department so I took a technical theatre course. Since I was also a musician, I was sorted out to do sound. I enjoyed the entire theatrical "story-telling" process, and sound allowed me to apply skills I already possessed. I also pursued directing for a while and studied with the great twentieth-century director, Herman Shumlin. I chose sound design over directing for several reasons:

   I. It is more difficult and more labor-intensive to find work as a director.
  II. Though you can pre-plan future projects, a director can only work on a single project at a time. A designer can have several projects in varying degrees of development going on simultaneously. My personal record is working in three different cities in one day for three different projects.
 III. If done *correctly*[1] directing is the least creative job in theatre as the director serves as the guide for those who actually create the various elements of the project (though don't ever mention this to a director).

What is most challenging about designing sound?

Many important challenges are shared with all of the creative members of the production team. It's important that anyone pursuing a career in theatre understands that every job in the theatre is essentially the same with each creative discipline bringing its specific craft to bear on the project. We're all telling the same story together.

"The Challenge of the Blank Page" is the big one. Of course the page is not entirely blank as we are usually provided with a script, but a way to physicalize that script must be found. Well-written scripts are extremely easy to design. Their "Commanding Form"[2] tell you almost instantly how to tell the story. When the scripts aren't so well written, that's when directors can (and MUST) become creative.

Besides the shared storytelling, a major challenge somewhat unique to sound design is designing for the venue. Theatrical sound design, more so than any other design discipline, is venue specific. The physics of the space and the desired effect of sound on the audience in *that venue for that project* must be taken into account.

For example, when designing a musical you first need to determine the style of the sound design. "Tommy" and "Tarzan" are "rock"-based shows so you would tend to use a "P.A."[3]-style sound system. Any of the Rodgers & Hammerstein or any other of the what-we-call "Book Musical" shows are usually better served by a reinforcement[4] style system.

After determining the style of the production, the physics of the sound in the performance venue then needs to be addressed as part of the design. I think it vital that as part of the craft a sound designer needs to be familiar with and know how to use the physics of sound to best advantage. There are two equal parts to every design: the storytelling and the engineering.

What is most pleasurable about designing sound?

For me the most pleasurable part of designing is when the three major components are in place: a good play, a good production, and working with good people. Nothing is more pleasing than helping to produce a successful production, knowing I've done my best, and that I helped create the atmosphere that allowed everyone else to do theirs.

If a student were interested in becoming a sound designer how might they begin?

There are no shortcuts. It takes a long time to acquire all of the required skills. A sound designer needs to be a storyteller, a musician, a physicist, an engineer, a technician, a computer "IT" expert, and a diplomat.[5] It also takes time to build a career and to get others to trust you with their productions. The way to begin is to design. Start with student productions and community theatre. If you can, find an established designer to mentor you. In the beginning you will make little if any money, but it's a great opportunity to learn the craft and build up your "trust" factor.

Finally, Herman Shumlin used to say: *"You only need two things to be successful in theatre—imagination and freedom from the fear of failure."*[6] This is great advice for anyone pursuing a career in any field.

Notes

[1] This depends on the quality of the script. The better the script, the less creativity required of the director.

[2] See Suzanne K. Langer's "Feeling and Form," Scribner Books, 1977.

[3] Not to get into design/engineering of sound systems, but briefly, a Public Address system is used where uniform coverage, high amplitude, and intelligibility are paramount.

[4] A reinforcement sound system does not provide the same uniformity of coverage nor amplitude of a P.A. system, but allows for better localization of source and a wider dynamic range.

[5] This is only a partial list.

[6] Well, these two things and everything in the above list.

Active Learning Assignment
"Bringing Theatre to Life"

I. **Designing Sound for Your Production**

In designing sound for your classroom project, first select pre-show, curtain call, and underscoring music that will compliment your production. Remember that sound effects, if needed, can be found on the Internet, in music stores, or in the library.

Many classrooms are equipped with speakers and compact disc players; if these are not available, a portable CD player can be brought in. Mark the sound cues in the script and assign an individual to operate the sound.

Hand Properties

Hand properties are important elements in the total stage design. Depending on the production, hand properties can be *practical* such as cups, saucers, food, plates, etc., that are actually used by the actors. Other props (properties) are intended to *dress the stage* (decorate the stage—curtains, pillows, and rugs). The property master will begin to design a production by researching and participating in production meetings. After the director has finalized the selection of props, the property master will begin to gather, make, or purchase the needed items.

Most established theatres have an extensive prop room from which to select props. But if a prop is not in storage, a "treasure hut" ensues. The property master will scour thrift and department stores and even private homes seeking the right props to complete the production. If the props cannot be found, they are constructed or purchased. Constructing a prop usually requires extensive research.

While the production props are being gathered, rehearsal props (substitute props that have a similar weight and feel to the production props) are given to the stage manager for the actors to use during rehearsals.

During the performance, actors take their hand props from one or two prop tables which are usually located off stage right and off stage left. It is extremely important that the props are replaced on the table after use, lest they be lost.

Some props are pre-set on the stage and a member of the props running crew is responsible for placing the prop on-stage before the audience arrives. The actors are responsible for checking their own hand props before the house opens.

Food and drink props that will be consumed by actors need extra attention. Liquids must not be sweet or they will coat the actors' throats and make it difficult for them to speak clearly. Food must be refrigerated, and dishes and utensils must be sanitized before every performance.

Properties Master Paul James Martin

Paul James Martin is Properties Master for the Oregon Shakespeare Festival. His duties include managing a shop of five crew members, organizing and producing furniture, hand props, weapons, set decoration, and draperies for half of the 11 shows produced annually by OSF. He has 31 years of experience in furniture construction, upholstery, drapery construction, welding and metal work, casting and mold making, sculpture and carving, painting and drawing, budgeting and scheduling, set decoration, and fabric dyeing. Paul James is a member of the Society of Prop Artisan Managers, an organization comprised of the Property Masters and Managers of Professional Regional Theatres throughout the United States. He became a member of the OSF Canon Club in 1989, having worked on the complete Shakespeare canon.

P.J. Martin in "Acts" class

Photograph Courtesy of Ashland Center for Theatre Studies.

Feature Section
An Interview with Properties Master Paul James Martin

What inspired you to become a property master?

In the beginning, while still in high school, I had planned to follow my father into the sheet metal trade, and as a result took every metal working, architectural drawing class, as well as art classes that focused on drawing and sculpting. I had already learned to weld from my dad at an early age. In my senior year one of my sisters was in a show where they needed help building the set for a show and the people in the cast of the show were sent home to recruit their siblings. In helping out on that show, I realized that this was what I had been training for all those years and sheet metal was in the past. Through the years, the more I delved into the process of preparing props for shows the more I became aware of the scope of possibilities available—as many possible levels to the work as I would be willing to commit to. I had been a Property Artisan at the Oregon Shakespeare Festival for a few years when the position of Property Master came available and I jumped at the chance to have more choice in the level of commitment to the shows.

What are your responsibilities?

I am responsible to the Production Manager, the Scenic Designer, and Director of a show, for coordinating the building/purchasing of all of the furniture, set decorations, soft goods (fabric goods), hand props, weapons, and for producing rehearsal versions of the all-of-the above needed for any of my part of the 11 shows of our season (there is another Prop Master whom I split the total show load with). I also share in the budgeting for the shows and the day-to-day management of the three-person building crew.

What is most challenging about your work?

Working within an ever-diminishing time frame between the time where the information about what is needed arrives and when the props are needed for the performances while adjusting to the changing needs as the rehearsal process proceeds—building and scheduling the building of the props while remaining flexible to the results of the rehearsal process.

What is most enjoyable?

The most enjoyable part of the process is the brain-storming with the building crew, problem solving the project challenges, using my 38 years of experience working in the theatre community, and seeing and using ideas from other people's backgrounds and perspectives. Seeing the results of the collaboration in the final results and then being able to add to my bag of tricks is always enjoyable and rewarding.

If a student were interested in becoming a property master what advice would you give them?

The skill set of a Prop Person is as varied as can possibly be. Really, any skill you may acquire is a useful addition to that skill set and the more skills you have the better. Learn how to sew, learn how to build furniture, how to sculpt, how to do a budget, how to work with others, how to weld. Develop as well-rounded a knowledge of Prop building techniques and work practices as you can. To be a good Prop Master you first have to be a good Prop Artisan. *The more you know how to do and the more of that that you are willing to pass on to others, the better of a Prop Master you will become.*

> ### Active Learning Assignment
> ### "Bringing Theatre to Life"
>
> I. **Designing the Props for Your Production**
>
> First, make a list of all desired props. Treasure hunting comes next. Search for the needed items in dorm rooms and in thrift and discount stores. Don't forget to return borrowed items after the performance.
>
> If food or drinks are needed, bring an ice-chest to prevent spoilage. Use clean plates, cups, and utensils. Iced tea can be used for any brown colored beverages—coke, ale, etc. Red dye can be added to water to create any red-colored beverage—juice, wine, etc.
>
> II. **Using Props During the Production**
>
> Lay out the props on a small table or on the floor so that they are easy to locate. Tell the actors to return them to the same place where they got them. Don't forget to pre-set any needed props. Remind the actors to check their props before the production begins.

Summary

Theatre designers—scenic, costume, lighting, sound, and properties—are more than technicians. They are theatre artists. Each artist, regardless of his or her specialty, begins the design process by researching the production and actively participating in production meetings. As a member of the artistic team, each designer must collaborate with the other designers and the director to insure the artistic continuity of the production.

Scenic designers communicate their interpretation of the director's vision through ground plans and three-dimensional models; costume designers create sketches, drawings, and collages; lighting designers make light plots and select colored gels and gobos; sound designers communicate via sound; and properties masters are often "treasure hunters."

Each of the designers works to bring a production to life and, as Tony Award-winning lighting designer Jennifer Tipton, says, " . . . if the chemistry between those people is 'just right,' it is a fantastic experience."

Getting an Audience

Publicity and Promotion

Most commercial and regional theatres have a marketing director on staff whose primary concern is selling tickets.

Most commercial and regional theatres have marketing directors on staff whose primary mission is selling tickets. The marketing director must know the types of plays that interest the potential audience as well as the most effective way to communicate with that audience. Toward this end, marketing directors usually begin by conducting surveys of the community. Some of the information gathered might include the age, race, economic status, careers, hobbies or interests, and means of transportation.

The marketing director will typically place advertisements in the local newspapers as well as attempt to entice a reporter to write a feature article.

The marketing director will usually place advertisements in the local newspapers and attempt to entice a reporter to write a feature article. Other marketing devices include television commercials, posters, postcards, and the Internet. The marketing director may also form an alliance with local businesses to promote production. Of course, good theatre is also promoted by "word of mouth."

Marketing Director John Zinn

Other marketing venues include television spots, posters, postcards, and the Internet.

John Zinn

John Zinn is Acting Director of Marketing and Communications at Steppenwolf Theatre Company in Chicago. His previous positions include a stint as Marketing Manager at Broadway In Chicago, and he was Marketing Director/Associate Artistic Director of Chicago storefront favorite Uma Productions for six years until they ceased producing in spring 2007. John has an MFA in Acting from The Theatre School/DePaul University. As an actor, his Chicago stage credits include numerous Uma shows, and shows with Signal Ensemble, Timeline and Collaboration, where he is an Artistic Associate. Originally from Oregon, John's West coast credits include shows at Artists Repertory Theatre and Tygres Heart Shakespeare. Film credits include the acclaimed short *The Fifth Horseman*, the independent feature *Into It*, and he has also done numerous commercial voice-overs.

FEATURE SECTION

An Interview with Steppenwolf Marketing Director John Zinn

What are your responsibilities at Steppenwolf?

I am currently the Acting Director of Marketing: responsible for single ticket sales and subscription sales for more than 15 productions annually in three spaces; crafting or shaping all outward-bound communication about Steppenwolf to insure mission, brand, and the heart of the theatre is in it; ultimately responsible for the visual look of all Steppenwolf materials, managing a staff of 15 and maintaining our status in the local and national theater community and making sure it reflects the current artistic state of the company.

What do you feel is most challenging about marketing?

Simply put, getting the message out that theatre is vital to being a citizen of the world. With the rise of the Internet, the decline of subscriptions and the shortening of attention spans, it can happen that theatre is thought of as stodgy or unable to be impactful. Thank God I live in Chicago where I can see every day of the week that isn't true. Theatre here is unruly, hilarious, in your lap, heartbreaking, shocking, extreme, tender, and life changing. I have seen shows all over the world, but the best shows I see year in and year out are here. There is a perceived trend of young people turning away from the classic arts: opera, symphony, and now theatre. I don't think that will ever happen completely for any of them, and I KNOW that it won't with theatre. We will ALWAYS crave that live performance, and seeing what I see here I know there will always be someone to give it to us.

What is most rewarding regarding marketing?

When you see someone come back for a second show, that is the best feeling in the world. You can get them to try anything once—when I see the second timer walk through that door, I know we got 'em. And building partnerships with publicity and marketing partners outside the usual scope of these things is really rewarding and it is truly what we all have to do next! For instance, regarding our friends in the press: if we find a publication that we feel adheres to certain standards (as we do!), that tries to tell the truth as much as humanly possible (as we do!) and that we believe actually does some very necessary advocating for this art form (as we feel we do!) then it is our responsibility to offer what we can of ourselves to further their mission, and to make no bones about asking them to further ours. There will be varying degrees of success in pulling off what we want to accomplish with our shows, there will be varying degrees of truly blazing insight in our productions, and there will be varying degrees of intuition, insight, and success in the reviews of these publications, also. But we should work together. And if we do, along the way, with every single show—everyone, we ALL get better.

What inspired you to become a marketing director?

I went to grad school at The Theatre School at DePaul (formerly the Goodman School of Drama) and got an M.F.A. in Acting. I gave the commencement speech right before August Wilson spoke. You don't forget a day like that, and I have both acted and marketed in Chicago ever since. I run the marketing department at one of the most important American theatres. I am a Chicago actor who works in theater, commercials, film, and voice over. I

was the associate artistic director and marketing director for Uma Productions, one of the stars of the Chicago storefront circuit for the past six years until we closed the books (in the black!) this spring. I love marketing and applied my desire to have the shows I was in play to full houses: I learned how to market them from the inside out (acting to marketing) and the outside in (marketing to acting). It is my contribution back, in a way, to the art that has given me everything. I have always wanted the great shows that I have seen in my life to be seen by everyone: if I was that affected, others must be too, right? And usually they were. The synergy between a full house and an engaged cast: it is the best feeling in the world, and it doesn't matter a bit which side of the lights you are on.

If a student was interested in becoming a marketing director how might they begin?

When you are working on a show: Be the one who makes a partnership with the corner restaurant for pre-show receptions, the one who takes the flier and poster design one step further, the one who takes time to invite not only the press but actual community leaders and tastemakers, be the one to make friends with the retail store who lets you put up posters, then provides costumes, then hosts events, then donates. Build those community partnerships, and you will have the best group of advocates possible: they love your work, they love you, and they will tell everybody else about it.

Programs (Playbills)

The program lists the names, biographies, and in most cases, a picture of each of the cast members, as well as the names and biographies of the production team.

As mentioned in Act I Scene I, programs contain information that will help you get the most out of your theatre-going experience. In most American theatres, the program is complimentary (although some theatres do sell full-color souvenir programs) but in European theatres, the playgoer must purchase a program. The program lists the names, biographies, and, in many cases, pictures of the cast members and the production team. A program also includes information about the production itself—the locale and time period, the title and author of the play, act and scene divisions, etc. The dramaturg or director may also include notes about the production.

Any financial sponsors are listed in the program and there might also be advertisements, some of which can include coupons. Nearby restaurants or coffee houses might offer discounts to theatre goers. The theatre itself may offer special ticket prices for upcoming production. Certainly, all plays that are or will be running in the theatre are listed.

Active Learning Assignment
"Bringing Theatre to Life"

I. Make a Program

Select one or two individuals in each group to make a program for the group's play. The program should include the names of the cast, directors, scenic designers, dramaturg notes, and other pertinent information such as time and location of the performance. The group should provide copies of the program to all of the audience members on the day of the performance.

The Wrap Up

This text has provided an overview of theatre history from its origins to the present day. It has examined some of the techniques used by theatre practitioners and pointed out how utilizing these techniques can enhance your life and career. The interviews with theatre professionals may even have inspired some of you to consider a new career path. During the course, you have had the opportunity to actively participate in the interactive art form that is theatre. These "hands-on" activities have perhaps given you a new perception of the art of theatre. If you have been inspired to see a play, keep in mind that professional houses (commercial and regional) are generally *dark on Monday*, meaning that there are no performances on Mondays. On the other days of the week, professional theatres usually have evening performances beginning between 7 P.M. and 8 P.M. and, quite often, there are also matinee performances. Community and educational theatres typically have limited performance runs—a production may run Thursday through Sunday evenings with a Sunday matinee. Occasionally, theatres provide audiences the opportunity to see a play at an unusual time. For example, it has become traditional to schedule a performance of *The Rocky Horror Picture Show* at midnight at least once during the run.

A program typically includes information about the production itself such as the location and time period that the production is set.

Partial Listing of Regional Theatres

For your convenience, most theatres sell tickets online. The following is a partial listing of regional theatres across the United States:

Baltimore, MD: **Center Stage Theatre**—http://www.centerstage.org/index.php
Cambridge, MA: **American Repertory Theatre**—http://www.amrep.org/
Chicago, IL: **Goodman Theatre**—http://www.goodman-theatre.org/
Chicago, IL: **Steppenwolf Theatre Company**—
  http://www.steppenwolf.org/
Cleveland, OH: **Cleveland Public Theatre**—http://www.cptonline.org/
Costa Mesa, CA: **South Coast Repertory**—http://www.scr.org/
Denver, CO: **The Denver Center for the Performing Arts**—
  http://www.denvercenter.org/home.cfm
Los Angeles, CA: **Center Theatre Group**—
  http://www.taperahmanson.com/
Louisville, KY: **Actors Theatre of Louisville**—http://www.actorstheatre.org/
Minneapolis, MN: **Guthrie Theatre**—http://www.guthrietheater.org/
Montgomery, AL: **Alabama Shakespeare Festival**—
  http://www.asf.net/asf/ticket/
New York, NY: **Manhattan Theatre Club at the Biltmore Theatre**—
  citytix@nycitycenter.org
New York, NY: **The Public Theatre**—http://www.publictheater.org/
Ashland, OR: **Oregon Shakespeare Festival**—http://www.orshakes.org/
San Diego, CA: **Old Globe**— http://www.oldglobe.org/
Washington, DC: **Arena Stage**—http://www.arenastage.org/contact/

See you at the theatre!

The Adding Machine, directed by Don Bristow. *Photograph courtesy of Nathan Braniff.*

Bibliography

Act I: Scene I

Viewing and Critiquing a Play

Ball, Robert J., and Oscar G. Brockett. *The Essential Theatre.* Belmont: Wadsworth, 2004.

Crane, R. S., W. R. Keast, Norman Maclean, Richard McKeon, Elder Olson, and Bernard Weinberg. *Critics and Criticism.* Toronto: Phoenix Books, 1966.

Greenwald, Mike. *Evaluating a Performance.* New York City: Pearson Education, Inc., 2002.

Grote, David. *Script Analysis Reading and Understanding the Playscript for Production.* Belmont: Wadsworth, 1985.

Jacobus, Lee A. *The Bedford Introduction to Drama.* Boston: Bedford Book of St. Martin's Press, 1993.

Kearney, Patricia, and Timothy G. Plax. *Public Speaking in a Culturally Diverse Society.* 2nd ed. Mountain View: Mayfield, 1996.

Smiley, Sam. *Playwriting the Structure of Action.* Englewood Cliffs: Prentice-Hall, Inc., 1971.

Act I: Scene II

Theatre: In the Beginning—The Development of the Western Theatre

Ball, Robert J., and Oscar G. Brockett. *The Essential Theatre.* Belmont: Wadsworth, 2004.

Butcher, S. H. *Aristotle's Theory of Poetry and Fine Art with a Critical Text and Translation of The Poetics.* 4th ed. New York City: Dover Publications, Inc., 1951.

Bywater, Ingram. *Aristotle on the Art of Poetry.* London: Oxford University Press, 1920.

Gassner, John, and Edward Quinn. *The Encyclopedia of World Drama.* New York City: Thomas Y. Cowell Company, Inc., 1969.

Gaster, Theodor H. *Thespis Ritual, Myth and Drama in the Ancient Near East.* New York City: The Norton Library, 1977.

Hamilton, Edith. *The Greek Way.* New York City: The Norton Library ed., 1964.

Hamilton, Edith. *Mythology Timeless Tales of Gods and Heroes.* New York City. The New American Library Inc., 1942.

Hamilton, Edith. *The Roman Way.* New York City: The Norton Library ed., 1964.

Kitto, H. D. F. *Greek Tragedy.* New York City: Anchor Book ed., 1954.

Kitto, H. D. F. *The Greeks.* Middlesex, Penguin Books Ltd., 1951.

McKeon, Richard. *Introduction to Aristotle.* New York City: Random House, Inc., 1947.

O'Brien, Patrick K. *Encyclopedia of World History.* New York City: George Phillip Limited, 2000.

Telford, Kenneth A. *Aristotle's Poetics Translation and Analysis.* Chicago: A Gateway ed. 1961.

Wickham, Glynne. *The Medieval Theatre.* 3rd ed. Cambridge: Cambridge University Press, 1987.

Act I: Scene III

The Renaissance (Italy, England, and France) Through the Restoration

Bellinger, Martha Fletcher. *A Short History of Drama.* New York City: Henry Holt and Company, 1927.

Brown, John Russell. *Shakespeare and His Theatre.* London: Viking, 1993.

Day, Barry. *This Wooden 'O'.* London: First Limelight ed., 1998.

Fernandez, Ramon. *Moliere: The Man Seen Through His Plays.* New York: Hill and Wang Inc., 1958.

Gossman, Lionel. *Men & Masks: A Study of Moliere.* Baltimore: The John Hopkins Paperbacks ed., 1969.

Gurr, Andrew. *William Shakespeare: The Extraordinary Life of the Most Successful Writer of All Time.* New York: HarperCollins, 1995.

Hartnoll, Phyllis. *The Oxford Companion to the Theatre.* 3rd ed. London: Oxford University Press, 1970.

Lea, K. M. "Italy." *The Oxford Companion to the Theatre.* 3rd ed. Edited by Phyllis Hartnoll. London: Oxford University Press, 1970.

May, Frederick. "Italy." *The Oxford Companion to the Theatre.* 3rd ed. Edited by Phyllis Hartnoll. London: Oxford University Press, 1970.

O'Brien, Patrick K. *Encyclopedia of World History.* New York City: George Phillip Limited, 2000.

Palmer, John. *Moliere.* New York City: Benjamin Blom, Inc., 1970.

Pickering, Jerry V. *Theatre a History of the Art.* St. Paul: West Publishing Company, 1978.

Sutherland, J. R. "England." *The Oxford Companion to the Theatre.* 3rd ed. Edited by Phyllis Hartnoll. London: Oxford University Press, 1970.

Act I: Scene IV

Romanticism and the Battle of the "ism" (Naturalism/Realism vs. Symbolism and Modern Experiments)

Artaud, Antonin. *The Theatre and Its Double.* New York City: Grove Press, Inc., 1958.

Bentley, Eric. *Modern Drama: From Ibsen to Brecht Theatre of War.* New York City: The Viking Press Inc., 1975.

Croyden, Margaret. *Lunatics Lovers and Poets: The Contemporary Experimental Theatre.* New York: Dell Publishing Company, 1975.

Esslin, Martin. *The Theatre of the Absurd.* Great Britain: Pelican Books, 1980.

Gordon, Joanne. *Stephen Sondheim: A Casebook.* New York City: Garland Publishing Inc., 1979.

Hartnoll, Phyllis. *The Oxford Companion to the Theatre.* 3rd ed. London: Oxford University Press, 1970.

King, Beatrice, rev. "Russia." *The Oxford Companion to the Theatre.* 3rd ed. London: Oxford University Press, 1970.

Mates, Julian. *America's Musical Stage: Two Hundred Years of Musical Theatre.* Westport: Praeger Publishers, 1987.
O'Brien, Patrick K. *Encyclopedia of World History.* New York City: George Phillip Limited, 2000.
Secrest, Meryle. *Stephen Sondheim: A Life.* New York City: Alfred A. Knopf Inc., 1998.

Act I: Scene V

Musical Theatre

Cockrell, Dale and Hugh M. Miller. *History of Western Music.* New York: HarperCollins Publishers, 1991.
Green, Stanley. *Broadway Musicals Show By Show.* Wisconsin: Hal Leonard Publishing Corp, 1994.
Grose, B. Donald and O. Franklin Kenworthy. *A Mirror to Life: A History of Western Theatre.* New York City: CBS College Publishing, 1985.
"Opera in America." http://www.pbs.org/wgbh/masterpiece/americancollection/lark/opera.html
McLamore, Alyson. *Musical Theatre An Appreciation.* New Jersey: Pearson Education, Inc, 2004.
Rosenstiel, Lèonie, ed. *Schirmer History of Music.* New York: Schirmer Books, 1982.

Act I: Scene VI

Theatre Around the World

Aikens, James. "Canada: 1. English." *The Cambridge Guide to World Theatre and Performance.* Ed. Martin Banham. New York: Cambridge University Press, 1998.
Allen, Rodger. *An Introduction to Arabic Literature.* New York City: Cambridge University Press, 2000.
Bharucha, Rustom. "India." *The Oxford Encyclopedia of Theatre and Performance.* Edited by Dennis Kennedy. New York City: Oxford University Press, 2003.
Carlson, Marvin. "Arabic Drama." *The Oxford Encyclopedia of Theatre and Performance.* Edited by Dennis Kennedy. New York City: Oxford University Press, 2003.
Conceison, Claire. "No Ordinary Days." American Theatre. May/June 2002:28–31, 77. Humanities International Database. EBSCOhost. Chambers Library, Edmond, OK. 15 March 2006. http://www.epnet.com/ehost/login.html.
Doucette, Leonard. "Canada: 2. French." *The Cambridge Guide to World Theatre.* Ed. Martin Banham. New York: Cambridge University Press, 1998.
Guy, Nancy. "China." *The Oxford Encyclopedia of Theatre and Performance.* Edited by Dennis Kennedy. New York City: Oxford University Press, 2003.

Hibbet, Howard S. *Japanese Drama. Collier's Encyclopedia.* New York City: Collier, 1997.
Kano, Ayako. "Visuality and Gender in Modern Japanese Theatre: Looking at Salome." *Japan Forum.* April 1999:43–55. Humanities International Database. EBSCOhost. Chambers Library, Edmond, OK. 15 March 2006. http://www.epnet.com/ehost/login.html.
Pires, Daniel. "Africa: Portuguese-speaking (lusophone)." *The Cambridge Guide to World Theatre.* Edited by Martin Banham. New York City: Cambridge University Press, 1988.
Rimer, J. Thomas. "Japan." *The Oxford Encyclopedia of Theatre and Performance.* Edited by Dennis Kennedy. New York City: Oxford University Press, 2003.
Wake, Clive. "French-speaking Africa south of the Sahara." *The Cambridge Guide to World Theatre.* Edited by Martin Banham. New York: Cambridge University Press, 1988.
Wake, Clive. "French-speaking North Africa." *The Cambridge Guide to World Theatre.* Edited by Martin Banham. New York City: Cambridge University Press, 1988.
Williams, Margaret. "Australia." *The Cambridge Guide to World Theatre.* Edited by Martin Banham. New York City: Cambridge University Press, 1988.
Woodyard, George. "Mexico." *The Cambridge Guide to World Theatre.* Edited by Martin Banham. New York City: Cambridge University Press, 1988.

Act I: Scene VII

The Theatre in You
Houchin, John H. *Censorship of the American Theatre in the Twentieth Century.* New York City: Cambridge University Press, 2003.

Act II: Scene I

Dramaturgs and Stage Managers
Stern, Lawrence. *Stage Management.* Boston: Pearson Education Inc., 2006.

Act II: Scene II

The Art of Playwriting
Barnett, Claudia. *Wendy Wasserstein: A Casebook.* New York City: Routledge, 1998.
Cole, Toby. *Playwrights on Playwriting.* New York City: A Dramabook, 1976.
Gelb, Barbara, and Arthur Gelb. *O'Neill.* New York City: Dell Publishing Company Inc., 1960.

Hellman, Lillian. *An Unfinished Woman: A Memoir.* Boston: Little, Brown and Company, 1969.
Roudan'e, Matthew C. *The Cambridge Companion to Tennessee Williams.* New York City: Cambridge University Press, 1997.
McFarlane, James. *The Cambridge Companion to Ibsen.* Cambridge: Cambridge University Press, 1994.
MacGowan, Kenneth. *A Primer of Playwriting.* New York City: Dolphin Books, 1962.
McLaughlin, Buzz. *The Playwright's Process Learning the Craft from Today's Leading Dramatists.* New York City: Back Stage Books, 1997.
Meyer, Michael. *Ibsen.* New York City: Doubleday & Company, Inc., 1971.
Miller, Arthur. *Timebends.* New York City: Grove Press Inc., 1987.
Plimpton, George. *Playwrights at Work—The Paris Review Interviews.* London: The Harvill Press, 2000.
Rutenberg, Michael E. *Edward Albee: Playwright in Protest.* New York: DBS Publications, Inc., 1969.
Schanke, Robert A. *Ibsen: In America a Century of Change.* New Jersey: The Scarecrow Press, Inc., 1988.
Sheaffer, Louis. *O'Neill Son and Playwright.* Boston: Little, Brown and Company, 1968.
Simon, Neil. *Neil Simon: A Memoir: The Play Goes On.* New York City: Simon and Schuster Inc., 1999.
Simon, Neil. *Neil Simon Rewrites a Memoir.* New York City: Simon and Schuster Inc., 1996.
Williams, Tennessee. *Tennessee Williams Memoirs.* New York City: Doubleday & Company, Inc., 1975.

Act II: Scene III

Producing and Directing the Play

Ball, William. *A Sense of Direction: Some Observations on the Art of Directing.* New York City: Drama Book Publishers, 1984.
Bloom, Michael. *Thinking Like a Director: A Practical Handbook.* New York City: Faber and Faber Limited, 2002.
Brockett, Oscar G., with Franklin J. Hildy. *History of Theatre.* Needham Heights, Allen and Bacon, 1999.
Fernald, John. *Sense of Direction the Director and His Actors.* New York City: Stein and Day Publishers, 1969.
Hodge, Francis. *Play Directing Analysis, Communication, and Style.* Boston: Allen and Bacon, 2000.
Jory, Jon. *Tips for Directors.* New Hampshire: Smith and Kraus, Inc., 2002.
Langley, Stephen. *Theatre Management in America Principle and Practice Producing the Commercial, Stock, Resident, College, and Community Theatre.* New York City: Drama Book Specialists (Publishers), 1980.
Pick, John. *Arts Administration.* Chicago: E. F. N. Spon, 1980.
Reiss, Alvin H. *The Arts Management Reader.* New York City: Marcel Dekker Inc., 1979.

Act II: Scene IV

Whether or Not You Want to Be an Actor, Achieve Your Personal Best

Hodge, Alison. *Twentieth Century Actor Training.* London: Routledge, Taylor Francis Group, 2002.

Bloom, Ken. *Broadway Its History, People, and Places and Encyclopedia.* 2nd ed. New York City: Routledge, 2004.

Chekhov, Michael, and Deirdre Hurst du Prey. *Lessons for the Professional Actor.* New York City: Performing Arts Journal Publications, 1985.

Goudsouzian, Aram. *Sidney Poitier Man, Actor, Icon.* Chapel Hill: The University of North Carolina Press, 2004.

Magarshack, David. *Stanislavsky on the Art of the Stage.* New York City: Hill and Wang, 1961.

Olivier, Laurence. *Confessions of an Actor and Autobiography Laurence Olivier.* Middlesex: Penguin Books, 1984.

Spoto, Donald. *The Definitive Biography of the Greatest Actor of Our Time: Laurence Olivier—A Biography.* New York: Harper Paperbacks: A Division of HarperCollins Publishers, 1993.

Smurthwaite, Nick. *The Meryl Streep Story.* New York: Beaufort Books, Inc., 1984.

Stanislavski, Constantin, and J. J. Robbins. *My Life in Art.* New York: Meridian Books, 1959.

Act II: Scene V

Designing

"Color Your World." *Edmond Sun.* Edmond: 7 January 2006: 12.

Koch, Polly, Don Quintance, and Deborah Velders. *Between Taste and Travesty: Costume Designs by William Ivey Long.* North Carolina: Cameron Art Museum, 2007.

Larson, Orville K. *Scene Design in the American Theatre From 1915 to 1960.* Fayetteville: The University of Arkansas Press, 1989.

Oenslager, Donald. *Stage Design: Four Centuries of Scenic Invention.* New York City: The Viking Press, 1975.

Waaser, Carol. *The Theatre Student Sound and Music for the Theatre.* New York City: Richards Rosen Press, Inc., 1976.

Act II: Scene VI

Getting an Audience

Langley, Stephen. *Theatre Management in America Principle and Practice Producing the Commercial, Stock, Resident, College, and Community Theatre.* New York City: Drama Book Specialists (Publishers), 1980.

McArthur, Nancy. *How to Do Theatre Publicity.* Ohio: Good Ideas Company, 1978.

Newman, Danny. Subscribe Now! *Building Arts Audiences through Dynamic Subscription Promotion.* New York City: Theatre Communication Group Inc., 1980.

Reiss, Alvin H. *The Arts Management Reader.* New York City: Marcel Dekker Inc., 1979.

Glossary

Absurdism   the language that characterized the plays was disconnected, filled with pauses and monosyllables; used metaphors and symbols as a means of creating an existential void

Actors Equity Association   the professional organization that was started in order to protect actors and actresses from unfair and unsafe working conditions

Actors' Equity Association   is the actor's union

actors/actresses   the individuals (male or female) who portray different characters on stage and in film

advertisements   signs or notices that are used to gain the attention of the public; typically found in newspaper, magazines, posters, postcards, or television; used by a marketing director to promote theatre productions

agent   an individual who represents an actor or actress and finds them acting jobs

American Company, the   eventually renamed the Old American Company, the company became America's first popular and successful theatre companies

amphitheatres   outdoor theatres, some have canopies to protect the audience from inclement weather

arena stage   a stage configuration in which the audience sits on all sides of the stage

Art of Poetry   written by Horace; one of two manuscripts upon which Italian literary theory was based during the Renaissance

audience   an individual or a group of individuals who attend and view a play, musical, or other theatrical event

auditions   the part of the production process where actors and/or actresses give a trial performance to the director so that the director can see which actors or actresses might work best for the production

Australian Elizabethan Theatre Trust   this trust was created in 1954 in an effort to give Australian artists some prominence

avant-garde   a broad term for artistic movements that push the boundaries of what is the accepted norm

black box stage   a flexible stage configuration; this configuration is most often used for intimate or experimental works

blackface   a practice in which white actors would paint their faces black with shoe polish or black make-up in order to portray African Americans on stage; this practice is taboo in modern theatre though still occasionally used in satirical works

blind casting   the act of casting a non-Caucasian in a role that has been traditionally portrayed by a Caucasian; also referred to as non-traditional casting

blocking   a term used to describe the director's direction of stage movement *book musicals* created when a storyline became the focal point of the production

Bunraku the doll theatre of Japan; all of the characters are represented by puppets

burlesque a humorous, provocative stage show that began in America with Lydia Thompson's all-girl troupe performing *The Black Crook* in New York City in 1866

carpenters members of the artistic team responsible for building the scenery

censorship the restriction of certain plays, musicals, or other artistic endeavor by the government, individuals, or groups of individuals

central character the focal character in a play

characters the individuals within the play or musical

characterization how the actors create and individualize their characters through vocal and physical differentiation

choreographer creates all the dances for the production. Focusing on supporting the storyline

City Dionysia the spring festival honoring Dionysus; it featured ancient Greek tragedies

climax the highest peak of the dramatic action during which the characters make final attempts to achieve their goals

collage poetry a device used by experimental groups; created by the members of Dada; characterized by three or four people who talk, sing, or whistle at the same time

comic opera this type of popular opera included popular songs stolen from other works and set to new lyrics and were typically presented as part of an evening of entertainment

Commedia Dell'Arte derived from the Roman Atellan farce; developed into an art form in Italy in the sixteenth century; the two traits indicative to commedia are stock characters and improvisation

composer and lyricist compose the music and lyrics, respectively

concept musicals tells a story based on an idea or theme

costume designer the member of the artistic staff responsible for designing the costumes

costume running crew members of the production who are responsible for costume changes, handling costume emergencies, and other costume details such as cleaning and ironing

costume sketches the drawings or renderings of what the costume designer has designed for a production

costume technologist the member of the artistic team responsible for overseeing the construction of costumes

costumes the clothing that different characters wear during a play

crisis an event or discovery which ends in a final resolution

dada for members of this artistic movement, dada meant anti-art, anti-reason, and anti-thought; this movement was responsible for "collage poetry"

De Architetura written by Sebastiano Serlio; contained three types of stage sets each for a different dramatic genre

denouement or falling action the section of a play when everything "falls into or out of place" giving the story sense of closure

designer a member of the artistic staff responsible for the design elements such as sound, lighting, scenery, properties, or costumes

development or rising action the characters strive to accomplish their objectives despite seemingly insurmountable obstacles

dialogue the words and phrases that characters within a play will express to one another

Dionysus the Greek god of nature; ancient Greeks worshiped Dionysus by performing dithyrambs and, eventually, tragedies at annual festivals

director is in charge of the artistic vision for the production

Dithyrambs passionate lyrical poems that were sung and danced by choruses of 50 men or boys to honor the god Dionysus

dramaturg a crucial member of the artistic staff; deals primarily with dramatic literature; responsibilities include researching, developing, and advising

drapers members of the artistic team responsible for draping

draping the act of laying a piece (or pieces) of fabric on a life size body form and manipulating (cutting and pinning) the fabric into the desired shape

English Cycle plays a series of religious plays outlining the Church's plan for salvation

exposition introduces us to the characters in the play and relationships that they have with one another

Expressionism This movement set out to "express," rather than depict, what was ugly, bizarre, and decadent

folk dramas derived from Celtic and Teutonic rituals, were adapted to Christian beliefs, and continued as a popular form of entertainment until the twentieth century

foreshadowing a technique used by writers and playwrights that indicates, to the audience, something unfortunate is soon to occur and involves planting information early on in the play; creates and maintains suspense and believability in a play

glee an uplifting musical number found in the Yoruba opera

gels   specialized "cellophane-like" plastic that, when inserted in front of the lamp, changes the color of the light

gobos   pieces of metal that have been cut into a shape, perhaps a window frame, which when illuminated will cast the shadow of the shape

griot   the focal person in African religious ceremonies who sang, told stories, and was thought to have wisdom of the past while also being receptive to the community's immediate concerns

hand properties (or props)   items that actors or actresses may use during a performance, such as a candlestick, handkerchief, or book

happenings   an art form that formalizes technological shapes, sounds, and people as objects and redefined them as works of art; based on the theory that humans are subjected to constant technological stimulation

intermezzi   lavish productions filled with visual spectacles which included colorful costumes, scenery, lights, exciting special effects, music, and dance

juke box musical   uses the music of today or one particular music artist and forms a script around the songs

Kabuki   Kabuki plays are composed of several emotionally charged incidents, each of which comes to a dramatic end when one of the principle characters sustains a *mie* or stylized pose; the scenic elements are always symbolic rather than realistic

kenosis   a seasonal ritualistic activity that involved fasts and mortification which symbolized the end of the previous "lease on life"

laboratory theatre   a small experimental theatre group founded in Poland by Jerzy Grotowski in 1959

lazzis   physical comedy routines that were typically based on basic human needs such as hunger, bodily functions, and material and physical desires

Lenaea   the winter festival honoring Dionysus; it spotlighted ancient Greek comedies

librettist   writes the spoken word or script to the musical

light cues   the point in the production that lighting instruments will be turned off or on; programmed into a lighting control board

lighting designer   the member of the artistic staff responsible for designing the lighting

lighting plot   indicates where the lighting instruments will need to be positioned in order to create the desired effects

Living Theatre, The   an experimental theatre group founded by Judith Malina and Julian Beck in 1947 in New York City

Maharashtra   a region in west central India

mansions provided the audience with a visual representation of the play's location; large enough to contain some properties and costume pieces, but they were too small to accommodate the actors; constructed of wood and fabric, brightly colored and elaborately decorated

marketing director the individual responsible for selling tickets and promoting the productions at the theatre

mechane a large crane that was capable of raising actors into the air so that they could "fly" as if they were gods; used in ancient Greek theatres as a special effect

melodrama the elements that characterize a melodrama are specific character types, suspenseful plots, musical interludes, and elaborate special effects

miracle play plays based on the lives of martyrs or saints

morality plays allegories which began to develop in the fourteenth century and remained popular throughout the sixteenth century

music director teaches the performers the music

musical theatre storytelling through acting, song and dance

musical reviews selections of songs usually written by the same composer and lyricist

musical theatre performers are the actors, dancers, and singers who perform the show

musicians play the music the orchestrator has provided

mystery plays short dramas that demonstrated the entire Biblical history from Creation to the Last Judgment; also known as Cycle plays

naturalism This movement sought to create drama founded on acute observations of an objective world

networking the exchange of information between and among members of the theatre and/or film industry for mutual support and assistance in gaining jobs within the theatre or film industry

Noh Noh plays are rooted in Zen Buddhism which was brought to Japan from India and China in the sixthe century A.D.; usually includes ghosts, demons, or humans that are still obsessed with and tormented by the earthy desires of the living world; the most traditional and structured form of Japanese theatre

non-verbal communication communications without the use of spoken language; typically represented by facial expressions, gestures, or body language

objective what a character (in a play) wants to achieve

obstacles/conflicts the persons, things, or circumstances that hinder a character from achieving his or her objective or goal

opera include large epic themes, difficult music and no spoken dialogue

operettas light comic opera

orchestra   a large flat circular area at the base of a hill in ancient Greek theatres

pageant wagon   mansions were mounted on these wagons in England during the Cycle plays

paradoi   the entrances into an ancient Greek theatre located on either side of the skene

playwrights   individuals who write plays; sometimes referred to as authors, writers, or poets

plerosis   a seasonal ritualistic activity that symbolized the renewal of life through ceremonial mass mating and special incantations intended to promote human fertility and to bring rain and sunshine to grow food

plot   the structure of the dramatic action which constitutes the play

Poetics, The   written by Aristotle; analyzes the function and structure of tragedy; defines tragedy as possessing the following elements: plot, characters, thought, diction, melody, and spectacle

Poetry Out Loud   this group strived to draw forth the most talented and imaginative artists to reconstruct the Mexican theatre; it lasted from 1956 until 1963

point of attack   where the story in a play begins

practical lights   lights operated by the actors on-stage, example: table lamps

practical sound cues   sounds that are cued by the actors or actresses on stage, such as an actor turning on a stereo and music playing

producer   producer find donors and raise money, hire the production team, and rent the theatre space. The producer many times has final say on any element of the production from artistic to box office sales

production meetings   the meetings in which all members of the artistic staff meet to discuss the production and inform the director of the progress and designs for the design elements

program   the booklet that contains the names, bios, and pictures of the cast and the names and bios of the production members; may also contain advertisements and occasionally coupons from sponsoring restaurants and businesses near the theatre

prologue   invented by Euripides; relays to the audience what has happened between the characters up to the point when the drama begins

property master   the member of the artistic staff responsible for designing, creating, and/or finding props for the production

proscenium arch stage   an indoor stage configuration in which the stage appears to have a picture frame around it, similar to a movie theatre

rehearsal   the act of practicing in preparation for presenting the public performance of a play; rehearsals usually occur most days of the week for four to six weeks prior to the performance

rehearsal props   items that are used in place of the real props during rehearsals prior to performances

Renaissance   began in Italy in the fourteenth century and made its way to England by the early sixteenth century; the period marks the beginning of modern science and geographical discovery and it is defined by a renewed interest in and study of classical works

rock musicals   tells a story with little or no spoken dialogue and music that reflects the rock and roll era

romanticism   this movement sought out to create art that epitomized a time when humans lived in nature free from stifling governmental laws

sangeet natak   Indian musical theatre

Sanskrit drama   one of the earliest forms of drama in India

scenic designer   the member of the artistic staff responsible for designing the scenery

scenic painters   members of the artistic team responsible for painting the scenery

script   the text or manuscript of a play, musical, or other theatrical event

shop foreman   the member of the artistic team responsible for overseeing the carpenters building the scenery

skene   a small building in the back of the orchestra that served primarily as a dressing room in ancient Greek theatres

sound designer   the member of the artistic staff responsible for designing the sound needed for a show, including pre-show, after-show, intermission, underscoring, and sound effects

sound effects   sounds other than music or dialogue; for example, a door creaking

stage manager   a vital member of the artistic staff; responsible for organizing and managing the entire production from early production meetings through post production

staged-reading   a public performance, in which the actors, although familiar with the characters and the dialogue, read from the script

stitchers   members of the artistic team responsible for sewing the costumes

surrealism   an artistic movement that can be described as "pure" thought

swatch   a small piece of the actual fabric a costume designer may use when presenting designs to the members of the artistic staff

symbolism   this movement revered beauty in the indescribable

technical director   the member of the artistic team responsible for overseeing the creation of the scenic designers scenery designs

Theatre, The   the first theatre in London, built by James Burbage

Theatre of Cruelty   an artistic movement created by Antonin Artaud; Artaud championed the ideal of unconventional theatrical methods which were intended to trigger violent reactions from audience members so that they may experience a psychological catharsis

theatron   the hill above the orchestra where the audience sat in ancient Greek theatres

theme   the overall subject of a play

Thespis   considered to be the "father" of drama since he introduced the first lines for an actor into one of his plays, which included a traditional chorus and its leader

The Ziegfeld Follies   created by Florenz Ziegfeld Jr. (1867–1932). The Follies consisted of beautiful dancing girls with elaborate costumes combined with vaudeville acts

thrust stage   a stage configuration in which the audience sits on three sides of the stage

ticket   a piece of paper that grants an individual admission to a play, musical, or other theatrical event

underscoring   sound, such as music, that is played underneath the action of a play in order to enhance the action

University Wits   playwrights who were graduates of universities such as Oxford or Cambridge during the Elizabethan era

Wakefield Cycle   originally called the Towneley cycle; the best known collection of English Cycle plays; includes 32 plays along with production notes and on indicating the specific guilds that produced the plays

Yoruba Opera, The   one of the most beloved contemporary forms of Nigerian theatre; created by Hubert Ogunde; begins and ends with a glee

Index

A

Aboriginal theatre, 97–98
Aborigines, 95
The Absurdist Movement, 67
Actor/actress, 48
   getting an agent, 171–173
   in liturgical drama, 35
   networking, 171
   personal preparation, 168
   Roman, 31
   training, 174–176
Actor preparation, 168–171
Actors Equity Association, 125, 126, 173
Actor training, 174–177
   method, 175–177
   psychological gestures, 177
   qualities of movement, 177
   the System, 174–175
Adams, Jolene, 179–181
Advertisement, 230
Aeschylus, 27
African theatre, 92–94
   dance and song, 92
   "griot", 92
   language, 92
   in Lusophone, 94
   mime, 92
   national theatres, 93
   in Nigeria, 93
   in North Africa, 93
   Pan-African Festival, 93
   shadow theatre, 93
   vernacular, 92
   village drama, 92
   Yoruba opera, 93
Agents, 171–173
Albee, Edward, 142–144
Aldredge, Theoni, 215–216
Amphitheatre, 31, 203

Andrieni, Isabella, 48
Antoine, Andre, 63
Arabic theatre, 94–95
   contemporary, 95
   dance, 94
   in Egypt, 94
   language, 94–95
   satiric monologue, 94
   shadow puppetry, 94
Arena, 202
Aristophanes, 28
Aristotle, 29–30, 42
Artaud, Antonin, 66–67
   psychotherapy, 66
   Theatre of Cruelty, 66–67
The Art of Poetry (Horace), 42
Assemblage, 67
Audience, 3–4, 54
   etiquette, 3–4
Auditions, 124
Australian theatre, 95–98
   Aboriginal theatre, 97–98
   Australian Elizabethan Theatre Trust, 96–97
   censorship, 96
   contemporary, 97
   convict theatre, 95
   corroboree, 95
   European touring companies and, 96
   in New South Wales, 96
   women's theatre, 98
   youth theatre, 97
Automatism, 66
Avant-garde theatre, 62, 72

B

Ballad opera, 79
Baudelaire, Charles, 61
Beats, 175

Beck, Julian, 68
The Beggar's Opera, 79
Bernhardt, Sarah, 96, 100
Biomechanics, 65
Black box theatre, 203
The Black Crook, 79
Blackface, 114
Blind casting, 114
Blocking, 124, 157–158
Boleslavsky, Richard, 175
Book musicals, 81
Brecht, Bertolt, 71–72
   avant-garde, 72
   Brechtian acting, 72–73
Bunraku, 105
Burbage, James, 52–53
Burlesque, 79

C

Call-back list, 156
Canadian theatre, 98–101
   English speaking, 98–99
   French speaking, 100–101
Carpenter, 206
Casting, 156
Censorship, 26, 112–114
Central character, 132
Characterization, 4
Characters, 4
   naming, 135
   stock, 48–49
Chekhov, Anton, 64, 177
Chekhov, Michael,
Chinese theatre, 101–102
   cross-cultural international theatre, 102
   opera, 101–102
   zaju, 101
Chiton, 27
Choragus, 25, 26, 31. *See also* Chorus
Choreographer, 86
Chorus, 25, 26, 31. *See also* Choragus
City Dionysia, 25
Classroom, as theatre, 203
Climax, 4, 5, 132
Collaboration, 115–116
   flexibility, 115
   self-esteem, 116
   teamwork, 115–116
"Collage poetry," 65
Comedy of Manners, 56
Comic opera, 79
Commedia Dell' Arte, 47–49
   actresses, 48
   Atellan farce, 47
   financial rewards, 48
   improvisation, 47
   lazzi, 47–48
   masks, 48
   stock characters, 48–49
Commercial theatre, 230
Composer, 85
Concept musicals, 81–82
Conflict, 132
Constructive criticism, 7–8
Convict theatre, 95
Corneille, Pierre, 44–45, 100, 107
Corporeals, 71
Corroboree, 95
Costume design, 11, 213–216
   collage, 213
   costume technologist, 213
   draping, 213, 214
   running crew, 214
   stitchers, 213
   swatch, 213
   technical director, 206
Costumes, 27, 31–32, 35, 37, 54, 213–214
Costume technologist, 213
Crisis, 4, 5, 132
Critical thinking, 8
Critiquing theatre, 7–11
   concept, 10
   constructive criticism, 7–8
   critical thinking, 8
   ethics, 8
   familiarity, 9–10
   open-mindedness, 9
   production, for class assignment, 11
   writing, 9, 10–11
Cross-cultural international theatre, 102
Cunningham, Rick, 126–128
Cycle plays, 36–37
   actors, 37

costumes, 37
English Cycle, 36
guilds, 36
humanists, 42, 43
mansion, 35
pageant wagons, 37
spectacle of, 36–37
Wakefield Cycle, 36

D

Dada, 65, 66
De Architettura, 44
Denouement, 4, 5
Design, 202–211
Designers, 155, 156
Dialogue, 4, 5
   inner, 64
Dickens, Charles, 62, 98
Dionysian festivals, 25
Dionysus, 24–25
Directing, 154–156
   casting, 156
   history, 154–155
   rehearsal, 156
   research, 155
Director, 84, 86
Dithyrambic contests, 24–25
Dithyrambs, 24–25
Diversity, in theatre, 114
Doyle, John, 158–159
Dramatists, 27–29
Dramaturg, 120–123
Draping, 213, 214
Dressers, 214
Duke of Saxe-Meiningen, 154–155
DuSold, Robert, 88–89

E

Eastin, Steve, 193–195
Ellman, Bruce, 223–224
Empathy, 5, 7
Engelman, Liz, 121–222
   Yoruba opera, 93
England, theatre and, 51
Environment, 67
Environmental space, 203

Essentials of theatre, 3
Euripides, 28
Europe, medieval, 34
Executive director, 150
Experimental theatre companies, 73, 108
Exposition, 4, 5, 132, 134–35
Expressionist movement, 63

F

Falling action, 4, 5
Folk drama, 37–38
Foreshadowing, 135–136
French Revolution, 60
Freud, Sigmund, 63, 66

G

Gay, John, 79
Genre, 4
Gershwin, George, 80
Gershwin, Ira, 80
The Globe, 53, 54
Greek theatre, 23–26
   censorship, 26
   Dionysian festivals, 25
   Dionysus, 24–25
   selection of poets and actors, 25–26
   spiritual beliefs and, 23–24
   Thespis, 25
Green, Lorne, 99
"Griot", 92
Grotowski, Jerzy, 71, 104
Ground plan, 124
The Group Theatre, 175–176
Guthrie, Tyrone, 99

H

Hair, 82, 113
Hammerstein, Oscar, 81
Hand properties, 225–227
   property master, 225
   props, 225
Happenings, 67–68
Hart, Lorenz, 80
Hart House Theatre, 98
Hellenistic Age, 26, 29
Hellman, Lillian Florence, 139

Hopkins, Kaitlin, 190–193
Horace, 42
Hrotswitha, 34
Human condition, 5, 7
Humanists, 42, 43
Hurwitt, Robert, 14–17

I

Ibsen, Henrik, 137–138
Improvisation, 47
Inciting incident, 4–5
Indian theatre, 103–104
    contemporary, 104
    language, 103
    Maharashtra, 103
    National School of Drama, 103
    sangeet natak, 103
    Sanskrit drama, 103
Inner dialogue, 64
Instituto Nacional de Bellas Artes, 108
Intermezzi, 43

J

Japanese theatre, 104–107
    Bunruaku, 105
    chorus, 104–106
    contemporary, 106–107
    Kabuki, 106, 107
    Noh drama, 104–106
    shogun, 104
    Zen Buddhism, 104
Jarry, Alfred, 61
Jerrold, Douglas, 95
Joseph and the Amazing Technicolor Dreamcoat, 82

K

Kabuki, 106, 107
Kenosis, 22
Kiernan, Kelly, 171–72

L

"Laboratory theatre", 71
Lazzi, 47–48
Lee, Eugene, 207–211
Lenaea, 25
Lescarbot, Marc, 100
Lessac, Arthur, 178–179
Levey, Barnett, 95
Librettist, 79, 85
Light cues, 219
Lighting design, 11, 218–221
    gels, 218
    gobos, 218
    lighting plot, 218
    practical lights, 219
Liturgical drama, 34–36
    actors, 35
    in church, 34–35
    outside church, 35–36
    costumes, 35
    mansion, 35
    medieval cycles, 34
    platea, 35
    Praesepe, 34
    Regularis Concordia, 34
The Living Theatre, 68–70
Livius Andronicus, 30–31
Long, William Ivey, 214–215
Ludi, 30, 31
Lyricist, 80, 82, 85
Lysistrata, 113

M

Make-up, 11
Malina, Judith, 68–70
Mallarme, Stephane, 61
Mansion, 35
Marketing director, 230
Martin, Paul James, 226–227
Masks, 48, 105
Mechane, 27
Melodrama, 74–75
Menander, 29
Message, 3
Method training, 175–177
    the Groupe Theatre, 175–176
    Strasberg, Lee, 175
    subtext, 176

Mexican theatre, 107–108
  Aztecs and, 107
  Instituto Nacional de Bellas Artes, 108
  professional theatre, 108
  Teatro del Murcielago, 107
  Teatro Folklorico, 107
  traditional theatre, 107
Meyerhold, Vsevelod, 64–65
Miller, Arthur, 102, 141–142
Mime, 90
Miracle plays, 38
Moliere, Jean-Baptiste, 45, 46–47, 100, 107
Monologue, 5
Morality plays, 38–39
The Moscow Art Theatre, 64, 174
Mummings, 38
Musical reviews, 80
Musical theatre, 77–90
  ballad opera, 79
  book musicals, 78, 81
  comic opera, 79
  concept musicals, 81–82
  contemporary trends in, 84–85
  influences on, 82–83
  musical reviews, 82
  opera and operettas, 78–79
  pre-opera, 78
  rock musicals, 82
  team, 85–86
Music director, 86
Musicians, 86
Mystery plays. *See* Cycle plays

N

National theatres, 93
National Theatre School of Canada, 101
Naturalist movement, 61–65
Nemirovich-Danchenko, Vladimir, 64, 72
Neoclassical ideals, 42–43
Neroni, Bartolomeo, 44
Networking, 17–18, 170
New Comedy, 28, 29, 33
Noh drama, 104–106
Non-cycle plays, 38–39
  miracle plays, 38
  morality plays, 38–39
Nonverbal communication, 169

O

Objective, 132
Obstacles. *See* Conflict
Oklahoma!, 81
Old Comedy, 28, 29
Olivier, Laurence, 185–186
O'Neill, Eugene, 113, 138
Opera, 43, 75, 78–79, 101–103
Operettas, 78–79
Orchestra, 26
Originality, of playscript, 5, 6–7
Ouspenskaya, Maria, 175

P

Pageant wagons, 37
Palmer, Scott Aaron, 159–162
Pan-African Festival, 93
Paradoi, 27
Performers, 3, 86
Persona, 31
Personalization, 175
Peruzzi, Baldassare, 44
Petitclair, Pierre, 100
Pickford, Mary, 98
Plasticity, 64
Plastiques, 71
Platea, 35
Plautus, 32–33
Play. *See* Playscript
Playbill. *See* Program
Playscript, 4–5
  characters and characterization, 4
  dialogue, 5
  genre, 4
  impact of production on, 5
  plot, 4–5
  theme, 5
Playwrights, 132–140
  French, 44–47
  lifestyle of, 146
Plerosis, 22
Plot, 4–5, 136

Plummer, Christopher, 99
The Poetics (Aristotle), 42
Poetry Out Loud, 108
Point of attack, 4, 5
Poitier, Sidney, 187–190
Porter, Cole, 80
Praesepe, 34
Pre-opera, 75
Producer, 83, 150–52
   interview with, 151–152
   role in production, 150–151
Production, 5, 32, 54, 150–151, 155
   critiquing, 11
   designing, 204
   meetings, 156
   playscript and, 5
   theatrical conventions, 6–7
Program, 232
Prologue, 28
Promotion, 230
Property master, 225
Props, 225
Proscenium arch, 165, 202
Psychological gestures, 177
Publicity, 230
Puritan Revolution, 55–56

Q

Qualities of movement, 177

R

Racine, Jean, 45
Regional theatres, listing of, 233
Regularis Concordia, 34
Rehearsal, 124–125, 156, 157–158
Renaissance, 39, 42
   intermezzi, 43
   Italy, 42–44
   neoclassical ideals, 42–43
   opera, 43
   scenic design, 43–44
Research, 120, 155
Resolution, 132
Restoration, 56–57
Ricardo, Cita, 73–74

Rising action, 4, 5
Rituals, as early theatre, 22
Rock musicals, 82
Rodgers, Richard, 80, 81
Roman theatre, 30–34
   actors, 31
   amphitheatres, 31
   costumes, 31–32
   Livius Andronicus, 30–31
   ludi, 30, 31
   playwrights, 32–34
   production, 32
Romanticism, 60–61
Roscius, 30
Running crew, 125, 214
Run-through, 158
Russian Revolution, 65

S

Salgado, Luis, 195–197
Sanskrit drama, 103
Satiric monologue, 94
Scene, 134
Scenic artists, 205
Scenic design, 11, 43–44
Scenic designer, 207–211
Script, 136
Sentimental Comedies, 56
Serlio, Sebastiano, 44
Shadow puppetry, 94
Shadow theatre, 93
Shakespeare, William, 51–54, 134, 159, 160, 185
Shaw, George Bernard, 99
Shogun, 104, 106
Shop foreman, 206
Sidaway, Robert, 95
Silver, Nicky, 144–146
Silverberg, Larry, 181–184
Simon, Neil, 142
Skene, 26, 27
Skenographia, 27
Soliloquy, 5
Sondheim, Stephen, 81
Sonnets, 51–54

Sophocles, 28
Sound design, 11, 222–224
   practical sound cues, 222
   sound effects, 222
   underscoring, 222
Spisto, Louis G., 152–153
Stage, 26–27
   mechane, 27
   orchestra, 26
   paradoi, 27
   skene, 26, 27
   skenographia, 27
   theatron, 26
Stage design, 206
Staged readings, 136
Stage managers, 123–128
   blocking, 125
   interview with, 127–128
   rehearsal, 124–125
   responsibilities, 124–126
Stanislavsky, Konstantin, 64, 174–175
Stitchers, 213
Stock characters, in Commedia Dell' Arte, 48–49
Strange Interlude, 113
Strasberg, Lee, 175
Stratford Shakespearian Festival, 99
Streep, Meryl, 186–187
Subtext, 175, 176
Surrealism, 65–66
Suspension of disbelief, 6, 170, 176
Symbolist movement, 61–65
The System, 174–175

T

Teatro del Murcielago, 107
Teatro Folklorico, 107
Technical director, 206
Technology, theatre and, 154
Terence, 33
Theatre
   created by specific groups, 114–115
   defined, 2–3
   diversity in, 114
   Elizabethan practitioners, 53
   essentials of, 3
   financial classifications of, 150
   jargon, 4
   permanent, 52–53
The Theatre, 52–53
The Theatre Guild, 113
Theatre of Cruelty, 66–67
Theatrical conventions, 5, 6–7
   empathy, 7
   human condition, 7
   originality, 6–7
   suspension of disbelief, 6
   unification, 6
Theatrical ritual, 22–23
Theatrical spaces, 3, 202–203
   amphitheatres, 203
   arena, 202
   black box, 203
   environmental, 203
   proscenium arch, 202
   thrust, 202
   traditional, 202
Theatron, 26
Theme, 4, 5, 155
"Theme" musicals, 80
Thespis, 25
Thrust stage, 202
Ticket sales, 230
Tipton, Jennifer, 220–221
Tolstoy, Leo Nikolayevich, 62
The Tony Awards, 86–88
Touring companies, 96
Tragedy, 25

U

Unity, 5
University Wits, 51

V

Village drama, 92

W

Wagner, Richard, 154
Wasserstein, Wendy, 144

Weitzenhoffer, A. Max, 151–152
Williams, Tennessee, 139–141
Writing, critiques, 9, 10–11

Y

Yoruba opera, 93

Z

Zaju, 101
Zen Buddhism, 104
Ziegfeld Follies, 80
Zinn, John, 230–232
Zola, Emile, 62

About the Author

Daisy Nystul is chairperson of the Department of Theatre Arts at the University of Central Oklahoma where she teaches acting, voice, and movement for the actor. Ms. Nystul also directs at UCO. Among her recent productions are *Metamorphoses, La Perichole,* and *Pterodactyls.* Out of 1,300 college productions from across the United States, *Pterodactyls* was chosen by the selection team of the Kennedy Center American College Theatre Festival as an alternate production to the national KCACTF festival in Washington, D.C.

Ms. Nystul is a member of Screen Actors Guild, Actors Equity Association, and The Lessac Training and Research Institute. She is a Certified Lessac Trainer (voice, speech, movement, and acting). Ms. Nystul is the recipient of the Vanderford Distinguished Teacher Award—Excellence in Teaching for the UCO College of Arts, Media & Design.